D1563413

The CPR
A Century of Corporate Welfare

By the same author

Right-of-Way: Passenger Trains for Canada's Future

Quebec: A Chronicle 1968-1972
(with Nick Auf der Maur)

The CPR
A Century of Corporate Welfare

Robert Chodos

James Lewis & Samuel, Publishers

ISBN paper 0-88862-046-2
ISBN cloth 0-88862-047-0

Cover design by Christer Themptander
Design by Lynn Campbell

James Lewis & Samuel, Publishers
35 Britain Street
Toronto

Printed and bound in Canada

Contents

1 A mari usque ad Japan: 1
   The myth of the CPR

2 The alliance: 9
   The CPR and the State

3 With enemies like this,   27
   who needs friends?
   The coming of the CNR

4 Where seldom is heard   41
   a discouraging word:
   The CPR and the West

5 Head 'em off at the   59
   Crow's Nest Pass:
   A contract and its implications

6 Passengers in the baggage car   73

7 Up up and away: 89
   The rise of CP Air

8 Phasing out people: 103
   The CPR and its employees

9 The shy and timid old lady: 117
   The CPR becomes
   a conglomerate

10 Life at the top: 133
    The men behind the CPR

11 The myth revisited: 147
    And a modest proposal

    Appendices   156

    Footnotes   160

    Index   171

for Jim Callaway
1926-1971

The careful reader will note that, although this is a book about Canadian Pacific, my strongest criticism is reserved not for officers of that company but for officials of the government of Canada. The reason for this is simple. As long as Canadian Pacific is allowed to exist as a private company, then it is the job of its officers to try to make as large a profit as they can, by all the means open to them. According to all evidence, successive generations of Canadian Pacific managers have been very good at carrying out that job, and one cannot criticize them for it. Government officials, on the other hand, are supposed to represent the people who elected them, rather than the shareholders of Canadian Pacific. From the very beginning of Canadian Pacific's corporate existence, our representatives in government have shown a regrettable tendency to act as if the interests of the two groups of people were the same. As a result, they have not served their constituency nearly as well as the company's managers have served theirs. In proposing nationalization of Canadian Pacific. I don't really expect it to be carried out except by some future government with a whole new attitude toward the relationship between government and business; without such a new attitude I doubt that nationalization would have much point.

In the course of researching this book, I had occasion to seek help from the public relations personnel of Canadian Pacific and many of its subsidiaries; I found them uniformly courteous and co-operative and would like to thank them collectively. Equally important was the aid and encouragement I received from officers and employees of the railway unions, and I am equally grateful to them. Emil Bjarnason, Donald Gutstein, Leo Johnson, Karl Jaffary, Tom Naylor, Bernard Nayman, John Sewell, Ben Ward and Joe Zuken all gave freely of their time, as did others too numerous to mention, notably the many librarians and archivists who must have found my impatience somewhat trying, but never showed it if they did. Finally, I owe special thanks to Homer and Grace Stevens, Bob and Anne Parkins, Ken and Rosemary Bolton, and Bill and Bobbie Gillespie; the nery nature of the book made travel across the country a necessity, and that would have been impossible had it not been for their kindness and hospitality.

Robert Chodos

1 A mari usque ad Japan: The myth of the CPR

*Official mythologies are common to all countries.
All countries cherish one or two particular periods
of their histories, which they ennoble and
embellish, to justify and give meaning to their
present and to give a purpose to their future.
This habit may be merely useful or ornamental
to great, old, and solid nations. It is extremely
important to recent and ramshackle ones.*

Luigi Barzini
New York Review of Books, 1972

Barzini was writing about Italy, but his words strike a responsive chord in other recent and ramshackle countries, for instance Canada. Of the stories we choose to tell and retell, the periods we ennoble and embellish, that of the construction of the Canadian Pacific Railway stands out most prominently. We have numberless histories of it, most of them of the "romance of railway-building" variety; songs by such as Gordon Lightfoot and George Hamilton IV; and even an epic poem, by that genius of a myth-maker, E.J. Pratt. The Americans contributed a grade-B Hollywood feature. Pierre Berton's two-volume narrative with its assorted spin-offs has surpassed all of these in public acceptance, but it is part of the same tradition.

To say that the story of the construction of the CPR is a myth is not to suggest that it is necessarily untrue. It is simply to suggest that truth is not a major criterion in deciding what the components of the myth will be. "He told the truth, mainly," Huckleberry Finn says of Mark Twain's portrayal of him in *Tom Sawyer*: "There was things which he stretched, but mainly he told the truth." There are things which get stretched in the story of the CPR too. They do not get stretched maliciously, and not without some suitably high purpose. "What we once did we can do again," said Pierre Berton in an article in *Maclean's* magazine attending the publication of his *Last Spike* in 1971. "Once again, the time seems ripe for a common endeavour that will hold us together." He picked out Expo 67 and the two world wars, along with the building of the CPR, as instances when Canadians "pursued and achieved the impossible," and suggested that now we should direct a similar outpouring of energy into a "massive and carefully thought-out program to regain this country for the use and the benefit of Canadians, both French and English-speaking."[1]

Berton's books have so far not spurred this particular activity, but they have, significantly, coincided with a new rise of Canadian nationalism. Berton wishes us to take the CPR as our nationalist model, and he can bring sound historical arguments for doing so. In many ways November 7, 1885, the day on which the last spike was driven on the CPR line, is a more appropriate point from which to date our existence as a country than July 1, 1867. All that happened at Confederation was that three British colonies in the northeastern corner of North America got together and set up a new level of government. The idea of Canada as a nation made little sense without the great North West, and Canada's hold over the North West was extremely tenuous without a railway. That there would be a country, and what kind of country it would be, was really only decided on November 7, 1885. "Like a gavel," in E.J. Pratt's words, the driving of the last spike "closed off debate."[2]

If the CPR had not imposed an artificial east-west connection, the natural north-south connections would have prevailed. The prairies of Manitoba and Saskatchewan would have been drawn into the orbit of the great American plains, the mountains of British Columbia would have been merely an extension of the mountains of Idaho and Washington state. If there had been no CPR, neither the settlement of the North West under Canadian authority nor the development of a Canadian industry in the east would have been possible. Perhaps there *are* parts of the argument that are stretched. Perhaps, as some revisionist historians have maintained, the CPR could have been postponed ten years without massive damage to Canadian nationhood. But the argument is basically sound, and it has served its purpose well through the years. The myth of the CPR has been a basic component of the residual nationalism that its original authors, the Conservative party, never seem to be able to shake off entirely. When they proclaimed "No truck or trade with the Yankees" in 1911 and swept Sir Wilfrid Laurier out of office, when they established a national radio network in the 1930s against the same odds that a national railway had faced fifty years earlier, when they refused to accept American nuclear warheads in 1963, the Conservatives were fleetingly pursuing the same vision that had driven them in the 1880s. This ornery, mulish perversity has been the only factor in Canadian life that has enabled this country to withstand American expansionism in whatever form it has appeared. "For Italy," wrote Luigi Barzini, "the myth of the *Risorgimento*[3] has been almost literally a matter of life and death."[4] So, for Canada, the myth of the CPR.

Nationalism is one essential component of the CPR myth, and there is one other. This is the concept of the public-spirited capitalist, the businessman whose activities, while perhaps providing profits for himself, are principally directed toward benefiting the great masses of people. Such men are the heroes of the CPR myth: flawed heroes often, but heroes nevertheless. Gordon Lightfoot sings of the railway being constructed so that others could "build the mines, mills and factories for the good of us all."[5] Pratt writes of the Scots bankers "who would one day climb from their Gaelic hideouts, take off their plaids and wrap them round the mountains"[6] and of William Van Horne, the dynamic general manager of the construction period whose "bugles knew only one call—the summons to advance against two fortresses: the mind, the rock."[7] Berton's speciality is physical descriptions, the kind of descriptions that are designed to leave you in awe of the subject. Here's Donald A. Smith, the future Lord Strathcona, whose interests extended to most of the major institutions of Canadian finance, commerce and industry: "At fifty-eight, his face leathered by the hard glare of the Labrador snows, his sandy locks and flowing beard frosted by the years, Smith had the look of a biblical patriarch."[8]

Or one of Smith's associates in the CPR syndicate, James J. Hill, who later built the Great Northern Railroad in the United States: "A stocky, powerful man with a massive, leonine head, the hair almost down to the shoulders, a short-cropped beard, a face scorched by the prairie sun and that single black eye—a glittering orb that like the Ancient Mariner's burned itself into the listener's consciousness."[9]

We are on somewhat shakier ground with this concept of entrepreneurship than we were with nationalism; the history of the CPR is the story less of public-spirited capitalists than of private-spirited politicians. And we are particularly vulnerable when we try to combine the two components of the myth. The idea that a privately-owned corporation could be effectively used as an instrument of national policy was perhaps a forgivable delusion in the 1880s—although it is worth noting that there were some even at the time who had the prescience to question it. But any attempt to put that idea into practice inevitably leads to the question of who is an instrument of whom. This question is of limited importance when the purposes of the company and those of the state coincide, and for a long time the corporate policy of the CPR and the national policy undertaken by Prime Minister Sir John A. Macdonald in 1878 and ratified by subsequent governments were thoroughly compatible. More recently, however, there have been increasing strains between national policy and Canadian Pacific policy. It would be an oversimplification to say that Canadian Pacific has always prevailed, but even on occasions when political necessity has dictated otherwise, Canadian Pacific has always managed to be well compensated for its pains.

There have been a number of trends in the twentieth century that have made companies such as Canadian Pacific less susceptible to control by the imperatives of national policy. The first of these has been the tendency toward the concentration of economic power in fewer and fewer hands. The era of wide-open capitalism, when anyone could go into business and with the right combination of skill, luck and greed make it to the top, never really existed in this country. Our nineteenth-century "entrepreneurs" were generally friends of the government in power (or members of it), who succeeded in wheedling railway charters out of the legislature and monies out of the public treasury. Still, such concepts as competition, entrepreneurship and the free market once bore some distant relationship to reality. If one group of dominant businessmen took control, it was still possible for another group to challenge it. But Canada's business community in the 1970s is a small elite with a tight hold on the areas of activity that have been left to it by the foreign owners who control most of the economy. Its members are united by the schools they went to, the clubs they join, the companies they own stock in and the attitudes they hold.

There is no room for any mavericks. Competition is eliminated by common interest, mutual respect and forbearance. Although actual monopolies have emerged in only a few industries, whole sectors of economic life are monopolized by this business class.

The position of Canadian Pacific in this web of business connections is central. Its directors also occupy positions on the boards of the other major corporations in Canada—companies such as Inco, Stelco, Dofasco, MacMillan Bloedel, Bell Canada, Brascan and, perhaps most significantly, the major banks. It sits right in the middle of the largest pool of capital in the country. A government trying to impose its will on Canadian Pacific has to deal not simply with one company but with the entire hard core of Canadian business.

A second trend that has increased corporate power has been diversification. In simpler times, railway companies ran railways, paper companies made paper, and mining companies dug metals out of the ground. If a company did get involved in secondary activities, they were usually more or less directly related to its primary one: a railway might own hotels to accommodate its passengers, a steel company might mine the coal that it needed. Now, however, a new type of corporation, the conglomerate, has grown up. The conglomerate is not a specialist in any particular industry. It operates in any business where it can make a profit. There is no relationship between an international pulp-and-paper giant and a rent-a-car service, but both are under International Telephone and Telegraph, nor between a brewery and an electric-power supplier, but both are under Brascan.[10] Even corporations such as General Electric that are not generally thought of as conglomerates have strayed far from their original base.

Diversification protects the company from some of the usual economic pressures that provide a brake on untrammelled corporate independence. If a union strike shuts down its plant, the conglomerate can view the scene with lordly indifference; profits from its other activities will allow it to ride out the storm. If a government wants to take over the giant's railway or airline or power company, that's fine: just pay us handsomely for it, so we can invest the money in something else. Since diversification is undertaken with an eye toward the investments that will yield the greatest profit, it also tends to provide a substantial boost to the net incomes of corporations that successfully undertake it: Brascan has seen its profit skyrocket since it started aiming to become a conglomerate, and Canadian Pacific has harvested similar results from its own massive diversification program.

The third, and probably most important, trend has been the emergence of the multinational corporation. Every shopper has seen some of the manifestations of this development: Fords built in Britain, RCA Victor television sets made in Taiwan, Spalding baseball gloves made in Japan. The multinational corporation is not constrained by union demands in any individual country, or by the policies of any individual government. If wages are too high, government subsidies too low, pollution standards too tough, the political climate too unstable, it will pack up and go somewhere else. It will make one part of its product in one country, another part in a second and then assemble it in a third; if the arrangement becomes inconvenient for one reason or another, then countries are easily interchangeable.

Canada has by and large been on the receiving rather than the dishing-out end of the multinational corporation. Foreign-ownership statistics have been recited in this country until they are as familiar as hockey records, and their significance has penetrated the national psyche at least far enough to generate a debate on the subject. A phenomenon less generally considered is the multinational corporations we have spawned ourselves. Their numbers are few and they are mostly fairly small by world standards, but they are there, standing as a bulwark against the notion that Canada is purely an exploited colony. Our own multinationals are quite adept at exploiting the resources of other nations, and it is also dangerous to ignore them here at home. One person who did no such thing was Arthur Cordell, a researcher for the Science Council of Canada. In his study of multinationals for the Science Council, Cordell found that Canadian multinationals were no more likely to pursue Canadian economic goals than corporations based in a foreign country. For Canadian multinationals, "increasing segments of the operation have been and continue to be transferred to the most active market area—the United States."[11] It was the head of a Swedish-based multinational who said that "we have come to the point where the company has outgrown the country,"[12] but like Barzini's remarks about Italy, the insight applies with little modification to Canada.

Even in the ranks of Canadian multinationals, Canadian Pacific takes a back seat to Alcan, Brascan, Massey Ferguson and some of the banks, but then it has only recently begun to put on the big push in this area. Its petroleum subsidiary explores in Italy and the North Sea, the railway operates in the United States, the mining company has interests in Australia and Spain, and now the hotel chain has expanded to Mexico, France and Israel. One of the most promising of the new Canadian Pacific subsidiaries is incorporated in Bermuda, builds ships in Japan and then mans them with British officers and Spanish crews. Canadian Pacific may be only a small multinational, but it has the right idea.

In one of the remarkably few biographies of Donald A. Smith, Lord Strathcona, an early-twentieth-century writer named W.T.R. Preston attempted to sum up the career of his subject. "Lord Strathcona," he said, "had great qualities—his foresight and his perseverance amounted to genius. He could have succeeded in any walk of life . . . . But he chose personal power and wealth for Donald A. Smith. That opportunity also was there in a large degree only possible in the western United States and Canada forty years ago [the 1870s]. He took the chance Fortune offered him, played for enormous stakes with the weapons that the circumstances of the time permitted him to forge. And he won. He deserved to win.

"He gained enormous fortune, immense power, high honours for himself—exceeding in all these particulars any romantic dreams that he might have indulged in. But just in the degree that Lord Strathcona succeeded for himself, it is a question for history to finally decide, whether he did not fail in the larger test—that of true and noble patriotism."[13]

We might, in the 1970s, have different criteria for just what "the larger test" is. But we could well entertain the same doubts as Preston did, not only about Donald A. Smith, but also about other men like him and about the institutions, such as Canadian Pacific, that they set up. In most of the aspects that we will discuss, Canadian Pacific is not unique, and in many of them, it is not even unusual. But if there is or was a Canadian capitalism, then Canadian Pacific is its proudest product, and that is perhaps why the CPR myth looms so large. When Canadian Pacific is found to have warts, that reflects badly on the whole, and if the myth of Canadian Pacific is hollow, then that casts doubt on the soundness of the whole economic structure. That Canadian Pacific has power is an observation on which both its defenders and critics of all political tendencies agree.

The remainder of this book will examine the nature of that power, the ways in which Canadian Pacific has obtained such might, and the purposes for which the company has exercised its strength. It will look at the extraordinary deals with public authorities that have made that power possible. It will show how this power is exercised unequally in different regions of the country. Different aspects of Canadian Pacific's operations—freight traffic, passenger service, air service, mining, oil and gas, real estate, and shipping—will be analysed in terms of their relation to the company's strength. This book will ask for whose benefit Canadian Pacific's power is being used. And it will question whether, at this point in history, Canadian Pacific ought to continue to be allowed to exist.

2 The alliance: The CPR and the State

As for government, the responsibility of corporate bodies is to conduct themselves in harmonious fashion with government.

Duff Roblin, President,
Canadian Pacific Investments,
September 1972

Although Canadian Pacific Limited, as the parent holding-company has been known since 1971, is the second largest corporation in Canada in terms of assets, its power and importance cannot be explained by size alone.

For Canadian Pacific has always been able to supplement its own considerable resources by an unparalleled degree of access to the resources of an even larger entity—the government of Canada. On the simplest level, this takes the form of a steady flow of cash from the federal treasury to the treasury of Canadian Pacific, at the rate of at least forty million dollars a year. On another level, Canadian Pacific has an indirect but evident influence on government policy in areas concerning the company, to an extent matched, if at all, only by Bell Canada—the single corporation that exceeds it in size. On a third level, Canadian Pacific maintains a curious relationship with the government-owned entry in the railway field, Canadian National, according to which the one is not allowed to behave quite like most public corporations, and the other is not required to behave quite like most private corporations.

The exact amount of the annual federal subsidy to CP Rail is difficult to determine. The government announces each year a total figure for subsidies to "the railways": $158 million in the 1972 fiscal year, an estimated $145 million in the 1973 fiscal year.[1] But the total figure obscures the fact that a subsidy to Canadian Pacific and one to Canadian National are very different things. A subsidy to Canadian National is a book-keeping device, a transfer of money from one public pocket to another, a polite fiction that allows CN to run a service in the red and still show a profit at the end of the fiscal year. There is no form of government expenditure in this country with a clearer purpose or a more solid philosophical underpinning. It is the responsibility of a national government to provide a national system of communications, and particularly so in as geographically scattered a country as Canada. Hence the federal government spends money to maintain a national radio and television network, a post office, a national airline and system of airports—and a national railway.

When we come to Canadian Pacific, we are dealing with another matter entirely: a payment from the government to a private corporation. Now there is nothing unusual in this either, although the philosophical basis is a bit more questionable. In 1972 New Democratic Party Leader David Lewis introduced the phrase "corporate welfare bum" into the Canadian political vocabulary; while the phrase was new, the concept was not. There have been corporate welfare bums in this country almost as long as there have been corporations, and none has collected as much money over as long a period of time as Canadian Pacific.

The current round of subsidies did not come about at Canadian

Pacific's bidding. Testifying before the most recent in a long series of royal commissions on transportation in 1960, Robert Emerson, then a CPR vice-president and later its president, declared himself opposed to government subsidies. They were, he said, a "flagrant misuse" of federal money. What he wanted was for Canadian Pacific to be left alone to run its railway as it liked.[2]

But for the federal government, there were drawbacks to that way of doing things. Because the entire Canadian railway system—and not just Canadian National—is important for the maintenance of national communications and the national economy, the necessity for the government to use that system as an instrument of policy is not lessened by the fact that a large part of it just happens to be in private hands (we will get to how that happened to come about a little later on). So, the government had three choices. One was to let Canadian Pacific have its way and determine its own corporate priorities, deciding, as corporations generally do, on the basis of what provides the best return on investment. This would have had serious implications. It would have meant, for instance, that Canadian Pacific would not haul grain at rates western farmers could afford to pay. It would have meant that it would not provide passenger service. It would have meant that it would not haul freight from the Atlantic provinces except at rates that would price goods from those provinces out of the market. It might have meant that Canadian Pacific would have decided not to run a railway at all, investing all its money in its other interests instead. So long as the federal government thinks that these services should be maintained, this choice is closed.

The second choice was simply to require Canadian Pacific to provide all the services generally associated with running a railway, at prices that people would be willing and able to pay. The only problem with that was there was nothing in it for Canadian Pacific. Everyone else would be happy, but Canadian Pacific would be running its railway at a loss, or at a profit so slight that it would be far better off in another business. Canadian Pacific would have complained, and power relationships being what they are, sooner or later it would have gotten its way.

Hence the need for a third alternative, one that combined the best features of both, that required Canadian Pacific to provide necessary services and yet allowed it to have its railway profit. Fortunately for the government and Canadian Pacific, precisely such a possibility did exist. Provide the services, said the government, and don't worry about losing money. We'll make it up. We'll make sure you have your profit. And that, of course, is what happened. There have been some years in which federal subsidies have exceeded Canadian Pacific's railway profit. There have been others in which the profit has exceeded the subsidies. By and large, in the last six years virtually all of the CPR's railway profit has come from government subsidy.

There are five separate provisions in federal legislation for subsidies to the railways. One is the Maritime Freight Rates Act, on the books since 1928, which provides for a subsidy on freight carried out of the Atlantic provinces. The other four are part of the National Transportation Act, passed in 1967, and require the government to pay:

- A subsidy equal to the losses on railway branch lines determined to be "uneconomic," in the quaint language of the Act.
- Eighty per cent of the losses on uneconomic passenger-services.
- A subsidy for hauling grain through eastern Canada to Montreal and ports east of it for export.
- A declining general subsidy, which started at a level of $110 million in 1967 and phases itself out at a rate of $14 million a year. Thus, payments under this provision in 1973 are $26 million.

Administration of this last subsidy is complex. If it is greater than the total of the specific subsidies under the Act in a given year, then only the general subsidy is paid. If the specific subsidies are greater, then only they are paid, but the general subsidy is still given to the railways as an advance on the specific payments, which are always made at least a year late because of delays in claiming and calculating losses. The specific subsidies are now greater in the case of both the Canadian National and the Canadian Pacific, so that in 1972 the government paid the railways for their 1971 losses, plus the general subsidy as an advance on further payments to be made in 1973.

In March 1973, Les Benjamin, the New Democratic Member of Parliament for Regina-Lake Centre, put a question on the Commons order-paper asking for a breakdown of all these payments, by railway and by type of subsidy.[3] The question was answered two months later, but a curious anomaly remained. The figures in the government's breakdown add up to considerably less than the total quoted in the yearly estimates. In 1973, for example, the railways were entitled to $105 million as payments for 1972 losses; $30.7 million of this belonged to Canadian Pacific. Of the $105 million, $40 million would already have been paid as an advance in the form of the 1972 general subsidy; by the same token, $26 million would go to the railways in 1973 (approximately $11½ million to Canadian Pacific) as an advance on 1974 payments. In addition, payments under the Maritime Freight Rates Act are estimated at $13.3 million—Canadian Pacific's share of that subsidy is $1.5 million.

This means that subsidy payments in 1973 should total $104.3 million, instead of the $145 million reported in the estimates. The Govern-

discrepancy exists in the 1972 figures). In any case, it seems safe to say that Canadian Pacific is at this point receiving a federal subsidy of roughly $40 million a year, if not more; the exact figure must remain in the realm of speculation. For purposes of comparison, Canadian ment has as yet offered no explanation of this difference (a similar Pacific's net profit on rail operations was $45.8 million in 1971, $57.6 million in 1972.

As the specific character of government subsidization of Canadian Pacific has changed over the years, the public rationale for it has changed as well. The report of the MacPherson Royal Commission on Transportation, issued in three volumes in 1961 and 1962 and embodied in the National Transportation Act five years later, provided the most recent justification, which, somewhat surprisingly, was a return to the hoariest catch-word of nineteenth-century laissez-faire capitalism: competition. But there was a new twist on the classical economic model. The Royal Commission was not talking about different corporations in the same field competing for the customer's favour; it was not so bold as to maintain that Canadian National and Canadian Pacific could or would seriously compete with each other. The competition of which it spoke was not between the different companies but among different modes of transportation. Railways, the Commission reported, were competing with trucks, planes, ships, buses and the private passenger car. And, it noted, the railways were coming off rather badly.

This competition was by no means totally a fabrication of the Commission. The railway had once been by far the dominant mode of transportation in Canada but, by 1961, it was dominant no longer. In 1928, 83.8 per cent of the country's freight and 38.3 per cent of its passengers had gone by rail; by 1953, this had declined to 60.5 per cent for freight and 11.3 per cent for passengers.[4] But there was an element to this competition that the Commission ignored. Canadian Pacific was aware that the pattern of transportation was changing, and had done something about it. Starting as a northern bush line in the early 1940s, Canadian Pacific Air Lines had developed an extensive network of international routes and had by the 1950s entered the lucrative transcontinental field. In 1958, Canadian Pacific had bought up a large eastern Canadian trucking firm, Smith Transport, which together with the growing Canadian Pacific Transport in the west, made it Canada's largest operator in the field of highway truck transport. And Canadian Pacific had been involved in ship-transport since the 1880s. One might expect few benefits to accrue to the consumer out of any competition where the competing airline, railway, trucking firm and shipping line were all responsible to the same management and board of directors.

No matter; in the past, the shipper and passenger had been protected by government regulation, and now they would be protected by competition. The Royal Commission set as the goal of transportation policy the creation of "conditions which will permit each mode, and each firm within each mode, to obtain that share of the growing volume of traffic which, on the basis of inherent competitive advantage, it is entitled."[5] As a consequence, "the regulation of transportation in Canada should be minimized as much as possible, consistent with the protection of the public interest." If the railways were to be able to adapt properly to the "new competitive environment"[6], they had to be released from the comfortable but inhibiting bondage of regulation.

The Commission recognized that this would not always work, that what it called "national policy" would sometimes conflict with the play of competitive forces. In these cases, it laid the groundwork for the policy of subsidy later adopted by the Government. It said that "no particular form of transport should be singled out as an instrument of national policy if any burden is involved in the performance of the function, unless sufficient compensation is provided to that mode of transport to prevent distortions in the competitive transportation market."[7] More specifically: "Where, for national policy reasons, it is considered necessary to retain rail operations such as unprofitable passenger or branch line services, the railways should be entitled to payment from public funds to cover their deficits on such services."[8] In a reference to its recommendation that the government should compensate the railways for hauling western grain at statutory rates, the Commission said that "assistance to transportation which is designed to aid, on national policy grounds, particular shippers and particular regions should be recognized for what it is and not be disguised as a subsidy to the transportation industry."[9]

This last came directly out of the brief presented to the Commission by Canadian Pacific which, it will be remembered, is opposed to subsidies to itself and prefers to see them disguised as something else. In fact, much of the Commission's report bore a distinct resemblance to Canadian Pacific's recommendations. Freedom from regulation, and reduced passenger service were major themes of the company's presentations to the Commission. In the area of statutory grain rates, the Commission's report supported a historic shift in Canadian Pacific policy: instead of calling for the abolition of parliamentary control of grain rates, as it had before previous commissions, the railway—and the MacPherson Commission—recommended government compensation.

The president of the Confederation of National Trade Unions, Jean Marchand, called the report "disturbing." He said that "transportation policy is closely linked to economic planning and as such must be linked to the common good and not the profitability of private enterprise."[10] But Marchand's was very much a minority view. Not only businessmen, who could hardly come out against competition, but most politicians and newspaper editorialists praised the report. It was regarded as a breakthrough, the final solution to Canada's transportation problem. Even some union leaders interpreted it only to mean that the railways would have more money to meet the next wage demand.

Despite the favour with which it was greeted, and despite its considerable length, the report left out a lot. Principally, it ignored one of the most important lessons of Canadian transportation history, which is that government has never been, and cannot be, a mere bystander in the transportation process. The early modes of transportation, the canals and railways, were built either as government projects or with substantial government aid. The later modes—bus, truck, car, airplane and pipeline—were equally dependent on government decisions. The bus, truck and car were made possible by the roads built with municipal, provincial and federal funds. As Depression projects, the federal government initiated the construction of a national system of airports and a Trans-Canada Highway. The first national airline, Trans-Canada Air Lines, was established as a public enterprise. The existence of the new "competitive environment" was not an accident, any more than the old monopolistic environment had been. The government had always been in a position to play a large part in determining the transportation environment. It had not always used that position wisely, at least partly because it had often placed the interest of private companies above considerations of national policy. Now the MacPherson Commission, in so many words, dismissed considerations of national policy as "an albatross around [the] neck"[11] of the railways, and proposed that such considerations be downgraded still further. This, like any other course the Government might choose to pursue, was bound to have far-reaching consequences.

In the area of passenger transport, for instance, the Commission was in effect recommending that the Government stop worrying about passenger trains; after all now there were cars and airplanes. The country would pay an increasingly high price for the emphasis on these new modes, both directly in the form of vast public expenditures on highways and airports, and indirectly in the form of pollution and accidents. In the late sixties, there would be a public reaction against their uninhibited growth. Planning against these eventualities should have been a higher priority of the Government than Canadian Pacific's profit margin—as the Commission itself suggested, there could be "a serious element of conflict between these two factors."[12] The Commission opted for Canadian Pacific's profit margin. The Government, in basing its new transport legislation on the MacPherson recommendations, agreed.

The new legislation did not have an easy passage. Jack Pickersgill, who took over the federal transport portfolio in 1964, spent almost the whole of his tenure trying to bring the national transportation bill into law. The first attempt ran into heavy seas in parliamentary committee, and finally died when Parliament was dissolved for the 1965 election. The second national transportation bill, Bill C-231, met some of the major objections to the first one. Instead of allowing for automatic abandonment of money-losing passenger services and branch lines, the new bill provided for such services to be kept alive, with government subsidy, if national policy considerations warranted. The railways were not to be directly subsidized for hauling grain at statutory rates, as the first bill suggested, although indirect compensation still existed, since most of the branch lines that would be subsidized were prairie lines used almost solely for carrying grain. The bill would also replace the outworn Board of Transport Commissioners with a new regulatory body of increased power. But it was still the basic MacPherson package. Instead of having to apply for freight-rate increases, as they did in the past, the railways had only to notify the new commission. And the bill contained a decided preference for the abandonment of passenger services and branch lines.

The passage of the National Transportation Act in 1967 was the crowning achievement of Jack Pickersgill's political career, and with that behind him, he promptly retired from politics and appointed himself to the powerful, $40,000-a-year presidency of the Canadian Transport Commission, the new regulatory body set up under the act. Even the staunchly Liberal Montreal *Star* was appalled at the appointment[13], but it was the sort of move observers of Jack Pickersgill had come to expect. He had first entered the Cabinet in 1953 after a remarkable career in the back rooms. In Parliament, his Liberal partisanship was so unvarnished that he succeeded in alienating even Toronto *Star* columnist Peter C. Newman.[14] By 1967, he had outlived his political usefulness. By 1972, he would outlive his usefulness as president of the CTC.

The clearest expression of the Pickersgill position on transportation came in a speech to the Canadian Manufacturers' Association on June 9, 1970. It was by and large a restatement of the MacPherson philosophy, and was sprinkled liberally with quotes from the MacPherson report and the National Transportation Act, in which he took a fatherly pride and which he said "showed a definite bias toward reliance upon the competition of the market place." But in this speech, Pickersgill went beyond what even the MacPherson Commission had dared say. He asserted that "the public generally, and business men specifically, must come to realize that it is just as moral, and just as praiseworthy to operate a railway, an airline, or a trucking firm at a profit as it is to make a profit manufacturing motor cars or packing meat or making steel.''

Later that summer Maurice Wright, counsel for the Canadian Railway Labour Association, made a motion that Pickersgill be disqualified from a hearing over which he was presiding, on the grounds that his June 9 statement had demonstrated his bias in favour of Canadian Pacific, which happened to be engaged in making a profit at all three of the transportation activities Pickersgill had mentioned. Pickersgill was somewhat taken aback at the suggestion. ''I must say,'' he said, ''that I thought that that statement was as safe as saying one was in favour of motherhood as one could come and not be accused of banality . . . . What I was seeking to do was to remove all bias of any kind, without raising a very large question, which I have no intention of raising, as to whether it is moral to make a profit on anything. I am sure that no one wants to debate this subject.''[15] Least of all Jack Pickersgill. In the eight years he was in a central position to determine Canada's transport policy, he had ample opportunity to show whether he felt it was moral to make a profit. Unless, of course, he consistently acted contrary to his own standards of morality, a suggestion one would not want to entertain.

Pickersgill's retirement in 1972 as president of the CTC was followed within a few months by the removal of his close political ally, Don Jamieson, from the transport portfolio. Pickersgill was succeeded by Edgar (Ben) Benson, another waning Liberal politician, while Jamieson's successor was Jean Marchand, who had once been disturbed by the MacPherson report, but had more recently, in a four-year stint as minister of regional economic expansion, displayed a new ability to get along with business. The early auguries of the new era were mildly encouraging. Marchand said early in 1973 that ''the railways aren't going to run this country,''[16] and suggested to the railways that a freight-rate increase they wanted was inadvisable. Although neither Marchand nor anyone else had the power to stop them, the railways withdrew the increase, for the time being at least. But there has been nothing yet to suggest that Marchand, or still less Benson, is ready to undertake the rewriting of a pattern of transport legislation and policy that has largely been drawn up by Canadian Pacific.

If they were to do so, they would be reversing one of the longest-held and firmest policy positions of the Canadian government. For neither Canadian Pacific's influence on the government nor its dependence on the public treasury for large portions of its profit is a new phenomenon. Both date back to the very corporate beginnings of the CPR, which postdated the beginning of the Dominion of Canada itself by only fourteen years.

As the story of the conception and birth of the Canadian Pacific Railway is usually told, the hero of the drama is not Donald A. Smith, the imperious Scottish financier who drove in the ceremonial last spike; not his cousin George Stephen, the first president of the railway and the man who attended to its often troubled finances, nor even William Van Horne, the organizational genius from Illinois who presided over its actual construction. The hero—Prime Minister Sir John A. Macdonald, master politician, far-sighted statesman and nation-builder who surmounted practical difficulties to realize his vision of a Canada stretching from sea to sea. According to this version, the story begins in 1871 with Macdonald making the apparently foolhardy promise of a transcontinental railway as bait to induce the remote Pacific colony of British Columbia into Confederation, descends into the Pacific Scandal and the simultaneous collapse of the first Pacific railway project and the first Macdonald government, continues on a low key through the succeeding Mackenzie administration and its obstinate refusal to adopt Macdonald's railway policy, picks up tempo with the return of Macdonald in 1878 and his discovery of George Stephen and his syndicate and the subsequent signing of the contract, develops the twin themes of the Herculean effort to complete construction in five years and Macdonald's repeated rescues of the company from financial distress, and ends triumphantly in the British Columbia mountains with the driving of the last spike on the seventh day of November, 1885.

The central role assigned to Macdonald is significant, for it indicates that from the beginning the Canadian Pacific Railway was not in any sense an ordinary commercial enterprise. According to pure capitalist theory, the entrepreneur takes risks in developing a new product or providing a new service. If the product or service meets with public acceptance, he reaps a reward in the form of profit for taking those risks. There have been attempts to apply that theory, or some variant of it, to the CPR. Buck Crump, then chairman of the Canadian Pacific board, used his address to the annual general meeting of shareholders in 1966 to answer criticisms of the company's policy of abandoning money-losing passenger services. As a result of the generous subsidies of land and cash given to the company by the Macdonald government, the critics said, the CPR had undertaken certain obligations which it was now trying to shirk. Crump was going to set the record straight on the exact nature of the original agreement with the Government. The Government, he said, had entered into the agreement because it was "worried about the level of taxation that might be necessary if it were forced on its own to continue building the railway." After the contract with the Stephen syndicate had been signed, "the federal government was now relieved of the obligations and risks, which were transferred to the shoulders of private enterprise."[17] This was why it had given the subsidies, and it had got good value for its money.

But the placing of the Pacific railway project in the hands of a private company did not relieve the Government of any risk. Macdonald pledged much of the government's financial capability, and all of its moral authority, to the Canadian Pacific Railway Company. "My own position as a public man," he wrote to Stephen in 1889, "is as intimately connected with the prosperity of the CPR as yours is, as a railway man."[18] Stephen himself held a similar view. "You will not forget the fact," he wrote to Macdonald in 1882, "that the Canadian Pacific Railway is in reality in partnership with the government in the construction of the national railway."[19] The concept of the CPR as a national enterprise is also one on which scholars agree. Donald Creighton, Macdonald's biographer and passionate advocate, referred to the railway as "a project of the Canadian nation."[20] Vernon Fowke, the economic historian of western Canada, saw parallels between the private CPR and the earlier, government-owned Intercolonial Railway:

> The Intercolonial Railway was built as a government undertaking as provided for in the British North America Act. The construction of the Pacific railway was attempted both publicly and privately and was finally completed by the Canadian Pacific Railway Company, a private syndicate. But this Company was well fortified by government grants of cash, land, completed line, an exceptional degree of freedom from rate control, and a monopoly clause. Legally, the Intercolonial Railway and the Canadian Pacific Railway emerged as distinct and sharply contrasting types of institutions—the one, state; the other, private. Functionally, they began and continued as substantially similar institutions—agencies of the state designed for the furtherance of the national policy.[21]

This comfortable relationship between government and private business is not peculiar to Canada. The early American transcontinental railroads were built with massive government aid; more recently, in the era of the defence contract, government favour has been a major factor in the growth of such corporations as Litton Industries and Ling-Temco-Vought. But, in Macdonald's time at least, there were stronger forces in the United States than in Canada critical of such arrangements. In 1885, just as Macdonald was contemplating yet another loan to the CPR to bail it out of its difficulties, the United States was inaugurating one of its trust-busting presidents, Grover Cleveland. Two years later the Cleveland administration piloted through Congress the Interstate Commerce Act, providing for an independent federal agency to regulate American railroads. No such body existed in Canada until the early twentieth century.

Business-government partnership had been a characteristic of the Canadian railway industry ever since the 1850s. It had helped compensate for the fact that the railways were rarely, if ever, profitable; most of the smaller lines were short-lived as independent enterprises, and even the Grand Trunk Railway, the most substantial of the early roads, was regularly on the verge of bankruptcy. To identify railways with politics, as did Allan MacNab, head of both the Great Western Railway and the government of the Province of Canada in 1854, was only to state the obvious.

No railway had government connections as extensive and intimate as the Grand Trunk, which maintained a continuing rivalry with MacNab's Great Western. It was a rivalry between the two chief commercial cities in the colony: the Great Western was based in Toronto, while the Grand Trunk, controlled by London banking houses, involved Montreal commercial capital. Among the government connections the Grand Trunk could claim were Francis Hincks, in 1853 Inspector-General of the Province of Canada and later, in the early years after Confederation, Macdonald's finance minister; George Etienne Cartier, the railway's solicitor, second only to Macdonald in the roster of the Fathers of Confederation; and Alexander Tilloch Galt, who entered the Government of Cartier and Macdonald in 1858 on the condition that it embody in its program the idea of a federal union of the British North American provinces, and also later served in Macdonald's early post-Confederation cabinets.

The line of succession from the Grand Trunk to the Canadian Pacific is direct. Montreal finance, centred in the Bank of Montreal, was heavily involved in both: Peter McGill, president of the Bank of Montreal, appeared on the original Grand Trunk board of directors in 1853; George Stephen was president of the Bank of Montreal until he moved over to the incipient CPR in 1880; and Donald A. Smith would become president of the Bank somewhat later. Both railways could also count upon the same kind of help from very similar governments. When the Grand Trunk, its favoured position in Ottawa threatened, was using its influence in the 1880s to prevent the Canadian Pacific from making inroads into the London money markets, it had an outstanding debt to the Canadian government of 3.5 million pounds, along with thirty-odd years of unpaid interest.

Railways can be seen as the physical bonds that augmented the political bonds created from 1867 onward by the growing Canadian Confederation. The proposal for an Intercolonial Railway between Halifax and the Grand Trunk terminus at Rivière-du-Loup, Quebec, was written right into the British North America Act in 1867. The promise of a Pacific railway was an integral part of the terms of union with British Columbia in 1871. Even tiny Prince Edward Island was lured into

Confederation in 1873 with the pledge that the Dominion would take over and complete its financially troubled trans-insular railway, and establish communication with mainland railway systems. However, one can also come to the conclusion that since so many of the Fathers of Confederation were railway promoters, the union of the colonies simply offered the opportunity for bigger and better railways. A railway to the Pacific was the biggest and best of them all.

The Grand Trunk had been based on the theory that Canada could capture a substantial portion of the trade of the burgeoning American Midwest; as such, it was a disaster—in 1860 it hauled only a fiftieth as much wheat to Montreal as the Erie Canal and the New York railroads did to New York City. It failed to bring much more trade to Montreal than the St. Lawrence waterway had already brought: of 12.2 million bushels of grain received at Montreal in 1862, 11.4 million came by water, only 800,000 by the Grand Trunk.[22]

During the American Civil War, some Canadian businessmen looked to the postwar South, if victorious, as a natural Canadian hinterland; the North's victory nipped that idea in the bud. It was becoming clear that the Reciprocity Treaty with the United States, signed in 1854, was going to be abrogated by the Americans. The Canadians were running out of places to look. Already, some of them had begun to see possibilities in the vast and unpeopled North West, then still under the direct control of the Hudson's Bay Company. George Brown, the Reform leader, had been the first politician of any influence to advocate western expansion, but in the 1860s, with the dreams of a profitable American trade evaporating, the idea gained increasing currency. It was necessary first to effect colonial unification in the east, so as to create a stronger base for the westward push. The Confederation of New Brunswick, Nova Scotia and the Province of Canada (divided into Ontario and Quebec) was only a prelude to the main event. With remarkable speed, British Columbia and the Hudson's Bay territory of Rupert's Land were absorbed into the new Dominion.

The program that gradually took shape involved three main elements. One was to stimulate manufacturing industries in central Canada. The second was to turn the Prairies, with their potentially rich, wheat-growing land, into a market for the products of those industries and a resource base for central Canada and Great Britain. The third was to realize the long-held dream of the British empire—the "all-red route" to the Orient. The fulfilment of the program required a protective tariff, a vigorous immigration policy to populate the western plains, and a Pacific railway; this was the policy that Macdonald adopted after 1878. To a large extent, the Canadians regarded themselves as junior partners in an imperial scheme. The prairie wheat economy was from the beginning primarily directed toward export to Britain. Meanwhile, the CPR quickly moved to establish both Atlantic and Pacific steamship connections: if the all-red route could also be an all-Canadian-Pacific route, then so much the better.

Along with the Grand Trunk, the most important spiritual forerunner of the CPR was the Hudson's Bay Company. Hudson's Bay rule of the North West was followed by Canadian Pacific rule after an interregnum of only sixteen years. The great fur-trading company sold its lands to the Dominion government for 300,000 pounds in 1869 (retaining the areas around its trading posts and one twentieth of the total for itself), and by 1885 millions of the most fertile acres of those lands had been handed over in turn to the Canadian Pacific as a grant for building the railway. Standing square in the middle was Donald A. Smith, with a substantial interest in both companies. Somewhere between 1870 and 1885 he had become the largest single shareholder in the Hudson's Bay Company; he was also, after 1874, its land commissioner. His interest in the CPR dated from the formation of the Stephen's syndicate in 1879; he was a silent partner at first because of his political unacceptability to Macdonald and his unpopularity in Manitoba, but he joined the board of directors in 1883 and by 1885 was sufficiently open about his involvement to pose over a railway spike for Canada's most famous photograph. Furthermore, he was a partner in the Canada North-West Land Company, which bought five million acres of the CPR's land grant for $13.5 million in the early 1880s. Smith was to die a Baron and Canada's richest man.

He was far from being the only person whom the CPR helped make wealthy. Largely because of the almost limitless aid provided by the Government to get the railway started, the CPR was at least a moderate success from the beginning. The total value of that government aid is impossible to estimate. There was $25 million in cash. Large portions of the transcontinental line were built by the Government and turned over to the company; those sections cost the public treasury $37.8 million. There were the lands: initially 25 million acres of land "fairly fit for settlement"; then when the railway decided to extend its line to the western end of Burrard Inlet, fourteen miles beyond the original Pacific terminus at Port Moody, it demanded and got an additional grant of 6,000 acres from the government of British Columbia, land so fairly fit for settlement that it is now the central part of the city of Vancouver. The company's prairie lands were valued at $1.50 an acre when it gave back 6.8 million acres in 1886 as partial payment of an emergency government loan; by 1916, however, the company estimated its net proceeds from land sales at $68.25 million, and carried its unsold lands in its accounts at $119.25 million.[23] Through its subsidiary, Marathon Realty, Canadian Pacific still owns roughly a million acres of land, including some of the most valuable urban land in the country.

There were other concessions as well, not quite as tangible but no less substantial. The lands granted to the company were to be free from taxation for twenty years or until sold. Properties used for railway purposes were to be free from taxation forever. All the necessary equipment for building the railway would be admitted into Canada duty-free. And the Government would for twenty years prohibit any competing road from being built south of the CPR's main line or within fifteen miles of the American border, ensuring the company a virtual monopoly of western traffic. This meant not only that the Dominion would not itself charter competing railways but that it would also use its constitutional power of disallowance if any province had the effrontery to do so—as, in the event, did Manitoba.

George Stephen hoped that the grants and concessions would be enough to allow the completion of the railway without the company assuming a huge funded debt, which was the bane of so many American railroads (and which was to force two later Canadian transcontinentals into bankruptcy). His hopes were realized, but not before he thrice more called upon his good friend Macdonald for help. The first time he asked merely for a government guarantee of part of the dividend on CPR stock, and offered to pay for the guarantee out of the CPR treasury. But this failed to accomplish its desired end of pushing up the price of the stock, and soon Stephen was back asking for more direct aid: a loan of $22.5 million. After some grumbling from Macdonald's reluctant colleagues, and a heated debate in the House of Commons, this too was granted, with the entire railway mortgaged to the government as security. Even this aid was not enough; scarcely six months later, in late 1884, the company was running out of cash again. Creditors were demanding their money. The men who were building the railroad, the navvies, were demanding their pay; at Port Arthur, they went on strike. The Government's generosity to the company had not gone unopposed, and any further loan was regarded as politically impossible.

Now, as in all good stories, a cloaked figure comes riding across the western plains to save the CPR and make heroes of Stephen, Macdonald and Van Horne. Fifteen years earlier, the transfer of lands from the Hudson's Bay Company to the Dominion had been punctuated by a rebellion of the Métis at the Red River colony, in what is now Winnipeg. The rebels had succeeded in winning their major demand: provincial status for the colony. As a result, the tiny province of Manitoba had been admitted into Confederation in 1870; but the advance of white settlement had forced the Métis westward out of the province that had been established under their leadership, into the North West Territories. Their claims remained unsettled, and the coming of the railway, the first settlers, and the North West Mounted Police threatened them with the extinction of their way of life. In 1884 the leader of the Red River rebellion, Louis Riel, returned from exile in Montana to act as a spokesman for his people. In early 1885, a second rebellion broke out in the North West.

From there, everything proceeds to fall into place. The story relates how, at Van Horne's initiative, the still-uncompleted CPR main line was used to transport a Canadian army to the North West. The rebellion was put down, and with the railway having thus proved its value to the nation, the Government guaranteed another CPR bond issue so that construction could continue. It was the finest moment of the government-CPR partnership in action. With the financial crisis resolved, the company went on to complete the road to the Pacific by November 7. Louis Riel was tried and convicted of treason by a Canadian court, and hanged at the prairie town of Regina on November 16. The partnership's mastery of the North West stood unchallenged.

How to measure the value of all that to the CPR? Perhaps the most accurate way would be to add up every penny of profit the Canadian Pacific has made since 1881, considering none of it would have been possible without the original government commitment. The power that was placed in the CPR's hands was enormous; the company was well aware of this, and ready to use this power in its own interest. It chose the names, shapes, sizes and locations of western towns from Brandon to Vancouver. In Calgary, it located its station—and thus the centre of the city—a couple of miles to the west of where a town had already begun to spring up, and took title to what would become the most valuable land in the city, after buying out its only resident, a Métis squatter named Ignace, for one thousand dollars.[24] With regard to the Vancouver terminus, Van Horne wrote to Major A.B. Rogers (he of the pass) in 1884 that "our object should be of course to give the greatest possible value to our own lands and therefore the least to any other."[25] In *The Last Spike,* Pierre Berton speculated that the very choice of the route through the Prairies was dictated by considerations of where the railway could exercise the most power: the CPR changed the route from the one the Government originally had had surveyed (which followed roughly what is now the Canadian National main line), for reasons that have never been made fully clear. Berton's explanation is that the original route already had settlers along it, and the CPR would not have been able to exercise the kind of total control it preferred. So, it opted for the uninhabited southern route, at the price of sending the railway through less favourable agricultural land (in large parts of which it refused to accept any of its land grant) and a more difficult passage through the mountains.[26]

Since this kind of power was implicit in the very purposes for which the CPR was set up, and since such large sums of public money were spent for its construction anyway, it seems surprising that Macdonald never even seriously considered the option of building the Pacific railway under public ownership. It was not a totally unknown concept at the time. Critics of the railways had long pinpointed private ownership—or at least some of the forms that private ownership took—as a cause of many of their ills. Thomas Keefer, the engineer and polemicist who had been one of the first to espouse the "philosophy of railroads", was an early critic of the Grand Trunk, and blamed what he called its "magnificent, complete, and disastrous" failure on the greed of British railway contractors and the venality of Canadian politicians.[27] Keefer noted that the original plan for a trunk line called for it to be built as a public work, with the hope of some aid from the British government, and suggested that one of the reasons the plan may not have been carried out was the offer to the Canadian negotiator in London, Francis Hincks, of "a *douceur* from the contractors, in the shape of 50,000 pounds in paid-up stock in the capital of the company, which, however, he repudiated when it was announced."[28]

Not long before Macdonald presented the agreement with the Stephen syndicate to Parliament for ratification in 1880, a pamphlet appeared called *Startling Facts!!: Canada Pacific Railway and the North-West Lands, also a Brief Discussion Regarding the Route, the Western Terminus and the Lands Available for Settlement.* It was written by the explorer Charles Horetzky, and dealt mostly with a controversy about the route. But Horetzky also attacked the policy of land grants to railway companies. He said that "the Dominion Government, were it at liberty to carry on the work in a common-sense manner, is perfectly able to build the prairie sections of the Pacific Railway as fast as necessary, without overburdening the tax-payers of the older provinces, while the construction of the British Columbian portion of the road could be deferred; but politics, and the Pacific Province being paramount over all other considerations, the entire North-West may shortly be sacrificed on that account, and find itself bound hand and foot under the domination of a gigantic and soulless monopoly, unless the people awaken to a sense of the impending danger."[29]

Macdonald would have been little inclined to take seriously such scribblers as Keefer and Horetzky. But he also had before him the example of the Intercolonial, which, containing little potential for profit and hence little interest for the capitalists of Montreal and Toronto, was built as a government railway. Perhaps most important, there was the railway policy of his rival, Alexander Mackenzie, who served as prime minister during the temporary eclipse of Macdonald that followed the Pacific Scandal in 1873. Whether Mackenzie believed implicitly that the railway should be a public project or whether his railway policy was a matter of expediency is a question on which historians differ. In any case, the actual construction of the Pacific railway was begun under his administration, as a government project; the 722 miles of line whose construction had been initiated by Mackenzie were later turned over to the Stephen syndicate by Macdonald. Mackenzie could not press any further with construction because he held office during a depression; it was the old boom-and-bust economy and this was one of the busts. It was economic necessity, and not public ownership, that dictated his go-slow policy on the railway.

Macdonald believed in the Tory version of the business ethic, which said not that you left business alone, as the Liberal version did, but that you helped it along if you believed that what it was doing was for the national good. And in Macdonald's mind there was no doubt that that condition was fulfilled. What was good for the CPR was good for the country. This was reflected in his personal attitude toward men like Stephen, whose company he came to prefer to that of many of his political colleagues. The two became not only partners in a great enterprise but confidants, just as present-day business-oriented politicians strike up friendships with the entrepreneurs who find them useful for their own ends. Thus former Newfoundland Premier Joey Smallwood got along very well with mining promoter John C. Doyle, and Richard Nixon's closest friend is a shadowy Miami wheeler-dealer, Bebe Rebozo.

Does Macdonald really fit the role of visionary in which he is so often cast? Was Mackenzie the honest but overly cautious Scot of Creighton's scorn and Berton's faint praise? A more accurate reading of the CPR's beginnings might reveal Mackenzie to have been a man of far greater vision than Macdonald. All he sacrificed by attempting the construction of the Pacific railway under public ownership was speed, and probably not even that. Speed was not of the essence; settlers did not pour into the Prairies in large numbers for fifteen years after the completion of the railway. What was of the essence was to ensure that the public interest was well protected in the opening of the new territory, and that its development was not entrusted to people whose primary motive was private gain. In this, Macdonald conspicuously failed.

3 With enemies like this, who needs friends? The coming of the CNR

Whenever someone tells me that Canadian Pacific should be nationalized, I say that first it would be necessary to really nationalize Canadian National.

Ed Finn, Research Director,
Canadian Brotherhood of Railway,
Transport and General Workers, 1973

Of all the assets, physical and political, that Canadian Pacific can boast, perhaps the least often recognized is the existence of its sister railway, the Canadian National. Early in this century, Canadian Pacific repeatedly agitated for all Canadian railways to come under its control; it was a concession that successive governments of Canada dared not make. No such agitation has been heard for some time now, for Canadian Pacific has grown quite happy with the present arrangement. Just as the existence of four large American car manufacturers instead of one takes some of the sting out of the cry of monopoly that would otherwise be heard much more insistently, so too does the existence of two large Canadian railways—especially when one of them is publicly owned.

We have already seen how the coexistence of the CNR and CPR helps fudge the issue of subsidies to Canadian Pacific, one of many such benefits, both direct and indirect. When Canada's pension legislation was revised in 1966, corporations were required to fund their employee pension plans fully, instead of just paying into the fund when money was required, as had been the wont of many companies, including Canadian Pacific. Private corporations were given twenty-five years to meet the requirements of the new legislation; Canadian National, as a Crown corporation, was given sixty years. Canadian Pacific demanded that it be given the same terms as Canadian National, and after four years, the Government finally agreed.

There are many different motives that might lead a government to set up a public railway system, and many different ways in which it could do the setting up. One way would be simply to nationalize the existing railway systems, which in Canada principally means taking over the CPR. As the largest and most successful of Canadian railways, the CPR would be the most desirable property for the government to have and the potential key to the effectiveness of any national railway. If a government of Canada tried to set up a public railway system without taking over the CPR, one would be forced to suspect that its motives were something other than the creation of an effective national utility.

A second method of setting up a public railway was described by Bernard Shaw in his *Intelligent Woman's Guide to Socialism and Capitalism*:

> The government could, no doubt, construct a network of State railways parallel with the existing railways.... The State could then undersell the separate private companies and take all their traffic from them. That would be the competitive method. There would then be two railways... one of them carrying nearly all the traffic, and the other carrying only its leavings and holiday overflows until it fell into hopeless and dangerous decay and ruin.

But can you imagine anything more idiotically wasteful? The cost of making the competing State railway would be enormous, and quite unnecessary. The ruin of the private railway would be sheer destruction of a useful and sufficient means of communication which had itself cost a huge sum. The land occupied by one of the railways would be wasted. What government in its senses would propose such a thing when it could take over the existing railways . . . . ?[1]

There is yet another course a government could follow, one that even Shaw, with his fine sense of the absurd, did not think of. With one private railway company operating profitably, the government could charter two new private railways to compete with it. When these two go bankrupt, as they inevitably must, since there is not enough traffic to sustain three roads, it could take them over and try to mould them into a workable national railway, leaving the first one alone to make its profits. Would any government in its senses propose such a thing? But we leap ahead of ourselves.

The relationship of the Canadian Pacific Railway with the government of Canada and the Conservative party continued and deepened after 1885. The railway was more than a visible achievement to which the Conservatives could point with pride. It was also a political machine that could be mobilized at election time in aid of the Tory cause. In addition to dipping generously into its treasury, the railway would attempt to ensure the political loyalty of its employees. "Our canvass is nearly complete," Van Horne, by then president of the CPR, wrote to Macdonald during the Tory chief's last election campaign in 1891, "and the CPR vote will be practically unanimous—not one in 100 even doubtful."[2]

These, however, were not vintage years for the CPR. Continuing agitation from the West led to the cancellation of the monopoly clause in 1888, and even that didn't put an end to western criticism of high freight rates. The railway's great protector, Macdonald, died in 1891, and at the next elections in 1896 the Conservatives went down to defeat at the hands of Wilfrid Laurier's Liberals. The mid-1890s were lean years everywhere, the expected flood of settlers failed to come in, and the CPR's profits remained at a modest level until the end of the decade. While the CPR weathered these misfortunes, the groundwork for future profits was being laid. In 1897, the CPR and the new Liberal government signed the railway's most important deal since the original contract, giving it access to one of Canada's richest mineral areas, southeastern British Columbia, in exchange for a reduction in freight rates.

With the turn of the century, the economic cycle turned as well; the settlers came in, Canadian Pacific's profit margin began to look extremely comfortable, and a heady mood struck the country the like of which has not been seen before or since. The twentieth century belonged to Canada; who could doubt it? The country's financiers and industrialists embraced the new climate with particular ferocity. It was a period in which the rich got richer, the powerful got more powerful, and the basic outlines of Canada's native business elite as we know it today first emerged. For the first time, Canadian businessmen did not stick to Canada, but plunged into large-scale ventures elsewhere as well, especially in the new and unsuspecting republics of Latin America. William Van Horne, who had graduated from the presidency to the chairmanship of the CPR in 1899, built a railway across Cuba, and then, in alliance with the United Fruit Company, turned to Guatemala. He was involved as well in setting up a Canadian utility empire in Mexico, where one of his partners was William Mackenzie, also the first chairman of Brazilian Traction, Light and Power—today known as Brascan. Meanwhile, back in Canada, Mackenzie was one of the principal figures in a new railway-and-banking octopus that was challenging the older one based in the Bank of Montreal and the CPR.

Mackenzie and his principal partner, Donald Mann, had started their careers as CPR contractors, and had acquired the first railway of their own in 1896. This was the Lake Manitoba Railway and Canal Company, consisting of a charter granted by the province in 1889, but never acted upon, for a 123-mile road from Gladstone on the Canadian Pacific main line to Winnipegosis. Mackenzie and Mann undertook construction of the line and after its completion were on their way. By obtaining charters—which usually carried with them at least some measure of public aid—and buying up other lines, they rapidly expanded their network on the prairies, and by 1902 the Canadian Northern, as the system came to be known, had reached Port Arthur, Ontario, with no intention of stopping there. As their railway grew, Mackenzie and Mann formed an important banking alliance, with the Canadian Bank of Commerce, and an equally important political alliance, with the Liberal party.

The time was ripe for a new Canadian transcontinental, but Mackenzie and Mann were not the only ones in the running. The Grand Trunk, with its substantial network of lines in the east, had abandoned its earlier doubts about transcontinental railways and was looking to move west. The Canadian Northern, as a western road looking to move east, was in precisely the opposite position. The logical thing was for them to get together, and the two railways began negotiations in 1902. Nothing came of them, to the dismay of Prime Minister Laurier, who had reasons of his own for wanting to see the railways come to an agreement. The success of the CPR-Conservative alliance had imbued the Liberals with the desire to make a similiar arrangement with a transcontinental of their own, and this appeared to be their chance. Laurier made a further attempt to get the Grand Trunk and the Canadian Northern together, but the second round of discussions was no more productive than the first.

Laurier, however, was unperturbed; if one new transcontinental could not be arranged, then why not *two* new transcontinentals? Was not Canada a land of endless possibilities? In 1902 a bill was passed allowing the Canadian Northern to extend its lines from Port Arthur to Ottawa, Montreal and Quebec City. In 1903 Laurier announced that the Grand Trunk Pacific, a subsidiary of the Grand Trunk, would build a railway from Winnipeg to Prince Rupert, B.C. The Government itself would undertake construction of another new road, the National Transcontinental, to begin at Moncton and link up with the Grand Trunk Pacific at Winnipeg. Upon completion, the National Transcontinental was to be leased to the Grand Trunk Pacific. Opposition to Laurier's policy focused primarily on the National Transcontinental, and particularly on the Quebec City-to-Moncton section, which was being built by the Government to compete with an existing government road, the Intercolonial. The minister of railways, A.G. Blair, resigned from the Cabinet over the decision to build that section. But the implications of the larger decision to give Canada a total of three transcontinentals had not yet hit home.

They would hit home only after 1913, when the economy took another dip, a setback the Canadian Northern and the Grand Trunk Pacific could ill afford. A year later, the outbreak of the First World War closed off European money markets to the railways. In desperate financial straits, the Canadian Northern and the Grand Trunk Pacific were left with only one source of funds, the same source that had bailed out the Canadian Pacific thirty years earlier: the government of Canada. As in 1884, the Government came through with repeated loans and guarantees. The Government was also stuck with the National Transcontinental; by the time the road was finished, costs had gone so far over the original estimates that the Grand Trunk Pacific reneged on its agreement to lease it, since the rental was to be based on the cost of construction. Both the Grand Trunk Pacific and the Canadian Northern were completed by 1915, but they were hollow achievements. Neither railway was in any position to stand on its own feet, and the Government's patience was finally beginning to wear thin.

The prime minister of the day was Robert Borden, under whom the Conservatives had returned to power in 1911, and he numbered among his friends Lord Shaughnessy, who had succeeded Van Horne as president and later chairman of the CPR.[3]

While in opposition in the early years of the century, Borden had been a vigorous critic of Laurier's railway policy. In the debate on the National Transcontinental, he had suggested that the Government buy the portion of the Canadian Pacific main line running through the sparsely populated, unproductive territory between North Bay and Fort William, and grant equal running rights over it to the CPR, the Canadian Northern and the Grand Trunk for a small annual rental. This would connect the northwest railhead of the Grand Trunk with the easternmost point of the Canadian Northern. The suggestion had first come from Shaughnessy, who had sat down and talked over the railway situation with Borden in August 1903. In comparison with Laurier's policy, it made a certain amount of sense from the point of view of the country. It also made sense from the point of view of the CPR. In the 1880s the syndicate's commitment to building the line through the barren and difficult country north of Lake Superior, so that the CPR would be an all-Canadian route, had enshrined Macdonald and Stephen in the nationalist pantheon. But Canadian Pacific was not so committed to the north-of-Superior line that it wasn't prepared to unload it onto the government if it got the chance.

It never got the chance. Laurier proceeded with his new transcontinentals, and Borden turned out to be somewhat more than just a mouthpiece for the CPR. He even made the suggestion, anathema to Shaughnessy, that the Government should build and run its own transcontinental. But Shaughnessy did not give up his attempts to influence Borden's policy, particularly after the latter became prime minister in 1911. The decisions Borden had to make after 1915 were crucial to the CPR. Government action of some sort in the matter of the Canadian Northern and the Grand Trunk Pacific could not be long postponed. There were a wide variety of suggestions being thrown around as to what the Government should do, among them that it should nationalize the Canadian Northern and Grand Trunk Pacific, integrate them, and run them as a government railway. It was an idea the CPR did not take kindly to. Two weak, privately-owned transcontinentals, with small reserves and little ability to compete, were no threat to the CPR. Their growth had had only a marginal effect on freight rates; in fact, it could be argued that they had helped keep freight rates high. The Board of Railway Commissioners, the regulatory body set up in 1903, had decided against a general reduction of western freight rates on the grounds that "rates based upon the Canadian Pacific's power to stand reductions would inevitably bankrupt not only the Canadian Northern and the Grand Trunk Pacific, but for the future preserve the western provinces to that company in so far as any new companies or new lines were concerned." The only exception to that, and one that might be able to compete with the CPR, would be a transcontinental that combined the lines of the Grand Trunk, the Grand Trunk Pacific and the Canadian Northern, and had the reserves of the government behind it.

Another suggestion made was that the Government should nationalize not only the bankrupt railways but the Canadian Pacific as well. This was based on the rather sensible conviction that it would not be fair for the public to bear the burden of the money-losing roads while the shareholders of the CPR reaped the benefits of that line. The *Grain Growers' Guide,* the magazine that throughout this era acted as the raucous voice of western farmers, said that "the C.N.R. and G.T.P. are short of money, short of rolling stock, short of equipment, short of management and short of success, while the C.P.R. is long on all of these essentials. To take over these poor roads will entail just as much responsibility and effort and graft as to take over the C.P.R. also. The C.P.R. is one of the finest railway systems under the sun. It is well financed, well operated and gives a good service with enormous profits to its shareholders, totalling last year [1916] $49,000,000. The loss on all the other railways was only $20,000,000. If all the railways of Canada were nationalized therefore and operated with the same efficiency as in the past there would be a profit from the outset. The present management of the C.P.R. is quite capable of managing a national system which would include all the railways. If the people of Canada are to become proprietors of the two lean railways there is all the more reason why they should take over the fat one at the same time."[4]

The CPR, opposed to nationalization of its rivals, was even more opposed to nationalization of itself—unless it could set its own terms. And this Shaughnessy attempted to do. On May 17, 1916, he submitted a memorandum to Borden outlining his own plan for a solution to the Canadian railway problem. The Grand Trunk Pacific, Canadian Northern and Canadian Pacific would be nationalized, and then all government railways would be placed under the existing management of the CPR. For its services, the CPR would receive "an agreed annual dividend" on its common stock, "to be guaranteed in perpetuity by the Canadian government."[5] Canadian Pacific's shareholders would retain ownership of the company's non-railway interests, which had already begun to assume considerable importance, and "from which," as Shaughnessy put it, "they would get some return."[6] The government would appoint some of the directors of the integrated railway, but not enough to threaten Canadian Pacific control.

The benefits of this plan, Shaughnessy said, were clear. He pointed out that it would eliminate the necessity of any further "shameful and indefensible raids . . . made on the public Treasury to evade Receiverships"[7] by the Canadian Northern and the Grand Trunk Pacific (rather an odd statement from a president of the CPR). There would be one management organization instead of four; maintenance and transportation charges could be reduced; duplicated and unnecessary lines could be abandoned. The "large earning power" of the CPR would eventually make the whole system profitable. And the Grand Trunk, which, according to Shaughnessy's plan, was to be left to its own devices (a position into which the CPR itself was extremely reluctant to be put) as a protection against the inevitable accusations of monopoly, would benefit "because in many districts where it divides its traffic with two competitors, it would, after the consolidation, have only one competitor."[8]

Shaughnessy's plan was not much different from the kind of relationship established between the government and the CPR both then and now. It was only a small step up from having the government pay most of the cost of constructing the railway and then turning it over to the CPR to run at a profit, as happened in the 1880s, or from having it subsidize the CPR for operating services it regards as necessary in the public interest, as happens in the 1970s. The formation in the early 1960s of an umbrella company for the CPR's non-transportation interests, Canadian Pacific Investments, indicated that holding on to those interests in the event that the government should ever take over the railway, was still very much a consideration in the minds of CPR managers. But Shaughnessy's proposal was a bit ahead of its time. Borden thought his memorandum "somewhat impertinent."[9]

In July 1916 Borden appointed a three-man Royal Commission to look into the railway problem, and in May of the following year the Commission submitted its report. The report was a divided one, with two of the commissioners ("more than might have been expected,"[10] was the *Grain Growers' Guide*'s unimpressed comment) favouring a government takeover of the Grand Trunk, the Grand Trunk Pacific and the Canadian Northern, and the third calling for a reorganization, but with retention of private ownership. This third commissioner was A.H. Smith of New York, the head of one of the largest American railroads. Said the *Guide*: "No one would have expected the president of the New York Central Railway to favour nationalization. If he favored it in Canada it would be pretty hard for him to oppose it in the United States where he is one of the biggest railway men at the head of the great New York Central system. However valuable Smith's opinion may be upon financial and operating questions, his views on nationalization would certainly be biased. No railway magnate that we have ever heard of would favor having his own business taken over by the government unless at a profit to himself."[11]

That the other two commissioners, Sir Henry Drayton, chairman of the railway commission, and W.M. Acworth, a British railway statistician, could have been induced to support public ownership was a testimony to the extremity of the situation. It was a conclusion they reached only after much pained reflection. The Drayton-Acworth report was filled with praise for the virtues of competition and private enterprise, and warnings of the dangers of parliamentary control of railways and political interference. But it was also filled with descriptions of the Canadian Northern's worthless, watered stock, of the neglected and dangerous condition into which the Grand Trunk management had allowed its lines to deteriorate, and of the general waste and foolishness of Canadian railway policy. It was only because "this is a case for generosity rather than strict justice"[12] that Drayton and Acworth could recommend more than very small compensation for the shareholders of the Grand Trunk, and only because "Governments in the past have not taken a stand on strictly legal grounds in their dealings with other companies" that Canadian Northern shareholders could expect any compensation at all.[13]

Even in prescribing public ownership, Drayton and Acworth made every attempt to disguise their recommendation. They headed the section containing their conclusions, "Government Operation not Recommended." And they said, "We desire to make a fundamental point clear. We express the conclusion to which we have come both in negative and positive forms. We recommend: (1) That the Government do not acquire or undertake to operate any further railways; but: (2) That these three railways, Canadian Northern, Grand Trunk, and Grand Trunk Pacific, be transferred by Act of Parliament to an independent Board of Trustees (incorporated as a company), constituted as we shall hereafter describe."[14]

They went on to describe an independent, non-political, self-perpetuating board, approximating as much as possible a private corporation, but—they could not avoid saying it—under government ownership. It was a clever compromise, but it could not be expected to satisfy Canadian Pacific's objection to a government-controlled railway, which was one of the reasons cited by Drayton and Acworth for their opposition to direct parliamentary control. Shaughnessy had continued his activities, but had gotten nowhere with Borden, who had considered his proposal seriously and had discussed it with members of Cabinet, but finally rejected it. Through his agent, Sir Thomas Tait, Shaughnessy had also presented the proposal to the Commission. The CPR president talked the situation over with Acworth too in December 1916, a conversation that had some influence on Acworth but, as soon became clear, not quite enough. After Borden made clear his intention to implement the Drayton-Acworth proposals, Shaughnessy even began to woo Laurier and his Liberals, marking the end of the historic special relationship between the CPR and the Conservative party. As late as 1921, when the Canadian Northern and the Grand Trunk Pacific had already been nationalized and the formation of the Canadian National Railways was well underway, Shaughnessy addressed a memorandum to the new prime minister, Arthur Meighen, outlining the same plan he had sketched to Borden five years earlier, down to the last detail of leaving the Grand Trunk to uphold the banner of competition and private enterprise.

The creation of the Canadian National thus appeared as a defeat for the CPR. But if aggressive competition was to follow, Canadian Pacific started out with a considerable advantage over its new rival. It had built up its own lines, always with its own interests in mind; it had a long string of profitable years behind it and a substantial reserve; it was well known and respected if not exactly loved. The CNR had only the makings of a sound transcontinental; it also had unnecessary lines, a huge funded debt and little public confidence—the legacies of the Canadian Northern and the Grand Trunk. Its best asset was the seeming willingness of Parliament to vote it all the money it wanted. At first, it did undertake to compete with the CPR, and tried to outdo the CPR in highly visible areas. It improved passenger service, introducing faster schedules and forcing Canadian Pacific to follow suit. Passenger competition included costly advertising campaigns and even extended to home delivery of tickets. Henry Thornton, the president of the CNR, was an active propagandist for his railway, and Edward Beatty, who had succeeded Shaughnessy at Canadian Pacific, was moved to respond; in the elegant language of Professor G.P. de T. Glazebrook, whose *History of Transportation in Canada* is still a standard work, "the presidents of both railways became peripatetic, explaining to audiences all over Canada their respective opinions on the railway situation."[15]

The most serious area of competition was the construction of new lines. It was the last great era of railway expansion in Canada, as the prosperity of the 1920s led to a revival of the optimism of the early years of the century. Again it was Canadian National that led the way, undertaking construction of the Hudson Bay railway, long desired in the West. On the Prairies both railways rapidly expanded their network of branch lines. In all, almost three thousand miles of new road were opened between 1925 and 1930.

The one area in which there was no competition was freight rates, which were heavily regulated by the Board of Railway Commissioners. After 1920, the Board had adopted Canadian Pacific as its "yardstick" railway—rates for all railways were to be set on a basis that would allow Canadian Pacific a "fair and reasonable" return. At least in part, this was done to meet the demands of shippers and provincial governments, since to use any other railway as the yardstick would have meant higher rates and far more than a reasonable return for the CPR; in 1917, a fifteen percent increase in freight rates authorized by the Board to breathe life into the dying Grand Trunk and Canadian Northern had proved an outright bonus for Canadian Pacific, and public pressure had forced the Government to impose a special tax on the CPR to wipe out its benefits. Now, however, the situation was different. If a rate that was high enough to allow Canadian Pacific the profit to which it had become accustomed was not sufficient for the Canadian National, then the difference could be made up from the public treasury. Everybody would be kept happy. Competition was fine for the periphery of railway activities, but when it came to the nitty-gritty this way worked much better.

In any case, the brief era of competition came to an inglorious end after 1929. For Canadian Pacific, the crash of that year and the onset of the Depression was a severe blow; for Canadian National, disastrous. The CNR had only begun to make a run at its older rival, and the efforts it had made in that direction had been expensive. Its funded debt, which had started out at a staggering $805 million in 1923, was up to $1.28 billion by 1931.[16] Revenue freight dropped from 69 million tons in 1928 to 31 million in 1933, passengers from 19.7 million to 9.4 million. An operating surplus of $48 million in 1928 declined to a deficit of one million dollars in 1933; after paying the interest on its debt in 1933, Canadian National had a deficit amounting to sixty million dollars.[17] The national railway was in trouble.

A Royal Commission that had been appointed in 1931 "to inquire into the whole problem of transportation in Canada" was not of much help. The Commission was presented with many proposals calling for the amalgamation of Canadian National with Canadian Pacific, which had also seen its large surpluses disappear. In the worst year, 1932, the CPR had a deficit after fixed charges of $424,000., and for five years during the 1930s it could not pay dividends on even its preferred stock. Amalgamation was an idea that the CPR itself still favoured, as it had since the heyday of Lord Shaughnessy. The plan CPR President Beatty presented to the Commission was a variation on the old Shaughnessy theme: the two railways would be consolidated, and the profits divided "in agreed proportions" between the Government and the owners of the CPR. "The agreed proportions would be ascertained," Beatty said, "by taking, for example, the percentage of each company's earnings to the total over a period of year, net."[18] In other words, by far the larger part of the profits would go to the CPR.

In the end, the Commission rejected all proposals for amalgamation and recommended "co-operation" instead. It decried the competition of the 1920s as "wasteful," and suggested mechanisms through which the railways could co-operate, instead of duplicating services and providing unnecessary frills. It was mild medicine for what seemed a serious disease, and it was watered down still further in legislation and hardly put into practice at all. Nevertheless, it marked an important milestone: it was the final nail in the coffin of the idea that the railways could be run in much the same way as any other business. The Commission's report legitimized practices that in any other industry would have violated anti-combines legislation. In so doing, it removed any possible justification for maintaining two separate railway systems in order to protect the public against the evils of monopoly. If they are to be allowed to behave as if they are a monopoly anyway, then it really does not seem to make much difference. The real justification for two separate railways was that they were there.

As late as 1935 Beatty was saying, "Experience with co-operation strengthens the view that unification alone offers an adequate solution to the Canadian railway problem. No other plan can eliminate the tremendous waste caused by maintaining duplicate services in a country that can no longer afford to pay for the duplication. Unification would also offer a solution to the unfair and dangerous anomaly of a Government-owned enterprise engaging in direct competition with private capital. The solution of the railway problem on fair and sound lines will produce benefits to Canada far in excess of mere operating savings. The Canadian Pacific, in complete co-operation with the Canadian Government—for that is what unification means—can achieve infinitely more for the future welfare of Canada than can the two railway systems separately within the present working limits of their statutory authority."[19]

Unification, on our terms. There is no clear point at which this stopped being the official position of the CPR. It just began to be heard less and less often, as the immediate reasons for unification became less pressing. After struggling through the Depression, the railways found unprecedented prosperity during the war years. Wartime traffic put the CPR's net profits back in the $40-million-a-year range, and the CNR had a profit of $35.7 million in 1943, even after making its interest payments.[20] Good times continued after the war when, for the first time in a generation, the railways applied for and got general increases in freight rates. These increases put the 1958 freight-rate level 120 percent above what it had been at the end of the war.

It was *the railways,* that curious amalgam of private and public institutions, that applied for the postwar freight-rate hikes. And when in 1959, the government of John Diefenbaker stopped the increases, authorized a federal subsidy instead and appointed a Royal Commission to look into the whole situation, it was *the railways* that were being subsidized, *the railways* that would be examined. Competition might show spasmodic signs of life, but only in peripheral matters. In the 1960s Canadian National decided that it would make an effort to attract the passenger trade, which both railways had spurned and which by this time represented only a small proportion of their traffic; it introduced faster trains, an efficient reservation system and red-white-and-blue fares to encourage mid-week and off-season travel. Canadian Pacific paid little attention, except to say that they thought the CNR was wrong, a view which Canadian National, after a few years, came to share.

The cosy relationship between the two railways papers-over a difference that is not only one of ownership but a functional one as well. Canadian Pacific is in business to make a profit and has never tried to obscure that fact, even when it goes begging to the government for large portions of that profit. Canadian National seeks profit too, but as a publicly-owned railway it can never quite escape the idea that its purpose is at least partly to provide a public service. Ventures that are unprofitable or very risky, but nevertheless desirable, tend to be the domain of Canadian National rather than Canadian Pacific. The foray into passenger service was one such venture. The Great Slave Lake Railway was another, and a particularly interesting one in that Canadian Pacific was a direct beneficiary of what Canadian National did. It is truly a tale of co-operation.

On the shores of Great Slave Lake, five hundred miles north of Edmonton, in Pine Point, N.W.T., is a mine owned by a company called, most appropriately, Pine Point Mines Limited. This mine produced 3.8 million tons of lead-zinc ore in 1972; it is one of the major suppliers of the lead-zinc smelter at Trail, B.C., operated by Pine Point's parent company, Cominco Ltd.—a diversified mining giant. Cominco first explored the Pine Point area in the late 1920s, but was unable to bring the mine into production until 1965, after a railway was completed to Pine Point from the Northern Alberta Railways' end-of-steel at Grimshaw, Alberta. The railway was built by Canadian National with a special federal grant of $86.5 million, only $20 million of which was to be reimbursed by Cominco—whose mine the railway was built to service.

All this would only be mildly extraordinary except for one additional fact: Cominco is the chief mining subsidiary of Canadian Pacific, which owns more than fifty percent of its shares. Cominco began with the Canadian Pacific's acquisition of the Trail smelter in 1897, and it has grown steadily since. The development of the Pine Point Mine was the central feature in yet another expansion. Millions of dollars were spent on improvements and additions to the Trail facilities to prepare them to receive ore from Pine Point. The one thing on which Canadian Pacific was not prepared to spend money was a railway to haul the ore out.

The Great Slave Lake Railway, as it is known, was a product of

John Diefenbaker's vision of the North, one of the few practical measures to come out of the soaring rhetoric that captured the country in 1958. When the idea of a railway to the North West Territories progressed from the dream stage to the status of a serious proposal in the 1950s, it was assumed that the road would be jointly built by the CNR and the CPR. Not only was it Canadian Pacific's mine that stood to gain, but the CPR was the joint owner, along with Canadian National, of the Northern Alberta Railways, of which the Great Slave Lake Railway would be an extension. As early as 1955, it was reported that the CPR and Cominco had turned down a federal proposal for a three-way sharing of costs among the railway, the mining company and the Government. In 1958, after Diefenbaker had come to power, the federal government was reported ready to give a grant of between $15 million and $20 million to the CPR and CNR to build the road. Northern Affairs Minister Walter Dinsdale was still talking about a joint CN-CP line on December 30, 1960. "I can't speak for the attitude of the railways," he said. "However, they were quite interested when this railway was first proposed and I would think they still are."[21]

But by the time the Great Slave Lake Railway proposal was actually introduced in Parliament in late 1961, Canadian Pacific had lost interest; or rather, it was still interested in having the railway built—by CN. It had cashed in on the vision of the West eighty years earlier by taking the federal government for all it was worth, and now it would do the same with the vision of the North. The profits were to be made from mining and smelting, not from the railway. In the House of Commons, Prime Minister Diefenbaker invoked the memory of his revered predecessor, Macdonald, scornfully comparing the depleted Liberal contingent's opposition to the Great Slave Lake Railway to Liberal doubts about the original CPR in the 1870s and the 1880s. A Liberal spokesman said Canadian Pacific was getting "a pretty big plum" without "putting up a plugged nickel"[22]; he was Jack Pickersgill, who would later prove no slouch at giving plums to the CPR himself. The bill passed without difficulty; even the CCF, which did not want to seem to be against northern development, voted with the large Conservative majority. The railway was begun in 1962 and completed two years later.

The net profit of Pine Point Mines Ltd. in 1972 was $7.3 million, down from $12 million in 1971.[23] But the overall value of the Pine Point mine to Cominco is difficult to estimate. The Trail smelter had for more than forty years depended largely on the Sullivan mine at Kimberley, B.C. for its ore; Pine Point now produces almost twice as much ore as the Sullivan mine. In all probability, Cominco would have eventually brought the Pine Point mine into production anyway. The Government, and Canadian National, just made it that much easier.

4 Where seldom is heard a discouraging word: The CPR and the West

In some ways we've been the authors of our own problems in the west.

Ian Sinclair,
(just after being appointed CPR president)

The classic CPR joke is the one about the western farmer who returns home one afternoon to discover that a hailstorm has destroyed his wheat crop, his farmhouse has been struck by lightning, and his wife has run off with the hired man. He raises his eyes heavenward, shakes his fist angrily, and yells, "Goddamn the CPR!"

The story is usually told by CPR propagandists to demonstrate the irrationality of western opposition to the railway. Ronald Keith, executive assistant to Canadian Pacific Air Lines President Grant McConachie until McConachie's death in 1965, told it in his adulatory biography of his ex-boss to show that western "resentments against the CPR . . . were usually illogical, since the company had spent millions in fostering settlement of the wheatlands, had assisted homesteaders with generous loans, and had written off $37 million in mortgages in the depth of the depression."[1] But the story has another point as well. For if the mythical farmer's perspective is distorted, the distortion nevertheless has very deep roots in reality, much as does that of the goldfish who finds proof of the existence of God in the fact that the water in its bowl is changed every day.

Westerners regard the East with many of the same suspicions that Maritimers hold toward Upper Canada, Newfoundlanders hold toward the mainland, Quebecers hold toward *les Anglais,* and northern Ontario residents hold toward the bureaucrats in Toronto who don't understand their problems. Only southern Ontario, and its satellite community of English Montreal, are free from this sort of regionalism, for the perfectly logical reason that they have benefited most from the interregional arrangements on which the country is based. But western Canada, and the Prairies in particular, are in a fundamentally different position from any other region. French Canada, the Maritimes and Newfoundland were all older civilizations that were unable to stand up economically to the newer, more aggressive society that grew up in southern Ontario (let alone the United States), and were drawn into its orbit. All three look to their original cultures and sets of values at least as much as they do to the ones that were imposed on them from Toronto and Ottawa.

In contrast, the only pre-Canadian western history of any significance is Indian and Métis history, and in the West, as everywhere else, the Indians and the Métis have been reduced to a remnant. The economic basis of western society as we know it today is a creature of central Canada, and its creation was carried out in central Canadian interests. If the western farmer began to find early in this century that the grain-marketing system, the transportation system, the banking system and the political system—the whole interlocking array of eastern Canadian institutions that put him on the land in the first place—did not operate in his interests, that was because they were never intended to. More than in any other region, strong voices in the West have expressed dissatisfaction with the economic relationships that exist in this country, but all the East would ever allow was a certain amount of tinkering with those relationships to remove only their worst effects.

The chief partner of the federal government in setting up those relationships, and the most visible representative of eastern interests in western Canada, has been the Canadian Pacific Railway. On the non-transportation side, Canadian Pacific participation in such other economic activities as real estate, mining, oil, and forest industries is particularly extensive in western Canada. But the railway itself is probably even more important; because of their agricultural economy and the distances that separate them from the eastern population centres, transportation questions are crucial in the prairie provinces, and the lack of water routes gives the railway a more central role than in the valley of the St. Lawrence. In central Canada freight rates are merely freight rates. On the Prairies freight rates are a visible manifestation of the unequal economic rules within which the West has to operate, and a convenient symbol to fight against.

In central Canadian newspapers, stories about freight rates are rare, and usually limited to a report on some western premier or MP complaining about them. In western newspapers, stories about freight rates are frequent and insistent. On December 11, 1969, the Calgary *Herald* reported "MP to fight freight rates setup." On May 12, 1970, the same paper said "Alter rail rates first, Saskatchewan suggests." On January 28, 1971, "Regina makes pitch for lower freight rates." On February 20 of the same year, "High freight, interest rates blamed for unemployment." On July 22, "Rail freight rate increase protested." On November 9, "Provinces urge rail rate probe." On March 11, 1972, "Railways blasted for 'blackmail, conspiracy.'" On July 26, "Blakeney demands freight adjustment." On August 30, "Lougheed predicts revival of big freight rate battle." And on January 19, 1973, it was "Those freight rates again."

The list is only partial, and a similar one could be compiled from any western paper. One would never know that the western freight-rate problem was supposedly solved in 1897 when rates on the most important western product, grain, were made the subject of a deal between the CPR and the Government that is still in effect: the Crow's Nest Pass agreement. There are a lot of commodities the agreement doesn't cover. And even in areas it does cover, freight rates are often still an issue—to the West. When the newest western glamour crop, rapeseed, first began to be grown in substantial quantities after the Second World War, its producers succeeded in having it made eligible for the Crow's Nest Pass rates. One result of this has been that the rapeseed-crushing industry has located largely in central rather than western

Canada, and western rapeseed-crushers have been struggling to survive. Rapeseed oil (an edible vegetable oil) does not come under the Crow rates, and hence it is considerably cheaper to ship unprocessed rapeseed east and crush it there than it is to crush the seed in the West and ship the oil and rapeseed meal (an animal feed) to the eastern market. The transportation cost for 100 pounds of rapeseed crushed at Lethbridge, Alberta, and then shipped as oil and meal by CP Rail to Montreal is 103.1 cents, while if the same 100 pounds of rapeseed is shipped from Lethbridge to Montreal to be crushed, the transportation cost is only 68.5 cents.

The western rapeseed-crushers took their case to the Canadian Transport Commission which, although highly critical of the railways' rate-making policies, gave the prairie producers only partial relief, ordering a reduction of the rates on rapeseed meal but not on rapeseed oil. The Commission's comments on the process by which the railways set rates on rapeseed products were revealing: "The railway companies seek to find a rate under which the shipper is prepared to deliver the traffic for carriage and which, at the same time, will give the railway companies the maximum revenue return. One railway witness in describing this process, after drawing attention to the requirement that the rate be such that the shipper will 'actually offer traffic for carriage, described it as charging what the traffic will bear."[2]

The rapeseed example also attracted the attention of an Edmonton economic consulting firm, Hu Harries and Associates Ltd., in a remarkable study done for the Calgary Chamber of Commerce in 1971. The study concentrated on the relationship between the freight-rate structure and the lack of secondary industry in the West; it noted that "in 1970 Canada Packers Ltd. announced plans for the construction of a substantial addition to its plant at Hamilton, Ontario for the production of rapeseed oil and meal," which could "displace virtually the total volume of rapeseed oil and meal sold to eastern Canada by all the present producers in the west."[3]

The four western provinces, the study estimated, have an annual nèt Canadian interregional trade deficit in manufactured goods of more than $2 billion: "This figure simply means that more than 100,000 jobs in the manufacturing industry are created in Ontario and Quebec to take care of the *net* western-Canadian demand. The manufacturing industry in the West is geared only to serving local markets except for the forestry industries of British Columbia. Railway freight rates combine with tariff policy and Canadian commercial policy to maintain the historic economic dependence of the West as a captive market for central Canadian industry."[4] The study also presented a figure of $18.5 million for the annual direct burden of freight-rate discrimination on western shippers.

Probably the most serious form of discrimination from which prairie shippers suffer, and certainly the most interesting, is long- and short-haul discrimination. To the logical mind, it would seem apparent that since Calgary is considerably closer to Montreal than is Vancouver, and is in fact on the way from Montreal to Vancouver on the CPR main line, it should be cheaper to ship goods from Montreal to Calgary than it is to ship the same goods from Montreal to Vancouver. This, however, is not always the case. There are many commodities which can be shipped by rail from central Canada to British Columbia more cheaply than they can be shipped to points on the Prairies. One of them is steel: for a commodity classification such as "steel plate—3/16 of an inch or over, plain, not corrugated, not bent, nor drilled, nor fabricated", for instance, the freight rate from central Canada to Vancouver is $1.12 per hundred pounds, while from central Canada to Calgary or Edmonton it is $1.98. For iron or steel "bars, not bent, drilled or fabricated; square, round or otherwise shaped in the drawing or rolling process", it is $1.61 per hundredweight to Vancouver, $2.46 to Calgary or Edmonton.

In practising long- and short-haul discrimination, the railways are not suffering from a lapse of logic. They are, rather, answering the dictates of a higher logic, the logic of what they can get away with. The historical reason for the discrimination is that the railways felt the need to reduce freight charges between central Canada and British Columbia to meet water competition from the Panama Canal route, while between central Canada and the Prairies there was no such competition and hence no need to reduce rates. Prime Minister Mackenzie King once said in reference to the Crow's Nest Pass agreement that "the East is protected by waterways, the Pacific by the Panama Canal, and the West by Parliament." But one need not look beyond its continuing tolerance of long- and short-haul discrimination to see why Parliament has rarely been taken seriously as a protector of the West.

The Harries study found other ways in which the freight-rate structure discriminates against the West. On a per-mile basis, rates between western points are generally higher than between eastern points; examples are legion. The west also suffers from the lack of freight-rate groupings. The whole central Canadian region from Montreal to Windsor is considered one location in determining freight rates to or from the West, but western towns a few miles apart often pay different rates. In Alberta, the same rates apply to Calgary, Edmonton, Lethbridge and Medicine Hat, but Fort Saskatchewan pays more, Red Deer pays still more, and Grande Prairie pays even more than that. The rate per hundred pounds for a minimum of 100,000 pounds of iron or steel is $2.33 from central Canada to Calgary, $2.38 to Fort Saskatchewan, $2.44 to Red Deer and $3.13 to Grande Prairie. Commented the Harries study, "In the absence of large rate-groups it is likely to be futile for either the Federal or Provincial Governments to spend money in attempts to diversify industry to all parts of Alberta. A few extra cents more on a freight rate can nullify a very large capital grant to encourage industry to go to a smaller center."[5]

Solutions to the specific problems are obvious enough. Long- and short-haul discrimination can be outlawed by an Act of Parliament—the Harries study suggested that such a clause be put into the Government's proposed Competition Act. The Canadian Transport Commission can require the railways to institute freight-rate groupings in the West. But the broader problems would remain—the dependence of the West on the railways, the close relationship between the railways and an eastern-dominated economy, the role of agricultural hinterland assigned to the West in that economy—and discrimination, in one form or another, would still be practised. In proposing solutions to those wider problems, the study called to mind the fact that the Calgary Chamber of Commerce is, after all, a chamber of commerce, and that Hu Harries was a Liberal MP. The study proposed that the Canadian Pacific Railway move its head office from Montreal to Calgary (a proposal to warm a chamber of commerce's heart), or alternatively, that the two railways create separate corporate entities under separate management (but not separate ownership) to run their operations west of Thunder Bay.

In discussing the idea of moving the CPR head office to Calgary the study said, "It is mere tautology to say that personal relationships are important in business and it is important to realize the extent to which on-the-spot decisions with a full knowledge of all local factors can pave the way to effective economic action. The railways of Canada are very large corporations and in spite of the best efforts to regionalize decision-making, it is still important to recognize the existence and location of the head office. For three-quarters of a century railway decision making has been two thousand miles from the center of western traffic.

"There is now no reason why the head office of one of the railways should not be in the west. The logical choice is Canadian Pacific. The relocation of the head office of Canadian Pacific to Calgary would do much to provoke reasonable freight rates for the west."[6]

In other words, if only Canadian Pacific understood our problems better and were more familiar with our needs, then all would be well. But Canadian Pacific has, on the whole, understood western needs only too well over the years. It is simply not in its economic interest to meet those needs. The federal government understands western needs too: it has on occasion introduced measures that defended western interests against the interests of Canadian Pacific. And the government has usually found it necessary to reverse its own course fairly soon afterwards.

The Turgeon Royal Commission, which reported in 1951, was unique among the astonishingly large number of commissions that have studied the railway situation in Canada. It alone examined the problem from the point of view of the people who depend upon the railways rather than from the point of view of the railways' balance sheets. Its findings, and their subsequent implementation in legislation, were regarded as "a great victory for the west,"[7] in the words of the Harries study. The contrast with the MacPherson report of ten years later is striking; in fact, the MacPherson recommendations represented a dismantling of the structure that had been put into effect as a result of the Turgeon report.

The Turgeon Commission proposed a series of measures designed to promote equal freight-rates for equivalent services anywhere in the country. Although its recommendation stopped short of outright prohibition of long- and short-haul discrimination, the Commission did conclude that this practice should be restricted, saying that rates to intermediate points should be limited to a maximum of one-third more than the long-haul rates. It recommended that the lonely stretch of track between Sudbury and the Lakehead be regarded as a bridge between eastern and western Canada, and that the federal government pay for the maintenance of that bridge. In effect, that meant a subsidy to Canadian Pacific—the idea that Canadian Pacific, rather than western shippers *or* the federal government, should be required to pay for the maintenance of the bridge was beyond the Turgeon Commission—but at least it was a subsidy designed to lower east-west freight rates and not to maintain the CPR's financial position.

The bridge subsidy, the one-and-one-third rule to combat long- and short-haul discrimination, and other measures were implemented. The railways quickly found their way around the one-and-one-third rule, using the mechanism of agreed charges, effectively a private contract between the railways and shippers. The province of Alberta obtained a hearing on this matter, with W.F.A. Turgeon himself as commissioner, but Turgeon found the railways to be within their rights in circumventing the rule. Meanwhile, the railways were applying pressure, in the form of constant increases in freight rates, for federal action that corresponded to what *they* wanted. The Diefenbaker government finally appointed another Royal Commission, and the MacPherson report and the National Transportation Act were the result. Since the passage of the Act, freight rates have been a hotter issue in western Canada then ever.

When ideas with western origins *have* become established parts of federal policy, these have generally been in the area of "western development," a distinction drawn by economist Vernon Fowke. In these areas, Fowke said, western advice "was most unlikely to favour the retardation of that development," and hence it "was often quite acceptable to eastern policy-makers."[8] Sometimes, in such cases, western interests and the interests of the CPR were more or less in harmony. Land policy is an example often cited by the CPR. Except in the very early days of the railway, when it sold some of its land grant for quick cash and gave some more of it back to the federal government as part of the cancellation of its debts, the CPR has looked to the long term rather than the short term to realize indirect profits from its lands. Once the initial financial crisis had passed, it could well afford to dispose of its land at relatively liberal terms to encourage settlement—since settlement meant traffic—and even to undertake an irrigation project in the dry belt of southeastern Alberta. The point the CPR is trying to make is that its rule of the West has been in the West's interests.

There is, however, another whole area of policy, the area that Fowke called "the question of national integration." Western advice in this area "was seldom found acceptable because it was most likely to be opposed to integration on eastern terms."[9] Western conflict with the CPR on this question is as old as the CPR itself. Before the Canadian Pacific Railway Act of 1881 had even been passed, the province of Manitoba objected strongly to article 15 in the proposed contract between the CPR and the federal government, which read: "For twenty years from the date hereof, no line of railway shall be authorized by the Dominion Parliament to be constructed South of the Canadian Pacific Railway, from any point at or near the Canadian Pacific Railway, except such line as shall run South West or to the Westward of South West; nor to within fifteen miles of Latitude 49."[10] This was the monopoly clause.

Macdonald answered Manitoba's complaints by saying that the purpose of the clause was to prevent American railroads from entering the North West Territories west of the Manitoba border, and nothing prevented Manitoba from issuing its own railway charters. Manitoba accordingly issued three of them. The CPR protested that this violated the contract, and the federal government promptly disallowed the charters. A battle was begun that would last until 1888. Railway charters kept being disallowed in Ottawa as fast as they could be issued in Winnipeg. When one Manitoba road, the Red River Valley Railway, threatened to cross a branch of the CPR, a footnote to Canadian military history was enacted. An army of 250 men was rounded up at Van Horne's orders and took positions behind an old locomotive. They were confronted by 300 volunteers from Winnipeg. As G.P. de T. Glazebrook described it, "Reinforcements were brought by both sides, and it was only a growing sense of reasonableness in both groups of partisans that prevented a fight."[11]

For the federal government, the situation was becoming untenable. The CPR was insistent that its monopoly be maintained. It was good for the CPR, it was good for the country, and a piddly little province like Manitoba couldn't be allowed to stand in the way. For a long time, the federal government accepted that position, but Manitoba's pressure was too insistent to ignore. On April 18, 1888, the Government bought its way out of the monopoly clause; the clause was cancelled and the Government agreed to guarantee the interest on a new $15 million CPR bond issue. But while Manitoba finally achieved victory in its struggle against railway monopoly, it was less successful in combating the corollary of monopoly, which is high freight rates. The original rates charged by the CPR were the same as those charged by the Government on the sections of road it had completed and operated, a straight mileage rate comparable to that prevailing in the East, with lower rates for many commodities. Then in 1883, with government approval, the railway announced a substantial hike in its western rates. The new rates were the cause of much discontent in the West, and neither the cancellation of the monopoly clause nor an investigation by a railway rates commission in 1895 offered much satisfaction. Not until the turn of the century, with the reduction of some rates by the Crow's Nest Pass agreement and the appointment of a regulatory body, the Board of Railway Commissioners, did the federal government offer any recognition that western freight rates were a problem.

The election of the new Liberal government in 1896 marked a ratification rather than a reversal of the national policy of protectionism and close co-operation with the CPR begun by John A. Macdonald in 1878. In 1905, Prime Minister Laurier told the Canadian Manufacturers' Association that the settlers then pouring into the Prairies "will require clothes, they will require furniture, they will require implements, they will require shoes—and I hope you can furnish them to them in Quebec—they will require everything that man has to be supplied with. It is your ambition, it is my ambition also, that this scientific tariff of ours will make it possible that every shoe that has to be worn in those Prairies shall be a Canadian shoe; that every yard of cloth that can be marketed there shall be a yard of cloth produced in Canada; and so on and so on . . . ."[12] If this meant business opportunities for the eastern manufacturer, it also meant higher prices for the western farmer. The two key elements of the national policy, the tariff and the railway, were becoming serious points of contention between East and West.

By this time, the foundations had been laid for probably the most significant political protest movement that has ever emerged in Canada.

As the population of the West grew after 1900, the protest movement grew with it. Under the banner of the United Farmers of Alberta, it captured the provincial government of that province in 1921. In the same year, another manifestation of it, the Progressive party, elected sixty-four members to the federal House of Commons, thirty-seven of them from the Prairies. In the 1930s it gave birth to the Co-operative Commonwealth Federation (CCF), and in the 1960s it was one of the elements making up the New Democratic Party. An aberration of it led to Social Credit.

The movement was not unique to Canada: the political culture that produced Tommy Douglas in Saskatchewan was the same one that produced George McGovern in South Dakota; moreover, the farmers drew much of their intellectual leadership from British thinkers. But the social condition out of which the movement developed was particularly acute in western Canada; the phrase "next year country" aptly expressed the mixture of disillusionment and hope that the prairie farmer felt. The Canadian plains seemed the last frontier in the civilized world, and if a person who wanted to work hard and improve himself couldn't carve out a good life there, then where could he go?

Parliamentary strength was only one expression of the agrarian protest movement; on the economic level it resulted in institutions such as wheat pools and consumer co-operatives. In the early years of the century, it also established an extraordinary monthly—and later weekly—magazine, the *Grain Growers' Guide*.[13] From the time its first issue appeared in 1908 until the mid-1920s, the *Guide* spoke with a clear and steady voice in favour of political power for farmers, public ownership, citizens' participation in government, co-operatives, women's rights, and the agrarian way of life; and against the protective tariff, eastern monopolies, the grain elevator companies (except the Grain Growers' Grain Company, owned by the farmers, with which it was associated), the two old parties (particularly the Conservatives), booze, and the railways—with special attention reserved for the largest and most powerful of them, the Canadian Pacific.

The *Grain Growers' Guide* discussed railway issues for the first time in its second issue, in September 1908, with an article—the first of many—advocating public ownership of all railways. The *Guide* believed in public ownership in principle, but it also had specific grievances against the railways. One, of course, was high freight rates. "And This a Civilized Country!" the *Guide* headlined one article in 1911 that attacked the CPR's policy of rate discrimination against western Canada. The article compared CPR rates on lumber for equivalent mileages in the East and in the West. Between Chapleau, Ontario, and Ste. Anne's, Quebec, a distance of 592 miles, the rate was 15 cents per hundred pounds; between Kenora, in northwestern Ontario, and Sutherland, Saskatchewan, a distance of 600 miles, the rate was 28 cents per hundred pounds. "Most of us have thought," said the *Guide*, "that the action of the lumber combine had put the price of lumber high enough but when the railways add another tribute like this it is easy to see where the consumer gets the heavy end of the load."[14]

Whenever freight rates were increased, a *Grain Growers' Guide* editorial was not long behind. In 1920 it directed its comments at a statement by J.D. Reid, minister of railways, in defence of a recent rate increase:

> Mr. Reid was very solicitous for the welfare of the CPR. He drew a dismal picture of this vast corporation failing to pay its usual dividends, discontinuing its glowing advertisements of Canada in foreign countries, and finally, coming to the Dominion government, cap in hand, begging to be saved from the hands of the official receiver. Mr. Reid laid it on with a trowel; no one would ever imagine from his remarks that the system he was eulogising had reserves of approximately $317,000,000, of which $116,000,000 had accumulated since 1910 . . . .
>
> The increase granted should allow the CPR to realize a surplus of something over $10,000,000 in 1921. It is quite true that nobody wants to see the CPR "go broke," but there is a vast difference between giving it a chance to meet all its expenses and pay its "usual dividends" and helping it to add a few millions to its already swollen reserves. If the country practically guarantees the dividends of the company, why should it be allowed to accumulate a surplus?[15]

Another continuing theme of the *Guide* was the shortage of boxcars for grain, which reached critical proportions in the season of 1911-12 and was the cause of disastrous financial losses to the farmers. The *Guide* saw the railways as being in cahoots with the grain-elevator interests; when a farmer could not find a car to load himself, he was forced to sell to the line elevator companies, which "were taking advantage of the farmers in three ways—in grading, in dockage and in price, and in some cases in weights—the elevators as a result making from ten to twenty-five cents over and above their usual profits."[16] Whether or not there was in fact a conspiracy, the farmers were unshakably convinced of it, and letters complaining of the car shortage poured into the *Guide* office from all over the Prairies.

The *Guide* also attacked the local tax exemptions received by the CPR, a loss of revenue which, the magazine charged, resulted in hardships and lack of services in many western localities. In 1915, it reported on a convention in Edmonton of the United Farmers of Alberta where "a resolution in favor of asking the Dominion Government to pay the municipal and school taxes of C.P.R. lands in order to allow schools to be maintained and public improvements to be made was brought... by H. Sorensen, of Strathmore. Mr. Sorensen said that in 1913, out of five schools he knew in the irrigation district, four were closed and the children went uneducated because of the C.P.R. exemption. When the Dominion government, in order to secure a transcontinental railway, gave a land grant and tax exemption it was not just to make that a burden upon the school districts and municipalities in the West. For one year the C.P.R. made a loan, but they would not continue it. A delegate outside the irrigation area said the odd sections in his district were owned by the C.P.R., and thru not being able to collect taxes on those lands, the school could only be open for four months instead of eight or nine. The resolution was carried unanimously."[17]

The solution the *Grain Growers' Guide* proposed for all these evils was nationalization. It was particularly tenacious in pressing the issue when nationalization of the Grand Trunk Pacific and the Canadian Northern was under consideration in 1918. "The nationalization of the C.P.R., which is the largest part of the whole problem, remains to be tackled," it said on December 4, 1918. Earlier it had commented: "It was said years ago at Ottawa that the C.P.R. was 'the government of Canada on wheels.' Under any possible method of dealing with Canada's railway problem which falls short of nationalization of the C.P.R. in addition to all the other railway systems, the C.P.R. is likely to become, proportionately at least, an even more powerful influence than in the past. The only way to solve the problem and prevent the possibility of 'a government of Canada on wheels' is for the people of Canada to nationalize the wheels." The *Guide* was so committed to public ownership that in 1921 it took seriously Lord Shaughnessy's proposal for nationalization under CPR management with a guaranteed CPR dividend, although it conceded that the plan had "obvious weaknesses."[18]

Some of the specific ills the *Guide* exposed were corrected, but the basic pattern remains, and the gutsy periodical's approach would find a ready audience in the West today. Its fate, like that of the larger movement it represented, was not altogether a happy one. The *Grain Growers' Guide* changed its name to the *Country Guide* in the late 1920s and as such it still exists, minus the political content. The Progressive party, which offered so much hope in 1921, was largely absorbed into the Liberals by 1926. The path that parts of the western movement took is perhaps best illustrated by the career of Charles Dunning. Born in England in 1885, Dunning came to Canada in 1903 and settled on the prairies, starting as a farm hand. As a farmer, he became active in the grain growers' movement: he was vice-president of the Saskatchewan Grain Growers from 1911 to 1914, and organized the Saskatchewan Co-operative Elevator Company, of which he was general manager until 1916. In that year, he ran successfully for the Saskatchewan legislature as a Liberal and was appointed to the cabinet; from 1922 to 1926, when he resigned to run for the federal House of Commons, he was premier of Saskatchewan. Under Prime Minister Mackenzie King, he held a number of federal cabinet posts, including the ministry of finance, until 1939 when he took up his third career, business, at which he was as successful as he had been at the first two. In the early forties he lent his name to a vicious campaign being carried on by a group of powerful businessmen to combat the rising CCF, the spiritual heir of the movement Dunning had been part of thirty years earlier. By the time he died in 1958 he was chairman of Ogilvie Flour Mills and a director of a whole maze of corporations, including the Bank of Montreal, Bell Telephone, the Steel Company of Canada, and the CPR.

Dunning was unique only in the prominence he achieved in his later life. But even if some of the people and institutions the western protest movement spawned did not live up to their early promise, the impetus of the movement itself was never lost. The growth of the Saskatoon-based National Farmers' Union in the sixties and seventies is a sign of its continuing vitality. On another level, so is the election of New Democratic Party governments in Manitoba in 1969 and in Saskatchewan in 1971. "The acquisitiveness of eastern Canada," wrote Harold Innis in his history of the CPR in 1923, "shows little sign of abatement."[19] Fifty years later, it still shows little sign of abatement, and as long as inequity persists, so will the regional consciousness and sense of grievance of the Prairies.

The fourth western province, British Columbia, is a different matter entirely: different historically, different geographically, different in its relation to the CPR. Born out of a gold rush, and nurtured by vast mineral and forest resources, British Columbia has always managed to maintain an aura of wealth. Farming has always been of relatively small importance in this most mountainous of Canadian provinces. Freight rates have never been a particularly contentious issue; B.C. is on the long end of long- and short-haul discrimination. In 1880 Charles Horetzky wrote, not without some evidence on his side, that the CPR represented the sacrifice of the Prairies to appease the Pacific province.[20] Yet no province has been more heavily under the influence of the CPR, or more thoroughly despoiled by it, than British Columbia.

The city of Vancouver, B.C.'s metropolis and the third largest city in Canada, is entirely a CPR creation, down to its name. There is a plaque at the corner of Hastings and Hamilton Streets in downtown

Vancouver that reads:

> HERE STOOD
> HAMILTON
> FIRST LAND COMMISSIONER
> CANADIAN PACIFIC RAILWAY
> 1885
> IN THE SILENT SOLITUDE
> OF THE PRIMEVAL FOREST
> HE DROVE A WOODEN STAKE
> IN THE EARTH AND COMMENCED
> TO MEASURE AN EMPTY LAND
> INTO THE STREETS OF
> VANCOUVER

There was a good reason why that job should have been done by the land commissioner of the CPR. The CPR owned the city of Vancouver, or at least most of what would become Vancouver. The land at the western end of Burrard Inlet had been held by the federal government just in case it needed it as a railway land grant, but when the terminus of the CPR had been established at Port Moody, at the eastern tip of the inlet, it had reverted to the government of British Columbia. Then, as construction proceeded, the CPR decided Port Moody wouldn't do as a terminus after all. At the request of the CPR, the obliging provincial government of William Smithe offered 6,000 acres of the land it had just received back from Ottawa to the company as an inducement to do what it would have done anyway—extend its line fourteen miles west to Coal Harbour and English Bay.

"The construction of the necessary docks, etc.," the CPR's Van Horne wrote to a federal Cabinet minister, "will involve a very large expenditure, and to provide for this the Government of British Columbia proposes to convey to the Company the tracts of land."[21] The docks were a good selling point. The federal government had already begun to build docks at Port Moody, which were to be turned over to the CPR upon completion. Since these docks would now be of very limited usefulness to the railway, the company proposed that the Government curtail its own construction and turn over the money it otherwise would have spent, directly to the CPR, to build the docks at Vancouver.

Van Horne was fully aware of the value of the land the company was getting. "I am told that a strong pressure is being brought to bear," he wrote to Premier Smithe in 1884, "to secure the extension of the timber limits on the Government property in the vicinity of Coal Harbour and English Bay for a long term of years, and I am

TOP: During construction, the CPR was always "shoving things", and labour was strained to the breaking point. Here, laying track on the lower Fraser Valley, 1881 (CPR photo, Archives of Saskatchewan). BOTTOM: Chinese construction camp (Public Archives of Canada).

TOP: Construction at the Chaudière (Public Archives of Canada).
BOTTOM: Memorial to men who died building the CPR (Provincial
Archives Victoria, B.C.).

TOP: After the official last spike ceremony, workmen drove in their own last spike (Archives of Saskatchewan). BOTTOM: Construction of the Crow's Nest Pass line, built by the CPR in the 1890s with a new government grant (Public Archives of Canada).

TOP: Railway through Centre Town, construction of Crow's Nest Pass line (Public Archives of Canada). BOTTOM: A North West Mounted Police constable guards CPR construction. This photograph was specially posed and may have been taken as late as 1930 (CPR photo, Archives of Saskatchewan).

TOP: Trestle construction, British Columbia (Public Archives of Canada). BOTTOM: First through transcontinental train at Port Moody, B.C., July 4, 1886 (CPR photo, Archives of Saskatchewan).

TOP: First through train on the Esquimalt and Nanaimo Railway at Victoria, B.C., 1888. When the CPR bought the E&N in 1905, it also got almost a quarter of Vancouver Island (Provincial Archives, Victora, B.C.). RIGHT: First through train at Vancouver, 1887 (Public Archives of Canada).

TOP: Prairie towns grew up where the CPR placed its stations. Here, the station at Carnduff, Sask. (Archives of Saskatchewan). RIGHT: CPR engine, 1905, with Engineer Fred Rowe standing (Public Archives of Canada).

TOP LEFT: Even the biggest cities in the West were largely CPR creations. Here, the freight yards at Winnipeg (Archives of Saskatchewan). BOTTOM LEFT: Train wreck at Saddle Rock, near Yale, B.C., 1909 (Provincial Archives, Victoria, B.C.). TOP RIGHT: For twenty years, the *Grain Growers' Guide* was the CPR's most vigorous critic. Here, cartoon, May 9, 1917 (Manitoba Archives). BOTTOM RIGHT: *Grain Growers' Guide*, August 10, 1910 (Manitoba Archives).

A POOR BUSINESS PROPOSITION

Royal Commission: —"Now, John, I'd like to see you buy these two small pigs. True, they're poor and mean and scrawny and the price is high and you'll lose money on them, but you ought to buy them."
John Canada: "Not much. I'll take all three or none."

HOW THE COUNTRY IS GOVERNED
The Real Rulers Send their Messengers to Meet the People

The Mercy of His Friends
TOP: *Grain Growers' Guide*, September 22, 1920 (Manitoba Archives). BOTTOM: *Grain Growers' Guide*, December 28, 1921 (Manitoba Archives).

TOP: Passenger service was once a matter of corporate pride if not profits. Here, an early CPR passenger coach (Provincial Archives, Victoria, B.C.). BOTTOM: The *Imperial Limited*, early transcontinental train (Public Archives of Canada).

TOP LEFT: CPR sleeping car, 1928 (Public Archives of Canada).
BOTTOM LEFT: CPR dome lounge sleeping car, 1954 (CPR photo,
Archives of Saskatchewan). TOP RIGHT: The *Dominion*, one of two
CPR transcontinental trains until the railway discontinued it in 1966
(CPR photo). BOTTOM RIGHT: The *Canadian*, the last remaining
CPR transcontinental train, about to leave Windsor Station in Montreal
(CPR photo).

TOP: The *Canadian* near Exshaw, Alta. (CPR photo). BOTTOM: The CPR's new look: a sulphur train near Lake Louise. At the back, the Alberta Superintendent's car and the President's car (CPR photo).

TOP: CPR freight train on the Prairies (CPR photo). BOTTOM: CPR unit train unloading coal onto a ship which will carry it to Japanese steel mills, Roberts Bank, B.C. (CPR photo).

With government help, CP Air has grown rapidly since the 1940s. TOP: Lockheed Lodestar, 1940s. MIDDLE: Britannia, 1950s. BOTTOM: DC-8, 1970s (CPR photos).

TOP: The smelter at Trail, B.C., became the heart of the CPR's mining empire, Cominco. Here, as it appeared under the ownership of F. Augustus Heinze, before 1897 (Provincial Archives, Victoria, B.C.). BOTTOM: After its purchase by the CPR, 1900 (Provincial Archives, Victoria, B.C.).

TOP: "Sim", mess and house cook, Trail smelter staff house, 1905 (Provincial Archives, Victoria, B.C.). BOTTOM: The smelter in 1929 (Provincial Archives, Victoria, B.C.).

TOP: The smelter with surrounding town, 1936 (Provincial Archives, Victoria, B.C.). BOTTOM: In the Sullivan Mine at Kimberley, B.C., the CPR found one of the world's richest lead-zinc orebodies. Here, surface buildings at the mine, 1938 (Provincial Archives, Victoria, B.C.).

TOP LEFT: No. 17 Conveyor and No. 1 Primary Ball Mill, Kimberley, 1923 (Provincial Archives, Victoria, B.C.). BOTTOM LEFT: Boring down in the Sullivan Mine, 1944 (Provincial Archives, Victoria, B.C.). TOP RIGHT: The CPR, through Marathon Realty, owns some of the most valuable urban land in Canada. Here, downtown Calgary showing Marathon's Palliser Square and Husky Tower (CPR photo). BOTTOM RIGHT: Containerization has increased efficiency and eliminated jobs in intermodal freight transport. Here, the Brunterm container terminal, Saint John, N.B., in which the CPR has a major interest (CPR photo).

TOP: Canadian Pacific (Bermuda) Ltd. is incorporated in Bermuda, builds ships in Japan, and mans them with British officers and Spanish or Hong Kong Chinese crews. Here, the T. Akasaka, launched at Yokohama in 1970 (CPR photo). TOP RIGHT: The CPR entered the trucking business on a large scale in the 1950s. Here, a CP Transport truck in the Regina railway yards, 1954 (CPR photo, Archives of Saskatchewan). BOTTOM RIGHT: The CPR controls 18 per cent of Panarctic Oils, a joint public-private consortium exploring for oil in the Canadian North (CPR photo).

TOP: Shopping centres are a major Marathon Realty activity. Here, the shopping centre at Yorkton, Sask. (CPR photo). BOTTOM: The older Canadian Pacific hotels are among the most imposing buildings in the country. Here, the Château Frontenac in Quebec City (CPR photo).

TOP: Dinner setting in the ballroom, Empress Hotel, Victoria, B.C. (CPR photo). BOTTOM: CP Hotels has now gone multinational. Here, the Château Royal, Mexico City (CPR photo).

TOP: The CPR was one of the first large corporations in Canada to introduce computers. Here, the computer centre at Windsor Station, Montreal (CPR photo). BOTTOM: Passenger liners, like passenger trains, have lost out because they don't make money. Here, the Empress of Canada, last of Canadian Pacific's passenger liners, which made its final voyage in 1971 (CPR photo).

George Stephen, first CPR president, friend of Sir John A. Macdonald, and financial brains behind the railway (CPR photo).

BOTTOM: Mrs. Stephen's drawing room, Montreal, 1884 (Notman Archives, McCord Museum). TOP RIGHT: William Van Horne, the gruff, union-busting general manager of the construction period and second president of the CPR (CPR photo). BOTTOM RIGHT: Lord Shaughnessy, third CPR president, who pressed for amalgamation of all Canadian railways under CPR control (CPR photo).

TOP: Buck Crump, who as CPR president and chairman turned the company from a railway into a conglomerate (CPR photo). MIDDLE: Cominco officials with friend—B.C. Premier W.A.C. Bennett (right)—Trail, 1957 (Provincial Archives, Victoria, B.C.). BOTTOM: Ian Sinclair, current CPR chairman (Canadian Newspaper Service).

also led to believe that it is the object of the parties in securing such an extension, to acquire rights that will have to be bought out; and I trust that this may be guarded against. In view of the probable rapid growth of the town when finally located and put upon the market and the certainty that manufacturing concerns of more or less importance will spring up all about it, and of the importance of being able to secure the location of such concerns where they will contribute best to the growth of the town, although they may not be directly upon the town site, it is very important that as much as possible of the property be immediately available for sale or lease.''[22]

While its Vancouver lands were probably the most valuable single piece of real estate the railway acquired in British Columbia, other choice properties all over the province were also obtained, as the generosity of the federal government was matched by that of successive governments of British Columbia. Between 1871, the year of B.C.'s entry into Confederation, and 1913, the province gave out 22 million acres of land to assorted railway companies. Much of this eventually came into the hands of the CPR, which zealously bought up smaller lines and acquired charters that had never been acted upon. Federal money and provincial land combined to sweeten the Crow's Nest Pass deal, through which the CPR also obtained the smelter at Trail and the beginnings of its mineral empire. By 1970, it was estimated that Canadian Pacific owned or controlled at least a billion dollars in assets in British Columbia, making it by far the largest corporation in the province. The number-two company, MacMillan Bloedel, had a mere $750 million in assets—and MacMillan Bloedel was slowly but steadily being bought up by Canadian Pacific.

The CPR's interest in MacMillan Bloedel, Canada's largest forest-products firm, dates back only to 1963, but the foundations for it were laid long before then. In 1905 Canadian Pacific bought the Esquimalt and Nanaimo Railway from the Dunsmuir coal interests; James Dunsmuir, lieutenant-governor and former premier of British Columbia, was accordingly made a director of the CPR in 1908. At that point the E&N was a 77-mile-long road running from Victoria to Wellington on Vancouver Island; the CPR gradually extended it to other locations on the island. Along with the E&N railway came 1.9 million acres of timber-and-coal-rich land, only slightly less than one-quarter of the whole area of the island, which had been given to James Dunsmuir's father, Robert, by Premier William Smithe in 1883 as a grant for building the railway. In proportion to the amount of track, this land grant exceeded even the original CPR bonanza.

On July 7, 1905, the Victoria *Times* reported on a speech to the local board of trade by one J.S. Dennis, land commissioner of the Canadian Pacific Railway. "Mr. Dennis, who was accorded the deepest attention during his remarks," noted the *Times*, "said that in accepting the invitation of the president [of the board of trade], his particular object was to explain the plan the C.P.R. had in view for the development of their interests on Vancouver Island. At the same time he advised that the people should not expect much from the company at once. Although the C.P.R., as all were aware, had recently acquired the E.&N. railroad and the land grant, they did not desire the latter. They already had six million acres in the province, and their experience had been that they paid out more on it than they had received. However, they hoped for a change of conditions in this respect, and no doubt it would come."

It did come. But the CPR held onto the E&N land grant for many years without doing anything with it. Then, in the 1940s, it began to sell the land, piece by piece, to the large paper companies: Crown Zellerbach, B.C. Forest, Rayonier, and the largest of them all, MacMillan Bloedel, which acquired big chunks of the E&N timber land between 1945 and 1955. In the early sixties, the paper companies negotiated to buy what remained of the land grant; the CPR said it would sell, but only for shares of the companies, and no agreement could be reached. Meanwhile, in accordance with a new corporate policy of developing all its assets to the fullest, Canadian Pacific in 1962 activated an already incorporated but dormant subsidiary, Pacific Logging, with the intention of carrying out its own logging operations on the remaining E&N lands.

However, two years later, Canadian Pacific sold 229,000 acres of that land to MacMillan Bloedel and Crown Zellerbach, for an estimated $56 million; $36 million of that, for two-thirds of the timberlands, was estimated to have come from MacMillan Bloedel. The sale was completed on November 26, 1964; on November 30, Canadian Pacific bought 750,000 shares of MacMillan Bloedel, which probably cost it $26 or $27 million, and which when added to the 250,000 shares the CPR had bought during the previous year, gave it a five-percent interest in the company.[23] Canadian Pacific's interest in MacMillan Bloedel has crept steadily upward since then, passing the ten-percent mark in 1968; on March 15, 1973, it stood at 12.33 per cent. Relations between the two companies have been becoming more intimate. J.V. Clyne, chairman of MacMillan Bloedel until his retirement in 1973, has been on the Canadian Pacific board of directors since 1959, but his presence there seems to be the result less of his specific MacMillan Bloedel connections than of the CPR custom of having one Vancouver representative on the board. More significantly, Buck Crump, chairman of Canadian Pacific, was appointed to the MacMillan Bloedel board in 1969, and when Ian Sinclair succeeded Crump at the top CPR position in 1972, he also succeeded him as a director of MacMillan Bloedel.

Just who controls MacMillan Bloedel is not entirely clear; the remaining shares of both the MacMillan and the Bloedel families are relatively small. The only interest with a larger share than Canadian Pacific is an American group known as the Wisconsin Corporation. If Canadian Pacific's share is not now a controlling one, it seems clearly interested in having such a share in the future, and there is no reason to believe it won't be able to attain its ambition. As well, Canadian Pacific had 300,000 acres of E&N land left over after completing the 1964 deal, enough to make a go of Pacific Logging, although the logging subsidiary feels itself something of an orphan. Most of the best timberlands in the E&N tract had been sold by 1962, and a further sale just as Pacific Logging was getting off the ground didn't do much for corporate morale. But in going after MacMillan Bloedel, Canadian Pacific was playing for higher stakes.

Sometimes known as British Columbia's Jolly Green Giant, MacMillan Bloedel holds a special place in the folklore of the province. H.R. MacMillan and later J.V. Clyne became symbols of its business wealth and power. Although the Jolly Giant's interests now extend as far afield as Malaysia and Spain, by far the bulk of its operation is still concentrated in B.C. A recent political history of British Columbia referred to its subject as "The Company Province."[24] If Canadian Pacific acquires control of MacMillan Bloedel, a future historian will be able to call it "The CPR Province" without much fear of contradiction.

5 Head 'em off at the Crow's Nest Pass: A contract and its implications

The Directors feel that they cannot too strongly urge the immediate construction of a line from Lethbridge to a connection with your Columbia & Kootenay Railway at Nelson, a distance of 325 miles, and anticipating your approval they have already taken steps toward commencement of the work on the opening of spring...

The interests of the country at large are so much concerned in this question that your Directors confidently expect reasonable assistance at the hands of the Dominion Government.

CPR Annual Report,
1896

"Sir William Van Horne, the famous Canadian Pacific president," Winnipeg *Free Press* columnist Maurice Western reported from Ottawa in 1959, "has been shabbily treated by the representatives of his own company at the current hearings of the Royal Commission on Transportation. For the sake of a subsidy, Sir William, the far-sighted businessman, the resourceful and imaginative empire-builder, has been thrown to the wolves. What we have in his place is a maker of bad bargains, Sir William the Chump."[1]

The bargain in question was one whose effects are still very visible in many facets of Canadian Pacific's operations: the Crow's Nest Pass deal of 1897. The postwar appearance of the ghost of Sir William the Chump to haunt the halls of Windsor Station did not signal any change in the pros and cons of that deal. What it did signal was a new resolution on the part of Canadian Pacific to alter those parts of the deal that it regarded as burdensome.

The ghost appeared again in *Canadian Pacific: A Brief History*, a company puff-piece written in 1968 by a former Queen's University professor named J. Lorne McDougall. "By the time the rate reductions had come fully into effect in September, 1899," said McDougall of the most controversial part of the agreement, "it was clear that prosperity was returning and the rising prosperity of each succeeding year to 1912-13 proved that, however desirable they may have been, the reductions of rates were not really necessary. Prosperity and a rapidly rising flow of settlers would have come, with or without.

"To state this fact is not to criticize the CPR officers who made the agreement. Their decision was made in the winter of 1896-97 in the light of facts which were known at the time. At that time a forecast of a stationary or declining price level was completely reasonable.

"It was also hopelessly wrong."[2]

Careful study of the myth of Sir William the Chump reveals several assumptions that deserve further examination. One is that the Crow's Nest Pass deal worked out, on the whole, to the disadvantage of the CPR. This assumption arises from Canadian Pacific's practice of looking at the agreement in isolation, without regard to the reasons why the company entered into it in the first place. A second assumption is that the Crow's Nest Pass deal has been the *only* reason why freight rates on grain have, in opposition to all price trends, remained at the level they were at in 1899, and slightly below the level of 1897. But this is contradicted by another CPR contention, which is that the Crow's Nest Pass agreement was abrogated when Parliament made the grain rates statutory in 1925. Even after the agreement was supposedly abrogated, the rates remained the same. The CPR in its time has entered into many agreements with the government of Canada, most of which served their purpose and were then forgotten. Why not this one?

The Crow's Nest Pass agreement between the Canadian Pacific Railway Company and the government of Canada had three main provisions:

- The Company agreed to build a railway line from Lethbridge, in what is now Alberta, to Nelson, B.C., crossing the Rockies through the Crow's Nest Pass.
- The Government agreed to subsidize the line to the extent of $11,000 per mile, which worked out to a total of $3,404,720.
- The Company agreed to reduce freight rates on certain specified commodities between eastern and western Canada, the most important of which were grain and flour eastbound to the Lakehead for export, and farm implements westbound to the Prairies.

The deal contained substantial plums for both parties. For the Government, there were strong nationalistic reasons for wanting the CPR to build the line. Otherwise, it was almost certain that an American rather than a Canadian railway would tap the mineral-rich valleys and mountain ledges in the Kootenay area of southeastern British Columbia. The CPR's chief American rival, the Great Northern, had already built feeder lines into the area, and only the construction of the Crow's Nest Pass line could effectively meet that competition. The Government also obtained freight-rate concessions that would placate the uneasy settlers of western Canada; freight rates had been a hot issue ever since 1883 and the Crow's Nest Pass deal could be expected to cool it down somewhat.

If tapping the Kootenays was a plus for the Government, it was a potential bonanza for the CPR, and Van Horne knew it; the CPR had been interested in the area for years. The cash subsidy, by comparison, was just a sweetener, nice work if you can get it, as it were. There was also a land subsidy coming from the government of British Columbia for building part of the line, and the deal with Ottawa made it possible for the CPR to take advantage of that. The freight-rate reductions, meanwhile, were not so onerous on the CPR that the rates on grain and flour could not be reduced ten per cent *below* the Crow level in 1903, and remain there for fifteen years. This was the deal that earned Sir William Van Horne the status of chump.

The geographical impediments to Canadian nationhood are nowhere more palpable than in southeastern British Columbia. From the Rockies on the east through the Selkirks, the Gold Range, and the Monashees, the mountains of the region are visibly powerful obstacles to east-west communication. The natural lines of communication are along the valleys that separate the mountain ranges from each other. The valleys, like the ranges, run north-south. It was not surprising that the early development of southeastern British Columbia occurred as a by-product of the development of the Pacific Northwest of the United States. As the province of Saskatchewan explained in its brief to the MacPherson Commission, written by Vernon Fowke, "the entire Kootenay-Columbia area is an integral part of the 'Inland Empire,' which is ordinarily and most mistakenly presumed to exist exclusively in the States of the Pacific Northwest with a northern boundary miraculously coincident with the 49th parallel of latitude. Spokane is the natural distributing point of the Inland Empire, to the north as well as to the south of the international boundary."[3]

From the beginning, the chief reason for interest in southeastern British Columbia was minerals. Gold was discovered there in 1885, and there was extensive gold mining by prospectors working from American territory in the 1860s. More significant mineral discoveries were made in the 1880s, and these finds led to the production of silver, copper, lead and zinc. Meanwhile, the first transcontinental railways had been pushed through to the Pacific: the Canadian Pacific ran to the north of the mineral area, and the Great Northern and Northern Pacific ran to the south. Of these, the Great Northern passed closest to the Kootenay region and had the greatest immediate potential for tapping it. A Great Northern feeder-line reached Nelson in 1895.

Two events marked the beginning of the Crow's Nest Pass railway project. In 1888, the British Columbia legislature, then in the midst of its railway spree, chartered the Crow's Nest and Kootenay Lake Railway Company, later renamed the British Columbia Southern. This charter was for a line from the provincial boundary in the Crow's Nest Pass to the Kootenays, and carried with it a land grant of 20,000 acres per mile, plus an additional six square miles of coal lands near the Pass. In the mid-1890s, it had still not been acted upon. The second event was the lease by Canadian Pacific in 1892 of the Alberta Railway and Coal Company line that ran from Dunmore, on the CPR main line near Medicine Hat, to Lethbridge. Canadian Pacific was only mildly interested in getting to Lethbridge, but as its 1892 annual report explained, "this line will be necessary to your Company in the event of the construction of a line through Crow's Nest Pass."[4]

The company also took other measures to penetrate the Kootenays. In 1889 it acquired control of the charter of the Columbia and Kootenay Railway Company, allowing it to build a rail line linking the navigable waters of the Columbia River with the navigable waters of Kootenay Lake. As a result of this, it was able to establish a rail-and-water connection between the Canadian Pacific main line and the Kootenay region. But this form of transportation was, at best, awkward; if the CPR was to attain a position of dominance in the Kootenays, it would have to build the Crow's Nest Pass line. The discovery of coal in the Pass only enhanced its interest in the idea.

By the mid-1890s the railway was dickering with the federal government to see if it could get any help for the line. In its dying days, the Conservative government of Charles Tupper came up with an offer: for each mile of road, there would be an outright subsidy of $5,000., plus a loan of $20,000 to be repaid at 3.5 per cent. Tupper was defeated in the general election of 1896, but the new Liberal government of Wilfrid Laurier proved just as receptive to the suggestion of a subsidy. Even though it contained the provision for a freight-rate reduction, the Liberal offer of an outright grant of $11,000 per mile was deemed the more generous of the two offers to the CPR by Government and Opposition alike. It was this offer that became the Crow's Nest Pass agreement of 1897.

One interesting aspect of the Government's defence of its offer was its refusal to be impressed by the statements of Canadian Pacific officials that the company would build the line anyway even if there were no subsidy. "I know," said Railways Minister A.G. Blair in the House of Commons, "that in the report of a meeting of the shareholders of the CPR . . . the statement appeared that if the Government did not assist the Canadian Pacific Railway they would take hold of the work themselves without assistance. But I believe that that statement was not so much the declaration of a fact within the knowledge of the company itself as a statement put forward perhaps for the purpose of creating an impression for other ends, it may be upon public opinion or the Government of the country, and not that the company was in a position to take up the very large outlay involved by the construction of the line; because I believe that neither the Canadian Pacific Railway nor any other company at this time is so well situated that it would be able, without our aid, to construct the work."[5] At any rate, the Government subsidized the line to the extent of almost 35 per cent of the construction costs.

As a result of the Crow's Nest Pass line, the CPR was eventually able to secure total economic dominance of southeastern B.C. "I grew up," said one native of the region, "thinking that the CPR was the only outfit in the world." The Crow's Nest Pass line provided the railway with an alternative route through the Rockies; CPR bought up other charters and lines in the area until that route stretched as far as the Cascade mountains, only a hundred miles or so from the Pacific. The first of these charters was the B.C. Southern, the terms of which the CPR fulfilled by building the Crow's Nest Pass line. The B.C. Southern charter brought with it a land grant of 3.75 million acres, which the railway eventually disposed of at a net profit of $1.8 million, according to its own records. Another of its purchases was the total assets of an entrepreneur named F. Augustus Heinze; these included a smelter at Trail, B.C., a narrow-gauge railway from Trail to the mines at Rossland, and a standard-gauge railway from Trail to Robson with a charter to build as far west as Penticton. In a third deal that worked out profitably for the CPR, in 1897 the railway pledged to the Crow's Nest Pass Coal Company that it would not itself mine coal in the area for ten years (it had received six square miles of coal lands as part of the B.C. Southern grant). In return, the CPR was promised a substantial traffic in coal and coke over the Crow's Nest Pass line. By 1901, the line was carrying 112,000 tons of coal and 199,000 tons of coke a year.

Of these agreements, the most important in the long term was the one with Heinze. The smelter that it received as part of that deal was the same one that formed the nucleus of Cominco, the CPR's worldwide mining empire. The CPR's protestations of hardship suffered as a result of the freight-rate provisions of the Crow's Nest Pass agreement lose much credibility in light of the circumstance that its lucrative mining interests came about as a by-product of that very agreement. The company, therefore, tries to minimize the connection between Cominco and the Crow's Nest Pass line, even to the extent of maintaining that there were two separate deals with Heinze, one for the railway and one for the smelter. However, its own annual report for 1898 indicated otherwise. "Arrangements have been completed, subject to the approval of the Dominion Parliament," it said, "whereby your company may acquire the Columbia and Western railway extending from Robson to Rossland (33 miles) for the sum of $800,000. With this property will be acquired the smelting works at Trail creek and about 270,000 acres of land in the vicinity, these being included in the purchase price named."[6]

It would be foolhardy to maintain that the CPR would never have entered the mining business if it had not been for the Crow's Nest Pass line and the Heinze deal. There are many activities, such as shipping, trucking and pulp and paper, that the CPR entered simply on the decision of its board of directors. But in the case of mining, its entry was handed to it on a silver, or rather a copper, platter. It was primarily copper that the Trail smelter was originally equipped to produce, although not long after acquiring it, Canadian Pacific added a lead furnace, the first of many expansions. A smelter standing alone, depending upon outside sources for ore, did not make particularly good business sense, and so Canadian Pacific began to buy up mines in the area. The final result was something it had perhaps never contemplated: not only was the CPR the chief carrier of the mineral output of the Kootenay region, but it was also one of the major producers of that output.

During the First World War there was for the first time a strong demand for zinc, which is always found along with lead; so, Cominco branched into that. In its search for mines to keep the Trail smelter going, Cominco happened upon the Sullivan mine at Kimberley, which turned out to be one of the world's great lead-zinc properties. The Sullivan mine would be the largest supplier of ore to the smelter until the mid-1960s, and still accounts for a substantial proportion of the company's production. By the early 1920s, Cominco was well on its way. It was itself becoming a highly diversified company. Since it was by far the largest customer of the West Kootenay Power and Light Company, it decided that it might just as well acquire the company as a subsidiary, which it did. Another diversification came about because, with Cominco's expansion, increasing quantities of sulphur were going up the smokestack at Trail and wafting over into neighbouring Washington state. In the mid-1920s, the complaints from south of the border became too insistent for Cominco to ignore; so, it began to recover the sulphur instead and went into the fertilizer business. In 1972, the fertilizer and chemical business provided Cominco with $86 million of its $374 million of revenue.

A map in Cominco's 1972 annual report showed dots, picks and crosses indicating the company's presence in more than fifty locations all over the world, including such unlikely places as Spain, Singapore and Brazil. "A lot of that is boasting," said longtime Cominco executive Howard Bayley,[7] but even accounting for some exaggeration Cominco is still the most geographically diversified firm in the Canadian Pacific firmament. Mining companies tend to be that way: they will go wherever the ore is and the politics are suitable—there being no point in going to all the trouble of developing a mine only to have it taken over by a government in an expropriative mood. Outside of Canada and the United States (where it has mines in Missouri and Montana, a nitrate plant in Nebraska, an electronic materials fabrication plant at Spokane and an ammonia plant in Texas), some of its more notable operations are its lead-zinc mine in northern Spain, another lead-zinc mine in Greenland, and a string of Australian mines controlled through the Aberfoyle group of companies. Major exploration efforts are underway in those countries as well as Mexico and South Africa.

When Canadian Pacific estimated for the MacPherson Commission the revenue it had received from Cominco since the latter was formed as a company in 1906, the total came to almost $250 million; since then, it has gone up to well over $300 million. Cominco's profitability is erratic, since despite its diversification it is still heavily dependent on lead-zinc production; if the market for lead-zinc is good, then Cominco has a good year, while if it is poor, as it was in 1971 and 1972, then Cominco has a poor year, making a net profit in the neighbourhood of only fifteen or twenty million dollars.

Brokerage-house reports on Canadian Pacific will often tout CP

Ltd.'s controlling interest in Cominco as one of the main reasons for the attractiveness of the company as an investment; it is much more important in this regard than the railway. Intended or not, it was by far the most spectacular result of the company's entry into the Kootenay region. But it is not the result most often discussed by either Canadian Pacific or its opponents. The very words "Crow's Nest Pass" do not evoke the mining company, the railway or even the actual pass itself. They evoke the reduced freight rates that Canadian Pacific agreed to in order to get the Government to close the deal.

When viewed in the context of the considerable benefits that the CPR got from the Crow's Nest Pass deal, the rate concessions it made have an impressive weight of economic logic on their side. This is especially true when they are looked at from the perspective of 1897, when the rate reductions were entirely reasonable, something the CPR might conceivably have contemplated undertaking even without the agreement. Van Horne and his colleagues no doubt believed that if the day ever came when the Crow rate levels became unreasonably low, then the agreement with the Government could easily be changed and the ceiling lifted. That was the way agreements between companies and governments usually worked.

The fortunes of the Crow rates in their early years tended to bear out that view. In 1902, as part of an agreement with the government of Manitoba, the Canadian Northern Railway reduced its rates on grain to well below the Crow level; the next year, the CPR made a similar reduction to meet the competition. Rates remained at that level all through the greatest era of expansion and prosperity on the Prairies; it was only in 1918 that the railways applied to the Board of Railway Commissioners for a rate increase. It was granted, subject to the terms of the Crow's Nest Pass agreement. Later that same year the federal government, acting under the authority of the War Measures Act, granted another rate increase in order to provide the railways with more revenue so that they could pay increased wages to their employees. This increase brought rates to twenty-five per cent *above* the Crow level. In 1919, the Government introduced legislation to put a formal end to the Crow's Nest Pass agreement.

At this point, however, the tide began to reverse itself. The legislation was passed by the House of Commons, but, as a result of opposition in the Senate, had to be amended so that the agreement would only be suspended for three years. When the three years were ended, the new government of Prime Minister Mackenzie King restored the Crow rates. Over the next few years, the rates were entrenched, with significant alterations in their scope, by successive pieces of legislation, Board of Railway Commissioners decisions and, in part, actions of the railways themselves. When the process was over, this was how the situation stood:

- Rates on all commodities other than grain and flour were restored to the normal processes of regulation.
- Grain and flour rates were set by parliamentary statute at the rates prescribed in the Crow's Nest Pass agreement.
- These rates now applied to export grain hauled not only to the Lakehead, as specified in the Crow's Nest Pass agreement, but to Pacific and Hudson Bay ports as well. They were also extended to cover all railways, instead of just the CPR, and to CPR lines built since the agreement was signed in 1897.

There has been some dispute over whether or not this new legislation constituted an abrogation of the Crow's Nest Pass agreement. The most authoritative opinion in favour of the view that it did, came from the Turgeon Commission, which said that "the real intention of the amendment of Section 325 of the Railway Act passed in 1925 . . . was to put an end to the Agreement of 1897 as between the parties to it (the Government and the Canadian Pacific Railway Company) and to prescribe instead a statutory stabilization of certain freight rates binding on all railways."[8] That opinion has, of course, been eagerly seized upon by the CPR, since it provides the means for looking at grain rates separately from the other provisions and effects of the 1897 agreement. That interpretation has also been seriously questioned, since it depends on a chance remark by George Graham, the railways minister of the day, that the primary purpose of the new legislation was "to get rid" of the Crow's Nest Pass agreement.[9] There is at least an equal weight of ministerial statements to the effect that the Government was in fact sticking to the very same agreement.

But it is indisputable that the legislation of the 1920s changed the whole context in which the Crow rates operated. For the first time, it became clear that the rates were not just a transitory phenomenon, which could be changed when the CPR wanted them changed, with only the usual amount of arm-twisting. Parliament had now separated rates on grain and flour from the general freight-rate structure. It had declared these rates to be its own responsibility, something it would watch over carefully. For a time, the Liberal party tried to make a partisan issue out of the Crow rates, pointing out that the rates had been suspended by a Tory government and restored by a Liberal one. The Crow rates were one of the main reasons for the Progressive party's support of the Liberals during the minority situation of 1925, and for that party's eventual absorption into the Liberals. In later years another, more significant division of opinion over the Crow rates occurred. On one side stood virtually all of western Canada, its spokesmen and organizations, and all politicians with any interest in maintaining electoral support in the West. On the other, stood the railways, and particularly the CPR.

It was not until after the Second World War that the CPR launched a serious attempt to get the Crow rates changed. The two postwar Royal Commissions both heard hours of essentially identical testimony from western spokesmen demanding that the rates be kept as they were, and more hours of equally repetitious testimony from the railways demanding that changes be made. However, the conclusions the two Commissions came to were very different. The Turgeon Commission seemed sympathetic to the western position, and found no evidence to support claims that the Crow rates were an undue burden either on the railways or on other shippers. The MacPherson Commission's basic sympathies were shown to be with the railways; since it would have been politically impossible to recommend that the farmers be forced to pay more, it recommended a government subsidy so that at least the railways wouldn't have to suffer.

The issue before the Turgeon Commission was whether rates on grain should remain under the control of Parliament. The Canadian Pacific Railway said they should not; the Canadian National agreed with its rival, but with reservations. Among the evidence presented by the CPR was a study that purported to show that for the year 1948, "while the exact dollar deficiency from the Crowsnest grain rates in Western Canada is not available, it will be seen that it is somewhere between $13,769,000 and $16,947,000."[10] The Commission didn't so much discount this study as dismiss it as irrelevant. "Whether or not these rates are in fact compensatory," it said, "is not of essential significance to the proposals the Commission intends to make concerning their future treatment."[11] What was important was whether Parliament still "looks upon Western Canada's production of grain for export as an industry requiring special consideration in the national interest."[12]

The Turgeon Commission's emphatic conclusion was that it should. It did not recommend that the rates should never at any time be raised, but simply that whether or not they should be raised should remain a decision for Parliament to make. If control of grain rates were shifted to the Board of Transport Commissioners, then it would have to be exercised, under the Board's terms of reference, "regardless of geographic or economic conditions." The only criterion the Board could apply was the so-called "reasonableness" of the rates. "The Commission does not believe," it said, "that the time has come to deal with this great export industry without regard to considerations which the Board cannot apply."[13]

As for any possible compensation to the railways for carrying grain at low rates, the Commission pointed out that the CPR itself had not maintained that the rates were a burden on the railways. It had maintained, rather, that they were a burden on other shippers. But if that were true, then where was the testimony of shippers to bear it out? Shippers from western Canada who had testified had supported keeping the Crow rates the way they were. Shippers in the Atlantic provinces were satisfied with the treatment they were getting under the Maritime Freight Rates Act. And shippers in central Canada were in such an advantageous position as a result of truck and water competition that by no stretch of logic could the Crow rates be called an undue burden on them. "On the whole therefore," the Commission said, "no justification can be found for the statement that the exemption of the Crowsnest Pass rates causes an undue burden upon shippers as a whole or upon any particular class of shippers."[14]

Ten years later the CPR got its chance to reopen the case. But it was the lasting achievement of the Turgeon Commission that the railway could not present its case again in quite the same terms. This time the CPR didn't even try to have the rates removed from the control of Parliament. Much as that would have appealed to the basic instincts of both Canadian Pacific and the MacPherson Commission, it was now out of the question. Nevertheless, the CPR's presentations to the two Commissions were similar in their details, right down to the accounting studies. Unlike the Turgeon Commission, however, the MacPherson Commission took the CPR's arguments seriously.

The question the MacPherson Commission considered most important was one that the Turgeon Commission had thought irrelevant: how much money are the railways losing by carrying grain? The railways said they had lost a total of about $70 million on grain in 1958. But in any attempt to apportion railway costs to specific commodities or services, there is a large amount of guesswork involved. This is because much of the cost of running a railway is constant whether any particular service is run on that railway or not—for instance the investment in track. This leads economists and accountants to talk about two distinct kinds of railway costs: there are variable costs, which are costs actually incurred in providing a service, and fixed costs, which are costs incurred whether the service is provided or not. The distinction is not absolute—an investment in boxcars, for instance, is fixed for the lifetime of those cars, but variable as soon as they have to be replaced—but it is a useful guide. For a railway to make money, revenues from a service have to contribute toward meeting fixed costs as well as cover its own variable costs. If the service were dropped, however, only the variable costs would be saved.

The MacPherson Commission recommended that the Government pay $9 million annually to the CPR and $7.3 million annually to the CNR to represent the share of fixed costs that should properly be borne by the grain traffic. In addition, if revenues on grain were less than variable costs, the Government would make up the difference; if revenues were greater than variable costs, then the difference would be deducted from the payment for fixed costs. In 1958, according to the Commission's own studies, revenue on grain had failed to cover variable costs by $2 million on the Canadian Pacific and by $4 million on the Canadian National. This seemed to cut the railways' claimed deficit of $70 million down to a total of only $22 million—the $16 million considered to be the share of fixed costs attributable to grain plus a shortfall of $6 million in the variable costs. However, the railways' figure had included the cost of operating branch lines "solely related" to grain, which the Commission proposed to subsidize separately[15]—as it was, this was the only subsidy actually paid. For the year 1971, the railways received $22.5 million as a subsidy for running unprofitable branch lines; all but one of the lines in question were on the Prairies and most of them were solely related to carrying grain.

That the railways were only able to get their Crow's Nest Pass subsidy in part and through the back door was due entirely to the persistence of western Canada on this issue. The government of Saskatchewan, in its testimony before the Commons transport committee when the implementation of the MacPherson report was being discussed, "opposed, without reservation, any payment by the federal government towards constant costs of moving western grain to export positions,"[16] and in addition "was not satisfied that there was actual out-of-pocket loss on the movement of export grain."[17] Its position was echoed by other western spokesmen, and the MacPherson proposal for this form of subsidy, which was contained in the first draft of the National Transportation Act, had to be withdrawn in the final version.

After all the argument and testimony, the question of whether the railways get their money's worth out of carrying grain remains moot. E.P. Reid, the economist hired by the MacPherson Commission to study the matter, would say only that "the traffic was remunerative until 1946 and . . . the shift to unremunerativeness came, if at all, during the last ten years [1950 to 1960] or so."[18] He concluded that "returns on statutory traffic are indeed grossly (if not uniquely) low"[19]—but not necessarily so low that the railways weren't making money. If the Crow rates were really such a heavy burden, then one possible indication might appear in the CPR's income statistics: a large wheat crop in a certain year might have some detrimental effect on the railway's earnings in that year. There is no evidence that that is so. In the decade 1962-1971, the year in which the CPR hauled the largest amount of wheat (12.1 million tons) was 1966. That was also the year in which the CPR had the highest net railway profit, $50.2 million. The next largest amount of wheat carried in a year was 11 million tons, in 1964. In that year, the railway earned $43.5 million, the third highest figure for the decade. The worst year for wheat was 1969, in which the CPR hauled only 6.2 million tons. That was also the CPR's second worst year for profits; it made a piddling $34.6 million. Its worst year for profits ($29 million) was 1962, which was its second worst year for wheat (6.7 million tons).[20] There are any number of factors that could account for the apparent pattern, and none of this proves that the CPR is in fact making money by carrying grain at the Crow rates; however, it does suggest that the CPR has failed to prove the opposite.

But as the Turgeon Commission pointed out, that is not the main issue. The main issue is whether or not the Crow rates continue to be important to the western farmer, and that is not in doubt. "Western Canada," said Harold Innis in his 1923 *History of the Canadian Pacific Railway*, "has paid for the development of Canadian nationality, and it would appear that it must continue to pay."[21] The best the Prairies could hope for was a reduction in the price they paid; that reduction took the form of the Crow's Nest Pass rates. As such, the rates were politically necessary, and that political necessity, and not the 1897 agreement, has been the real reason for their survival. Increased costs to the farmer would be only one effect of lifting the ceiling on grain rates. E.P. Reid found that in all likelihood the farmer would share the cost of increased rates with the buyers of his wheat. And that might mean that the buyer would not buy.[22] Growing wheat on the Prairies always has been, and is still, pre-eminently an export industry. The prosperity of the prairie farmer depends on his being able to sell his wheat abroad. One factor in his ability to do that is the low rate he pays to ship his crop to an export position.

The cost of shipping a bushel of first-grade northern wheat by rail from a typical Saskatchewan point to the Lakehead for export is 13.8 cents.[23] Lift the rate ceiling, and the cost would at least double—it could conceivably be tripled or more. If the cost doubled, that would mean that for the farmer to keep the same income, the wheat would have to be sold at 13.8 cents per bushel more. If the price were then reduced in order to keep the wheat competitive, the difference would be absorbed by the farmer. The logic is inexorable, and it has been well understood by the farmers and the politicians whose ear they have been able to get.

There has been much talk in recent years of diversification on the Prairies, of a move on one level away from wheat toward other crops, and on another level away from agriculture altogether. But as we have seen, the structures of Confederation and particularly the freight-rate structure are not set up to promote the growth of an industrial economy on the Prairies. The dependence of the Prairies on agriculture, set up by eastern interests for their own benefit, may not be as total as it once was, but it is still considerable. One sign of the continuing importance of the Crow rates is that agricultural diversification has often been toward crops, such as rapeseed, that are eligible for those rates. If the wheat economy is to be maintained, some people have always considered it reasonable that the chief corporate beneficiary of that economy, the Canadian Pacific Railway, should at least share in the cost of maintaining it.

One such person was Edward Beatty, a CPR president in the days before anyone in the corporation would have dreamed of labelling Sir William Van Horne a chump. Beatty said in 1938 that "Sir William Van Horne made an agreement with the Government for the Crow's Nest Pass rates. A great many people criticized that because they said he only got around three million dollars-odd in the way of subsidies for building that line, and in consideration for that made this very drastic reduction in grain rates, and certain other commodities westbound.

"I have always thought that Sir William Van Horne was 100 per cent right. . . . I think he went into that with his eyes open and undoubtedly made a good bargain. I think he made a good one for both the country and the railways. And that must have been the influence that actuated him in the matter."[24]

6 Passengers in the baggage car

Mr. Crump don't 'low no easy riders here,
Crump don't 'low no easy riders here,
We don't care what Mr. Crump don't 'low
We gonna barrel house anyhow
Mr. Crump can go catch hisself some air.

From an old Negro blues song

The consumer, in our private-enterprise society, has really only one protection against the large corporation, and it is this: the corporation wants him to come back. General Motors, having sold you a Chevrolet, wants you to buy another Chevrolet when planned obsolescence has taken care of the first one. The Kraft Corporation, having sold you a jar of Cheez Whiz, wants you to buy another jar of Cheez Whiz, which you will not be able to do if you have died of food poisoning in the interim. With advertising and oligopoly making a mockery of the idea of corporations' responding to public demand, this protection does not quite live up to the claims made for it by economic theory, but it does have some effect. The concessions that Ralph Nader and his troops have been able to wring out of the car manufacturers would not have been possible otherwise.

There are, however, situations in which even this small protection is lacking. There are corporations that do not want you to come back, that are not even indifferent to whether or not you come back, that are actively trying to discourage you from coming back. You would have to be pretty brave to buy such a corporation's product, or else extremely foolish. There aren't too many people who would continue to be so brave or foolish over a long period of time. If a corporation really wants to discourage people from buying its product, it isn't very difficult.

Take, for instance, the case of passenger service on the Canadian Pacific Railway. Canadian Pacific does not make too many bones about its attitude toward rail passenger service. Testifying before the MacPherson Commission in 1960, CPR Vice-President Robert Emerson said the railway planned to scrap about $64 million worth of its passenger equipment over the next twenty years. He doubted "whether it is fully realized the extent to which Canadian Pacific is now a freight road," and said that "passenger train service on Canadian Pacific is no longer required for the economic well-being of Canada." One might be forgiven the suspicion that what he really meant was the economic well-being of the CPR. "Canada and its rail transport industry," he said, "cannot afford the luxury of providing costly and unnecessary passenger services."[1] Eight years later, Buck Crump said that Canada's small population and tremendous land expanse made long-distance train travel impractical. "By 1980 eighty per cent of our population will live in urban areas," he said. "They won't need long-distance trains."[2] In 1970, at a hearing on the CPR's transcontinental *Canadian*, Thomas James, director of passenger service, did not disagree when a trade-union representative said the CPR is "desperately anxious to get out of the passenger business." James was asked whether the railway's proposed reductions on the *Canadian* were a step in that direction. "Yes," he replied.

On other occasions, as might be expected, Canadian Pacific officials have adopted a different tone, a more lamenting, almost wistful one. "It's not as if Canadian Pacific hadn't tried to make it work," cost analyst John Kelsall told the Vancouver *Sun* in 1970.[3] Interviewed at the same time, James said that "we always strove to give you the very best we could give you for your money. We feel the passengers have deserted us—we haven't deserted them."[4] But this gentler attitude has not, on the whole, been borne out by the CPR's actions. Early in 1973, passengers travelling on the Dominion Atlantic Railway, a CPR subsidiary, between Truro and Windsor, Nova Scotia, were startled to find that they had to sign a document acknowledging that they were travelling at their own risk. The reason for this was that the Canadian Transport Commission would not recognize the car provided by the railway as a passenger-carrying car. It was an old wooden caboose, tacked onto the end of a freight train which took about two and a half hours to complete the 59-mile run. The regular passenger coach used for the service was up for repairs and "there aren't any other coaches available," explained F.S. Champagne, CPR superintendent of passenger service. If passengers deserted the Dominion Atlantic Railway, it was hardly any wonder.

This was perhaps an extreme case, but other tales of CPR passenger service have been only slightly less hair-raising. In 1970, the Canadian Transport Commission brought down a decision ordering the Esquimalt and Nanaimo Railway, Canadian Pacific's Vancouver Island subsidiary, to maintain and upgrade its passenger service between Victoria and Courtenay. In examining the E&N run, the Commission had sent one of its officials, John Green, to ride the train and report what he saw. "Mr. Green's report," said the CTC in its decision, "was highly illuminating . . . .

"As it happened, there were 48 passengers on board leaving Victoria the day Mr. Green made his inspection. At Langford, a man with two children got on, and, as the passenger compartment was full, they were placed in the baggage compartment on [an] old station bench.

"At Shawnigan, five more passengers got on and were also put into the baggage compartment. They were followed at Cobble Hill by a lady with her arm in a cast. Passengers forced to stand in the baggage compartment have to hang onto racks on the walls, difficult enough for a person with two good arms. When Mr. Green observed what was happening, he instructed the conductor to place those standing in the passenger compartment, which was done."[5]

The CPR also operates ferry services between Vancouver and Nanaimo, and between Victoria and Seattle. The timetable folder produced by Canadian Pacific for its Pacific Coast ferry services advertised summer connections between Vancouver and Seattle via "the Scenic

Malahat Drive between Nanaimo and Victoria.'' The folder suggested that the traveller go from Vancouver to Nanaimo on the CPR ferry, from Nanaimo to Victoria by bus, and from Victoria to Seattle aboard the CPR's *Princess Marguerite*. ''Nowhere in this folder,'' said the CTC, ''is the existence of the E&N Railway and its passenger trains recognized.''[6] Even if a traveller knew about the E&N train from the north, it was scheduled to arrive at the railway station in Victoria at exactly the same moment that the *Princess Marguerite* was leaving from the harbour, making it impossible for anyone to make the ferry connection.

The total annual advertising budget for the E&N passenger train was $150, which, the CTC noted, all went toward ''producing a local timetable folder which gives the names of the stops, the times of arrival and departure of the trains, and very little else.''[7]

The E&N case was notable in that it was one of the few in which the CTC got tough with the CPR and ordered it to improve its services. More typical was the case of the Montreal-Ottawa run. The Montreal-Ottawa-Toronto triangle is the most heavily travelled route in the country. Two legs of that triangle, Ottawa-Toronto and Montreal-Toronto, were served for thirty years by CN-CP pool trains as a result of the ''co-operation'' that followed the Royal Commission report of 1932; on the third leg, Montreal-Ottawa, the two railways offered competing services. On October 30, 1965, Canadian Pacific pulled out of the pool agreement, establishing its own trains between Montreal and Toronto and between Ottawa and Toronto. Canadian National establish-ed the Montreal-Toronto *Rapido*, cutting the running time between the two cities to five hours. Barely two months later, on January 14, 1966, the CPR dropped its Montreal-Toronto and Ottawa-Toronto trains, leaving the entire field open to CN.

In 1970 Canadian Pacific turned its attention to the third leg of the triangle. It had five trains daily in either direction between Montreal and Ottawa, complementing four CN runs. The CPR was quite willing to take the burden of competition off CN's back, but legalities made it necessary to tread softly. The National Transportation Act had been passed three years before, and abandonment procedures now had to go through the CTC. Earlier in 1970, the CTC had heard its first aban-donment cases, and these hearings had been something of an embarrass-ment for the railways. At Guelph and Owen Sound, Ontario, more than seventy people had shown up to submit briefs on passenger service between those cities and Toronto, and all of them except the rep-resentatives of the railways had wanted the service maintained. CPR preferred to avoid such public hearings on its plans for the Montreal-Ottawa run.

Its first move was to institute a series of changes in this service.

A morning train was rescheduled from 8 a.m. to 11:30 a.m., making it useless for anyone who wanted to make a one-day trip. An eastbound evening train was rescheduled to pass through Montreal West station at 9:50—missing a connection for New York by five minutes. Meal service was curtailed, and prices were raised. A bacon-and-eggs breakfast that had cost $1.95 now cost $2.75 a la carte (including 20 cents for toast, 30 cents for marmalade or jam, and 40 cents for coffee). Instead of the average of 150 passengers per train they had attracted before, the trains now attracted only 40. Complaining that it was losing money, the CPR announced that it was cutting out three of the five trains daily in each direction. The only trains left in service would be the Montreal-Ottawa section of the *Canadian*, which it was running anyway, and a single, self-propelled Dayliner car that meanders along the north shore of the Ottawa River, taking three hours to make the complete run (as compared to two hours and ten minutes for the *Canadian* or CN trains); whatever its importance to the myriad small communities on the north shore, this train cannot seriously be claimed to be a Montreal-Ottawa service.

This was not, said the CPR, an abandonment. It was merely a reduction in service. And therefore the railway didn't need CTC permission to carry it out. There would be no necessity for any awkward hearings. There were many suggestions, from sources as diverse as the Canadian Railway Labour Association and the Montreal *Star*, that the CTC should not agree to Canadian Pacific's definition of its powers, but the situation didn't seem to bother the Commission. It uttered not a peep about the dropping of the trains. On August 1, 1970, the trains stopped running.

Canadian Pacific is trying to do the same thing with its most important, prestigious and expensive passenger train, the *Canadian*. Because the *Canadian* represents so large a proportion of its passenger deficit—of $22.2 million in Canadian Pacific passenger losses certified by the CTC for 1971, $16.3 million was for the *Canadian*[8]—it has been at the centre of the company's most recent attempts to get rid of its passenger service. Because it covers so large an area of the country and is endowed with such a substantial reputation and tradition, the *Canadian* has also been at the centre of the efforts being made to require the railways to preserve passenger service. If the CPR ultimately wins its battle to drop the *Canadian*, then the rest of the war will only be a mopping-up operation; if it loses, then a turnaround in the prevailing attitude toward passenger transportation in Canada may have been achieved.

Although its stainless-steel sleekness bespeaks modernity, the *Canadian* is a remnant of another era at Canadian Pacific, an era when passenger trains were still a matter of corporate pride if not profits.

Thomas James reminisced about it to the Vancouver *Sun* in 1970: "It was about 1951—Mr. Crump was then the vice-president of the company . . . . Well, we decided it was time we had a fleet of new cars. We got $44 million appropriated for them. We were thinking in terms of something grand. So Mr. Crump, Mr. [J.N.] Fraine, who is now head of the western region, and myself were made an equipment committee to decide what to get. We rode all the good passenger trains of the time . . . . I saw this dining car on the Burlington. I re-designed the kitchen. The Canadian National has nothing like it."[9]

The *Canadian* was introduced into service with great fanfare in 1955. In that same year, Crump was promoted to the presidency of Canadian Pacific, and brought with him a new corporate policy of looking beyond the railway for profits—to the CPR's interests, acquired over the years, in base metals, oil and gas, timberlands, urban real estate, and so forth. Money-losing rail passenger services didn't fit in. Crump answered, "It could well be," when asked in Vancouver in 1958 whether he thought the days of the great transcontinental trains were numbered. "You only have to go out and look at the activity at any airport to get the answer to that one," he said, although he would not predict how much longer the transcontinental trains would last.[10] In 1960, Robert Emerson was able to tell the MacPherson Commission that Canadian Pacific had abandoned about a hundred passenger runs between 1954 and 1959.[11]

Another wave of abandonments took place in late 1965 when, in addition to the Montreal-Toronto and Ottawa-Toronto runs, the CPR got rid of its second-string transcontinental train, the *Dominion*. The demise of the *Dominion* caused considerable furore at the time; parliamentary committees were still meeting about it months afterward. The CPR first announced its intention of abandoning the *Dominion* in August 1965, with D-day scheduled for September 7. On September 1, the Board of Transport Commissioners, predecessor to the CTC, ordered the CPR to "continue to operate the present passenger service provided by the *Dominion* until the Board orders otherwise."[12] As a result, the *Dominion* left Montreal for Vancouver on September 7 as usual—or almost as usual. The train consisted of an engine, a baggage car, and two coaches. Predictably, the number of passengers dwindled. On September 28 Canadian Pacific again asked for permission to drop the train; again the Board said no.

There were some doubts raised at subsequent public hearings about whether the post-September 7 *Dominion* constituted the "present passenger service" referred to in the Board's order, but Chief Commissioner Rod Kerr said the order was not meant to exclude such "seasonal changes in the consist of the train." Canadian Pacific said it had to cancel the *Dominion* because it needed the diesel power to haul the wheat the federal government had just sold to the Soviet Union, but this was evidently an afterthought, since Emerson, by now president of the CPR, admitted that the company had reached the decision to drop the *Dominion* before the wheat deal had been made. On January 7, 1966, the Board of Transport Commissioners authorized the CPR to abandon the *Dominion*; by January 11, the train had vanished without a trace. The House of Commons transport committee said on June 17, 1966 that a definite need existed for additional Montreal-to-Vancouver passenger service, and recommended that the CPR restore the *Dominion* in 1967 and support it with an adequate advertising and promotion campaign. The committee had decided not to recommend restoration of the train in the summer of 1966 because CPR president Ian Sinclair (Emerson had died in the interim) told it that that would be physically impossible.

Soon after that, the National Transportation Act was passed, making passenger trains eligible for either abandonment or subsidy if the railways could prove that they were "uneconomic." But before the section of the Act regarding passenger service could be put into effect, there were several matters of interpretation to straighten out. What, for instance, did the word "uneconomic" mean? Did it simply mean unprofitable, or did it mean that there would be a greater overall cost to the economy in maintaining the rail passenger service than in accommodating the people who used it through some other mode? If the second interpretation prevailed, then services that lost money could nevertheless be "economic." A second question concerned how passenger losses were to be determined. If a railway could prove that a service was uneconomic, but the Canadian Transport Commission decided that its retention was necessary in the public interest, then the government would reimburse the railway for eighty per cent of its losses. Determination of the loss thus became a matter of some importance, but railway costing is a highly complex process and it took the CTC until 1969 to decide on the cost criteria it would use—and even after that the CPR appealed the decision, unsuccessfully, to the Supreme Court, resulting in further delay.

In another part of that same decision, the CTC ruled on the meaning of "uneconomic." It said, "We agree that in the context of the Act the term 'unprofitable' is probably as close a synonym to 'uneconomic' as could be found," but went on to explain, "the principal difference in meaning lies in the emphasis which the word 'uneconomic' lays on the intrinsic or fundamental nature of unprofitability, as opposed to temporary unprofitability or unprofitability which could be eliminated through operating changes within the present capability of the railway system."[13] The CTC's ability to read the minds of the shapers of the National Transportation Act has been one of its greatest assets.

Its job has been made easier by the coincidence that the person primarily responsible for the Act was Transport Minister Jack Pickersgill, and the person primarily responsible for the Commission's early decisions was its first president, Jack Pickersgill.

In the fall of 1969, the railways submitted their first applications for abandonment (with the exception of one bizarre case that had been decided *before* the cost decision), and to anybody who had grown accustomed to thinking that the trains would run forever they came as something of a shock. Canadian Pacific applied to discontinue its entire passenger network, with the single exception of its Montreal commuter service, which makes money. Canadian National applied to get rid of thirteen of its passenger services, mostly serving out-of-the-way places like Churchill, Manitoba, and Senneterre, Quebec, where there are few if any alternative modes of transportation. One of the reasons for the wide sweep of the abandonment applications was the perverse phrasing of the Act: if a railway wants a service subsidized, it has to apply for abandonment first. Canadian National tried to apply directly for a subsidy on its transcontinental run, the *Super Continental*, but it was told that there was no such provision in the Act. In effect, then, many of the applications for abandonment were really applications for subsidy. But Canadian Pacific, and to a lesser extent Canadian National as well, would not have been particularly upset if all of the requests for abandonment had been granted.

The Commission has so far not been quite that securely in Canadian Pacific's pocket. It has, however, shown a disturbing tendency to look at rail passenger service strictly in terms of profit and loss. In a sense, the Act gave it little choice. The Act virtually forced the railways to consider their profit-and-loss statements first, even in the unlikely event that without the Act they would be inclined to consider something else. It encouraged them to exaggerate their losses, on which the subsidies were based, while giving them little incentive to make any improvements in service that might reduce those losses. The Act virtually forced the Commission to decide that "uneconomic" was synonymous with unprofitable, since to have done otherwise would have created the anomaly of having some unprofitable passenger services eligible for subsidy while others, more worthy of preservation in that they were "economic," were not eligible. Still, the Act did leave some leeway which some CTC president other than Jack Pickersgill might have taken advantage of. There was a clause that said, "in determining whether an uneconomic passenger-train service or parts thereof should be discontinued, the Commission shall consider all matters that, in its opinion, are relevant to the public interest,"[14] and the Act chose not to limit the definition of "the public interest".

Is there, then, any significant public interest that requires the retention of passenger-train services? Is all the noise and fuss that has been raised the clamouring of special interests—of trade unions trying to protect their members from the loss of their jobs, of town councils and boards of trade that would feel hurt if the milk train didn't stop there any more? If all the passenger trains in the country were to disappear tomorrow, wouldn't the few remaining people who use them be quite happy to travel by car, plane and bus, as most people do anyway? Is there not some truth to the railways' allegation that they have not abandoned the passengers, but the passengers have abandoned them?

That there has been a decline in the numbers of people using passenger trains is beyond dispute. The trend was already apparent when economist J.C. Lessard did his study of transportation in Canada for the Royal Commission on Canada's Economic Prospects in the mid-1950s. Lessard found that whereas in 1938, 38.3 per cent of the intercity passenger-miles travelled in Canada had been by rail, by 1953 this had declined to 11.3 per cent. The private car, meanwhile, had climbed from 59.5 per cent to 78.7 per cent, the bus from 2.2 per cent to 7.1 per cent, and the airplane from ground zero to 2.9 per cent.[15] Thirteen years later, the trend had accelerated: the passenger train's share of the market was only 4.6 per cent, while the car held 83.8 per cent and the airplane 9.2 per cent.[16] This in part relected the attractiveness of the new modes and the improvements made in them. A Toronto businessman going to Vancouver is unlikely to want to spend three days on the train when he can get there in four hours by air.

But it also reflected the investment decisions made by governments and by transportation companies both public and private. If money is spent on roads and airports, then people will be more inclined to travel by car, bus and plane. If money is spent on improving rail passenger service to make it more rapid, convenient and comfortable, then people will be more inclined to travel by train. The fuss over subsidies to the railways for their passenger services obscures the costs of other modes of transport. The Department of Transport spent $393.8 million on its air transportation program in the 1972-73 fiscal year, only $98.6 million of which was recovered in revenues, leaving it with a deficit of $295.2 million[17]—roughly five times what was spent to subsidize passenger trains. The total expenditure by the three levels of government in 1968 on streets, roads and highways was $1.738 billion. Of that, $1.321 billion was recovered in gasoline taxes, license fees and other user charges, leaving the taxpayer with a deficit of $417 million on road transport.[18] Even the largest passenger-train losses don't look so huge in comparison.

In addition, a large part of the passenger losses that the railways and the CTC calculate, are losses only in a restricted sense. They include both variable costs and a portion of fixed costs. They are not in any sense an estimate of how much would be saved if the services were abandoned. Even at eighty percent of the loss, the subsidy that the CTC provides to a money-losing passenger service may well cover considerably more than the variable cost of providing that service. In 1965, Canadian National calculated its overall passenger deficit at $46.5 million, but estimated that only $9.2 million of that consisted of expenses "controllable over the short term."[19] In other words, most of the money required to transport you from Montreal to Toronto by train has already been spent; it was, in fact, spent by the railways years ago. Much of the money required to transport you from Montreal to Toronto by plane, on the other hand, is being spent by the government right now, in the form of new airports for those two cities. "Every passenger who is attracted to a train rides on a capital investment already in place," wrote Toronto journalist Ron Haggart in *Saturday Night* in 1969, "but every passenger who is diverted to an airplane or car increases the need for public investment in airports and highways, and private investment in automobiles."[20]

Some of the other ways in which passenger trains are a more "economic" form of travel than planes or cars cannot be expressed so easily in dollars and cents:

- They are relatively non-polluting; if some of the money now being spent on airports and highways were spent on electrification of some of the major railway lines instead, the train's pollution advantage would be increased.
- They are relatively safe. Collisions at level crossings are the only common type of accident involving passenger trains, and they could be eliminated by eliminating the level crossings. In 1967, there were no railway passengers killed in Canada; in that same year, there were 5,240 people killed in car accidents.[21]
- They are relatively efficient users of land, particularly of valuable urban land. In his 1966 book *Megalopolis Unbound*, U.S. Senator Claiborne Pell of Rhode Island, one of the chief American advocates of rail passenger service, estimated that 60,000 commuters per hour could be carried in trains over a single set of transit tracks, while a single lane of urban expressway could accommodate only 2,860 people per hour.[22] Pell also estimated that the four airports serving New York City—Kennedy, LaGuardia, Newark and Teterboro—have a combined area equal to the space taken up by the entire Penn Central Railroad right-of-way linking New York and Chicago.[23]
- While the jet airplane and the superhighway are built for travel between one large city and another large city, the passenger train also serves smaller communities and is necessary for the preservation

of those communities. This is particularly true in those parts of Canada where climate makes highway travel difficult or uncertain for long stretches of the year. James Doak, a lawyer and businessman from Virden, Manitoba, told the House of Commons transport committee during its hearings on the *Dominion* that "we find on the prairies that rail transportation is not a luxury and it is not a choice. We speak of buses, but is there any choice in the winter when the roads are drifted or when they say, 'Stay off the highways'? Is the bus any choice in this type of country?"[24] The concentration of investment in airports and expressways is not only a response to the process of increasing urbanization; it contributes to that process as well.

● Rail transportation is available to people with relatively small incomes, while air transportation is not. A 1970 survey done of travellers in Montreal and Toronto found that more than 50 per cent of air travellers came from families making over $15,000 a year, while fewer than 20 per cent came from families making under $9,000 a year. For rail travellers, it was exactly the opposite: more than 50 per cent came from families making under $9,000, and in the neighbourhood of 20 per cent came from families making over $15,000.[25]

All of this is of some relevance to the planning of a truly "economic" passenger transportation system. None of it, however, is of any relevance to the investment decisions of Canadian Pacific. Passenger trains do lose money. At best, with a heavy injection of capital, they might be made to break even or turn a very small profit. Oil wells, shopping centres, container ships, and some freight trains all make money. They are, quite clearly, better investments. For Canadian Pacific to pump its resources into its rail passenger service is not worth the effort. From its point of view, it would simply be a misuse of capital that could be better applied in other places. If it can get away with putting passengers in a caboose, then so much the better.

The point of view of the Canadian Transport Commission is somewhat different. But because of the philosophy that prevailed during the regime of Jack Pickersgill, the CTC has found its point of view easy to reconcile with that of Canadian Pacific. That philosophy was expressed in a catchword that has been almost as pervasive with regard to rail passenger service as "competition" has been with regard to the transportation system as a whole—"rationalization." It is even harder to be opposed to rationalization than it is to be opposed to competition. Everybody wants things to be rational. So it was, in 1970, that the CTC turned down Canadian Pacific's application to drop the *Canadian*, and ordered it to come up with a plan to rationalize it.

Canadian Pacific had lots of experience with rationalization. It had rationalized the *Dominion* out of existence four years earlier. And its plan for the *Canadian* had a familiar ring—increase fares, cut out sleeping- and dining-car service, and reduce the frequency of the train from every day to three times a week except in peak periods. At a subsequent series of revealing public hearings, a bit more came out about the attitude that had gone into formulating the plans. Passenger-service Director Thomas James did not think that the reduction in frequency would result in "a serious loss to other modes if you're thinking in terms of air or bus or anything like that. I do think that a person who couldn't go today would go tomorrow because I think that train riders ride trains because they like to ride trains." It was a good example of the aggressive business thinking that has got the CPR's passenger service where it is today.

During the hearings, cost analyst John Kelsall was asked by Commissioner J.M. Woodard about the proposal to increase fares. Was it not possible, Woodard wanted to know, that Canadian National would decide to leave its fares exactly where they were and as a result the *Canadian* would lose some business to CN? "Well, I think we recognize that we don't operate in isolation," Kelsall said. "I would presume that if the CNR did not see fit to increase their fares, there could be a reduction in revenue, attributable to our operation." In other words, Woodard asked, was it not possible that the CPR might end up with more of a deficit than before? "Right," said Kelsall. "It is at this point that we recognize the world we live in. There are inter-relating factors between the two." And weren't there also inter-relating factors between rail fares and the fares on other modes of transport? "That is right," agreed Kelsall. Even if both CN and CP decided to raise fares, could that not affect both railways to their detriment? "It could."[26]

The CTC was disturbed by this sort of testimony and its decision on the *Canadian* was somewhat ambivalent. It rejected the CPR's rationalization plan, but it disclaimed jurisdiction over whether or not sleeping- and dining-car services should be provided on the train, giving the railway the green light to drop those services whenever it saw fit. At the same time, the *Canadian* became eligible for subsidy, and with a cheque for $13 million or so coming in from the Government each year, Canadian Pacific no longer feels quite as strongly about getting rid of it. The Commission said, however, that the subsidies would eventually be withdrawn from the sleeping- and dining-cars; as soon as that happens the CPR will have no further use for those services. The CTC has also recommended that the two railways get together and rationalize their transcontinental services jointly, but so far not much has come of that. The effect of the CTC's decision was to postpone the problem, but not to solve it. As long as it is guided by the same narrow "economic" criteria, it is only ensuring that there will be periodic public controversies until the last passenger train is gone and the last person who ever rode one has died off.

The *Canadian*, meanwhile, is still running, still a pleasure to ride although a bit seedier than before, almost but not quite the great passenger train it once was and could be again. Its decline is sad, and its abandonment would be the squandering of a national resource. But perhaps the saddest effect of Canadian Pacific's passenger policies has been their influence on the policies of the last railway in North America that actually *wanted* passengers—Canadian National.

In the early 1960s, inspired by an ebullient vice-president for passenger services named Pierre Delagrave, a strange mood took hold at Canadian National. It not only cut passenger fares, it advertised that it was cutting them. Commercials for CN passenger trains became as ubiquitous as those for cigarettes and beer. CN travellers could now play bingo in the club car or be entertained in the Bistro car. The red-white-and-blue differential fare plan encouraged people to travel during the off-season and the middle of the week. The introduction of the *Rapido* made CN by far the most sensible way to travel between Montreal and Toronto. Like the energetic, publicly-owned passenger railways of Europe and Japan, CN was ordering new equipment: United Aircraft's lightweight turbine-powered *Turbo* would cut the Montreal-Toronto running time to four hours, an hour less than the *Rapido*.

There was only one flaw in what Canadian National was trying to do. It had the unrealistic expectation, for public consumption at least, that it could make a profit from passenger service. "I cannot stress too strongly," Delagrave told the Moncton Board of Trade in May 1965, "that CN is in the passenger business to make a profit—sooner or later." The problem was that if it became clear that CN could not make a profit from passenger service, then that would be the go-ahead to downgrade and drop it. The attitude of railway officials elsewhere in the world that the purpose of railways is to provide services to the public was never accepted by CN. The railway even set the early seventies as the target date when passenger services should start turning a profit. But at least it was interested enough in passenger service to give it a try.

"I don't say I think they're wrong," said Ian Sinclair over at Canadian Pacific. "I know they're wrong."[27]

In the latter half of the sixties things began to go sour. Discouraged by the indifferent support he was getting from top management, Delagrave left CN for Domtar Ltd. in late 1965. The *Turbo* was introduced, but it fell victim to the rigours of the Canadian winter and had to be withdrawn in 1971; it made a brief return in 1973, but broke down and had to be withdrawn again. Passenger revenues went up dramatically—from $44 million in 1963 to $84 million in 1967,[28] but so did expenses, and the target date for profitability had to be pushed back. Then revenues dropped sharply after the Centennial boom, and CN began to lose heart. When the CTC came around with its abandonment formula, CN was only too happy to oblige.

It made its first request for abandonment in the fall of 1967, with the ink on the National Transportation Act barely dry. This was for its service between St. John's and Port-aux-Basques, Nfld., the train that CN called the *Caribou*, but everybody else called the Newfie Bullet.[29] Way of life, tourist attraction, tradition, institution, "the slowest crack passenger train in civilization"—it was all those things; if ever there was a train whose value could not be measured in dollars and cents, the Bullet was it. In July 1968, the CTC announced its decision: citing "a continuing decline in patronage and . . . a loss of over $900,000 in the year 1966," it would allow CN to drop the Bullet if the company could prove that its proposed bus service was an acceptable alternative. Although the application to abandon the Bullet was based on loss of revenue, this was the one case decided a year before the Commission determined the criteria by which losses would be calculated.

CN ran the train and the new buses side by side for half a year, an example of what intermodal competition generally amounts to in Canada. The buses were heavily advertised, the existence of the trains all but concealed; in fact, one traveller was told by CN in Toronto that there was no longer a passenger-train service in Newfoundland. Predictably, the buses won out. The CTC was satisfied that they were an acceptable alternative—although there have since been some problems with buses getting lost and being blown off the road—and on July 2, 1969, the Bullet left Port-aux-Basques for St. John's for the last time.

The demise of the Bullet has continued to be a matter of public controversy in Newfoundland, and in Ottawa Conservative MPs from the province have continued to press the issue. For the rest of Canada, it was the clearest sign yet that CN had been purged of its uppity notions of challenging Canadian Pacific and had reverted to its more accustomed role of willing partner. Its enthusiastic participation in the ensuing round of abandonment proceedings was still another sign. The imaginative marketing techniques that had characterized the recent past were gone. "Since 1969," according to the executive officers of a union local representing employees of CN's Customer and Catering Services in Toronto, "the CN management have been deliberately pricing themselves out of the market—purchasing suspect equipment, reducing maintenance, altering their schedules, slowing up trains, reducing equipment on trains, and anything that would discourage the public from using this mode of transportation."[30]

For Buck Crump and Ian Sinclair, it was a time of triumph. Railways were for making profits, and there wasn't any Crown corporation anywhere that was going to show them how to do that. How could anyone presume to know more than Canadian Pacific about the travel preferences of Canadians? Sinclair had had the final word on that back in 1966: "I'm not one to think Canadians are so sophisticated that we don't like our own cars. We still like the idea of ownership, and power underfoot, and the sense of well being that driving along the highway provides."[31]

One might almost have thought he was selling Fords.

7 Up up and away: The rise of CP Air

OTTAWA—CPR Chairman N. R. Crump has denied emphatically that his company is trying to abandon the railway passenger business to gain domestic air routes for its airline, CPA.

But he did admit to a Commons committee that while the CPR was discussing further cutbacks in its passenger service, its airline company was eager to expand its air routes.

John Walker,
Southam News Service,
March 4, 1966

In any list of great friends of public ownership in Canada, one would be surprised to find the name of Clarence Decatur Howe, who during the twenty-two years he was a powerful cabinet minister was as responsible as anyone else for the Liberal sellout of Canada's economy to foreign interests. Yet it was C.D. Howe who set up one of this country's most successful public institutions, and in later years took strong measures to protect it against encroachment from private business. In this, he ultimately failed, but he has to be given credit for trying. The institution was Trans-Canada Air Lines, now Air Canada, and the corporation Howe fought against, and finally gave in to, was Canadian Pacific.

The battle is still not over. For a generation after 1946, when Howe capitulated and accepted the existence of Canadian Pacific Air Lines as a rival to TCA, it appeared that there was no limit to the concessions the Government would make to CP Air. In the 1960s, when Jack Pickersgill was transport minister, the Government even worked out a formal division of domestic and international traffic between Air Canada and CP Air. But Jean Marchand, since his appointment as transport minister in late 1972, has shown some signs of balking at easy acceptance of the arrangement that had been developed. The immediate question concerned the new route to Milan and which airline would get it. Under the Pickersgill division, Milan should belong to Canadian Pacific; it is, indisputably, in southern Europe, and southern Europe is Canadian Pacific territory. Marchand, however, favoured awarding Milan to Air Canada. For twenty-six years, government air policy had encouraged private at the expense of public aviation; if Marchand's position won out, it might finally mark a reversal in that policy.

Like railways, airlines are natural candidates for public ownership—perhaps even more natural, since whether privately- or publicly-owned they require heavy public investment in airports, meteorological and navigational aids, and so forth. The government provides these services at a deficit of some $300 million a year, as we have seen (and will examine in more detail later). Despite this, setting up TCA as a public utility was not C.D. Howe's original plan. He wanted to have it jointly owned by the two largest transportation companies in the country, the CPR and the CNR, which would have made it half publicly-owned, a Liberal solution if there ever was one. That was his intention as late as March 4, 1937, when he gave notice in the House of Commons of a resolution to establish a national airline. But when the bill was introduced, Canadian National surfaced as the sole owner of TCA (although even then provision was made for the sale of minority shares to private interests, a step that was never carried out).

The reason for the change was the recalcitrance of Canadian Pacific. "Why the directors of the privately-owned railway withdrew from the open doorway," said Leslie Roberts in his biography of Howe, "has never been made clear. One cynical ex-aviator has suggested that 'they did not believe the airplane had come to stay.' A more likely explanation may be that they did not want to go into partnership with the government-owned railway in a new form of transcontinental transportation which would, in a sense, 'be competing with themselves'. Whatever the correct answer to rejection of participation may be, for many years a false propaganda ran through the country which implied that the Canadian Pacific had been 'frozen out' of transcontinental air transportation by C.D. Howe and permitted to run only north-south feeder lines. The suggestion was made repeatedly that Howe had been determined from the outset that the Government would be the only main line operator in the country. But it was never the truth.''[1]

Canadian Pacific spokesmen now maintain that the company withdrew because it was dissatisfied with the proposed composition of the board of directors: CP, CN and the Cabinet were each to appoint three directors to a board of nine. The reason for the presence of three government directors was that the Government was making a heavy investment in air services, but Canadian Pacific felt that, since it was putting up half the capital for the airline proper, it should be allowed to appoint half the directors. In any case, Canadian Pacific was not involved in Canada's initial venture into civil aviation, but far from believing that the airplane had not come to stay, it quickly set about finding other ways to get into the airline business. In the sprawling bush operations of the Canadian North, it soon found its opening.

The Canadian bush pilots of the 1920s and 1930s were at the same time explorers and entrepreneurs: George Stephen, William Van Horne and Chinese coolie all rolled into one. Their exploits in the air were the stuff legend is made of, but the pilots' originality in flying was at least equalled by that of their bookkeeping. Much of the traffic of the ten bush airlines was curtailed by the outbreak of the Second World War, and by the time these airlines were bought out *en masse* by Canadian Pacific in 1941, their normally rickety financial status had descended into virtual bankruptcy. For the bush pilots, the sale to Canadian Pacific meant that they had a solid financial base for the first time. For the company, the benefits of the deal were equally important: it now had the beginnings of an airline of its own, and it hardly intended to stop there.

"Trans-Canada's monopoly of main line and international air services," wrote Grant Dexter in the Winnipeg *Free Press* in 1943, "is being challenged by the Canadian Pacific Air Lines. If the challenge succeeds our international air policy would be profoundly affected."[2]

The Government had assigned feeder and pioneer services to private airlines, but CP Air never accepted that secondary role. The 1942 and 1943 annual reports of Canadian Pacific contained references to the airline's international ambitions. Conversely, Trans-Canada, with a mandate to be *the* national airline, inevitably expanded into territory where CP Air was operating. It was not a happy situation, but at first the Government gave strong backing to the public airline. Prime Minister Mackenzie King made a policy statement to that effect on April 2, 1943,[3] and a year later C.D. Howe moved to implement that policy.

On March 17, 1944, Howe said in the House of Commons that "the Government has decided that the railways shall not exercise any monopoly of air services. Steps will be taken to require our railways to divest themselves of ownership of air lines, to the end that, within a period of one year from the ending of the European war, transport by air will be entirely separate from surface transportation." One effect of this was that the CNR would have to relinquish formal ownership of TCA; Howe said he regretted this, since CN had "given splendid administration to Trans-Canada Air Lines."

However, he left no doubt that the order was really directed at Canadian Pacific. He noted that CP Air had "lost no time in challenging the non-competitive position of Trans-Canada Air Lines, and in reaching out for new lines . . . . It is becoming obvious that ownership of airways by our two competing railway systems implies extension of railway competition into transport by air, regardless of the Government's desire to avoid competition between air services. In the old days, competitive railway building developed pressure methods for obtaining new franchises. Such methods must not have a place in the development of our airways." Having two coast-to-coast air services in Canada, he said, would be "wasteful and unjustifiable. Service to the public must be the paramount consideration, and it seemed obvious [in 1937] that the cost of a non-competitive, non-profit service was the lowest that could be offered the public. An impartial analysis of the situation today leads to no other conclusion."[4]

The policy that Howe enunciated made sense on both a practical and a theoretical level. In theory, having airlines owned by railways, particularly privately-owned, profit-seeking railways, released the old spectre of transportation monopoly, with its connotations of manipulation and arbitrary power, and the divestment order effectively countered that. Similar legislation had been passed in the United States for precisely that reason. On the practical level, the order met the one serious threat that the public airline actually faced: the threat from Canadian Pacific. There was even less justification for competition in the air than there had been on the rails. The new transcontinental railways had at least had the effect of breaking a private monopoly, but in the case of the airlines, Canadian Pacific was trying to break a *public* monopoly. The policy statement of March 17, 1944, was almost unique in Canadian history. If the Government had carried it out, perhaps this one experiment in public ownership would have turned out differently from the others.

It did not. In August 1946 Stanley Knowles (CCF—Winnipeg North Centre) pointed out that the war in Europe had been over for more than a year, and that the deadline Howe had set for divestment had thus passed. What had happened, Knowles wanted to know, why had the railways not divested themselves of their air services?[5]

Not a man who liked to admit that he was wrong, Howe told Knowles that he still thought the divestment order had been the right thing to do. At the time. But now times had changed. TCA and CP Air were getting along fine. There was no longer any need to force Canadian Pacific to give up its airline. "All sources of friction have been removed as between the government authority and Canadian Pacific Air Lines and between Canadian Pacific Air Lines and Trans-Canada Air Lines," Howe said. "Today the two operations are working as an integrated system. At the time, Canadian Pacific Air Lines was ambitious to extend its territory into other parts of Canada. Today it finds it has a sufficient task to develop the parts of Canada for which it was then and is now responsible for giving service." He announced that the Government was postponing the deadline for implementing the divestment order one year, to give it time to pass new legislation that would repeal the original altogether.[6]

Ostensibly, Howe was saying that divestment was no longer necessary because CP Air had accepted the Government's position. But subsequent events were to show that Howe was being either naive or not entirely candid. The 1946 policy statement was the turnaround point for CP Air. Three years later, it had obtained its first international routes; one to Hawaii, Fiji, Australia and New Zealand, and another to Japan, Hong Kong and China. These were routes that TCA did not want. There was no prospect of an immediate profit from them. But Canadian Pacific, at this point, had something else in mind. TCA had been clearly designated by the government as its Chosen Instrument in international aviation; once Ottawa had signed an air treaty with another country, flights into that country were automatically assigned to TCA. The awarding of the Pacific routes to CP Air was the first breach in that policy, and once there was one breach, Canadian Pacific figured, there could be others.

Ronald Keith told an interesting, although probably somewhat exaggerated, story in his biography of Grant McConachie, a onetime bush pilot who was president of CP Air from 1947 to 1965.[7] It seems that when McConachie and other Canadian Pacific officials went to Australia in 1948 to obtain an operating license for CP Air to fly there, they were at first rebuffed by the Australian government. "I am sorry, Mr. McConachie," Keith quoted the Australian Transport Minister as saying, "but we are a government of labour. We are socialists. We believe in government operation of vital public services such as air transportation . . . . When we made the air agreement with Canada it was our understanding that your government service, Trans-Canada Air Lines, would be designated for the Australia route. We don't propose to issue an operating permit to a capitalistic corporation such as Canadian Pacific.

As Keith tells the story, even the help of the Canadian high Commission was to no avail. "It's a damn shame you gentlemen have been put to the trouble of flying all the way down here to Australia for nothing," the Canadian trade commissioner told the CP Air delegation. "I can assure you we have laid on all the diplomatic pressure possible, right up to the PM, but aside from straining international relations somewhat, it's had no effect." With nothing left but a farewell diplomatic luncheon the next day, the Canadian Pacific group was despondent. Then, according to Keith, it developed in the course of conversation that both the Australian Prime Minister and the Transport Minister had been railway engineers—as had Grant McConachie. Suddenly McConachie was struck with a Great Thought. "All is not lost, fellows," he said. "This luncheon tomorrow may not be a total waste of time after all."

Keith relates how the next day the Prime Minister said to McConachie that "we did not want you Canadian visitors to think of us as savages, even if we are socialists, so we have arranged this luncheon to get better acquainted," and invited him to tell the story of how he had come to be president of CP Air. McConachie, holding up his union card for effect, told how he had worked his way up from a humble railway hand to his present position as a Canadian Pacific executive. "As he spoke he could sense new warmth in his labourite listeners," Keith wrote. "He found the Australian politicians amazed and delighted to learn that in Canada, and particularly in the great Canadian Pacific organization, a man could rise from the ash pits of the rail yards to become a top executive, even as they themselves had come from humble origins to the highest political offices in the land."

The story ends happily, of course, with CP Air getting its operating license. If true, it casts some doubt on the Australian Labourites' credentials as socialists. But it also indicates how strange it appeared that Canada should be giving international routes to a private airline when it had a government airline of its own. It was a phenomenon Canadians would soon be getting used to. The entry into the international field paid off for CP Air. Although the South Pacific route was a money-loser for a long time, there was a brisk traffic on the run to Japan and Hong Kong. (China was lost to Canadian Pacific when the Communists seized state power there in 1949, and not regained until 1973.) As the result of a contract with the Canadian defence department, CP Air was able to fill its planes heading for the Orient with American soldiers off to fight the physically yellow but philosophically red peril in Korea. On the way back to Canada, the planes brought Chinese immigrants who had been smuggled out to Hong Kong, an appropriate business for a company whose railway had been partly built by another generation of Chinese immigrants sixty years earlier.

CP Air was also flying to Mexico City, Lima, Buenos Aires, Amsterdam, Lisbon and Madrid by 1957, and would later add Rome, Athens, Tel Aviv, San Francisco, Santiago de Chile and finally, in 1973, Peking. A 1961 application to fly from Vancouver over the North Pole to London was accepted by Ottawa and did not come to fruition only because the British government decided against it. The effect of all this was to give CP Air a considerably longer route pattern than Air Canada (as TCA has been known since 1964), although the most profitable international routes were still in Air Canada's column. CP Air showed a profit in only six of the twelve years preceding 1966; only four other major airlines—Air France, Lufthansa, Sabena and Varig—had records as bad or worse.[8] But by the late sixties CP Air was making a steady profit, and it avoided the worst effects of a slump that hit the airline industry at the turn of the decade. In part that was because the international routes were now showing direct results. But it was also because they had shown very important indirect results: they had given CP Air the credibility it needed to get into the transcontinental market, the most lucrative market of all.

Its first application for a transcontinental flight was made as early as 1953. In keeping with CP Air's policy of first trying to get permission to do things TCA had not done yet, this application was for an all-cargo flight, but there was widespread suspicion that this move was another foot-in-the-door operation. The application "is aimed at the idea there should be more than one transcontinental operator," TCA president Gordon McGregor said in Vancouver on November 4, 1953. "The federal cabinet has no illusions on this point. If CPA gets a cargo license they will fully expect to carry passengers in the not too distant future."[9] The Air Transport Board reached a similar conclusion. It found that to approve CP Air's application would involve a major change in government policy, and so it passed its report on to Cabinet without recommendation. Cabinet rejected the plan, noting, "Competition in transcontinental air cargo services in Canada at the present time would not be apt to achieve greater efficiency, lower costs and charges, and better service, but rather overexpansion of expensive facilities with division of the market amongst competing carriers leading to a heavier burden on carriers, shippers and taxpayers alike."[10]

Members of the Conservative party, traditionally Canadian Pacific's best friends, leapt to the defence of CP Air. Opposition Leader George Drew called the Government's policy "socialism in a silk hat"—this was 1953, and socialism of any sort was a serious accusation. "We have contended," he said, "that the government was displaying more and more monopolistic tendencies but this was stoutly denied. The Prime Minister has now dotted the i's and crossed the t's of a policy which means the end of free competition where the government has entered any business. It could mean the end of free competition generally . . . ." And what was this, Drew wanted to know, except socialism: "If this government is going to use its powers to decide what is good for business, that is socialism no matter what it may be called . . . . It is the policy which determines the doctrine, and the policies being followed by this government, and now enunciated so clearly, do constitute Socialist doctrine."[11]

Drew's words were echoed by one of his chief lieutenants, John Diefenbaker. "How far are we to go in this country along the road of state enterprise?" Diefenbaker asked. "Are we to be placed in the position where the future of Canada and its development is to be considered as the patrimony of the Prime Minister and his Cabinet?"[12] In another attack, Tory financial critic J.M. Macdonnell charged that TCA was a private monopoly of (who else?) C.D. Howe.[13]

For four more years CP Air bided its time and built up its international network. Then in 1957, the Liberal government was swept out of power. C.D. Howe went down to personal defeat in his home riding of Port Arthur. The Conservatives, under Diefenbaker, were the government of the country, and the omens were good for a new CP Air application. One was duly submitted to the Air Transport Board in November 1957, five months after the Conservative victory. On February 7, 1958, Transport Minister George Hees made the formal announcement of the change in policy. He said in a campaign speech in the northern Ontario town of Timmins that the objective of the new policy would be "introduction of competition on a gradual basis on domestic air routes where economic conditions warrant." He said British aviation consultant Stephen Wheatcroft would be imported to study how this might best be done, and warned private airlines not to expect to get the cream of the domestic routes while TCA was stuck with money-losing flights to out-of-the-way places.[14] Ronald Keith, at that point executive assistant to CP Air President McConachie, professed himself "delighted" with Hees's announcement.[15]

CP Air's enthusiasm had, in fact, run away with itself a little. The airline had applied for *five* east-west return flights a day, serving Vancouver, Calgary, Edmonton, Regina, Saskatoon, Winnipeg, Toronto, Ottawa and Montreal. The Government was prepared to allow competition, but it was not prepared for this—at least not yet. The Air Transport Board was also not impressed with the way CP Air had done its budgeting and had calculated its schedules, or with the fact that no traffic surveys had been carried out. The Board pared the airline's hoped-for five flights a day to one serving Montreal, Toronto, Winnipeg and Vancouver, and said it was granting even that only because it would "strengthen CPA in the international field by allowing it to penetrate the Canadian market."[16] It was a grudging concession and Canadian Pacific was not happy with it. Still, CP Air had succeeded in getting its foot in another door.

Again, there was more to come. In 1964, Transport Minister Jack Pickersgill issued a statement of aviation policy principles, one of which was that "in the domestic mainline field, while the principle of competition is not rejected, any development of competition should not compromise or seriously injure the economic viability of T.C.A.'s mainline domestic operations which represent the essential framework of its domestic services. In other words, there must not be the kind of competition that would put T.C.A. in the red; and, in the event that competition continues, the Air Transport Board should ensure an opportunity for growth to both lines above this basic minimum."[17]

That sounded somewhat less than startling. It sounded, in fact, as if the government airline was by and large being protected. But three years later, when Pickersgill put the principle into practice, it turned out that it meant nothing of the sort. In the interim, British aviation expert Stephen Wheatcroft had again been engaged to study Canada's air situation. He had found, according to another Pickersgill statement, that CP Air's one flight a day "had not shown any indication of producing either major improvements in efficiency or new traffic," but it "had led to a wider public satisfaction as a result of the availability of choice between two carriers. Moreover, while it had led to some diversion of revenue from Air Canada, it had not had the effect of preventing Air Canada from establishing a profitable position."[18] The conclusion was that there was plenty of room for CP Air to be allowed further inroads; it was immediately granted a second daily return flight, and promised future expansion of its transcontinental services until its share of the market had reached twenty-five per cent. Accordingly, three more CP Air flights were inaugurated in 1969, and an additional two in 1970 brought it up to the twenty-five-percent quota. Meanwhile, in the international field, another Pickersgill principle had divided up the world between the two airlines, giving the Caribbean, Britain and northern Europe (except for Amsterdam, which continued to be Canadian Pacific territory) to Air Canada, and the rest of the globe to Canadian Pacific, except for the United States, which was split up, and Africa, which was left open until somebody actually wanted to go there.

The last remnants of the policy of 1944 had been swept away. There were now, in fact and in name, two national airlines, one public and one private. If Canada's air system had avoided the insane early stages of its railway system, it had now developed along lines that were remarkably similar to the railways' illogical later stages, falling into precisely those mistakes that C.D. Howe had hoped would not be made. What had occurred was not so much "competition" as a division of the market. There was no price competition between Air Canada and CP Air. The kinds of planes they flew were similar. The schedules were similar. As with the railways, competition was restricted to the periphery: only on Canadian Pacific's Executive Jet between central Canada and Vancouver was the *Wall Street Journal* offered among the reading material, and CP Air's stewardesses were universally conceded to have sexier uniforms.

But what's wrong with that? Granted that CP Air's entry into the transcontinental field hasn't really helped anyone (except CP Air), can it be said that it has hurt anyone either? If the airlines are so close to being indistinguishable from one another, why should anyone care whether the company that's providing the service is government-owned or private? If Canadian Pacific can make a modest profit from its air services, why not let it?

To answer these questions, it is necessary to examine the nature of the profits that airlines make. Most industries benefit to some extent from government subsidies or services, but few depend on them to the same extent as the airline industry. The objective of the air transport program of the Department of Transport is, as described in the governmentese of the 1973-74 estimates, "to provide facilities and to foster the optimum development of the air mode of transport consistent with the protection of the environment, on a cost-recoverable basis to the maximum practicable extent."[19] The last phrase is the key one, for recovering costs from the provision of air services just doesn't appear to be very practicable. It is not a business that Canadian Pacific, for instance, would ever consider going into.

Of the estimated air services deficit of $377 million for 1973-74, $157.6 million goes to cover an item called "payments into the self-supporting airports and associated ground services revolving fund." The Montreal and Toronto airports are designated "self-supporting" and their expenses are covered out of a revolving fund instead of directly out of the departmental budget. However, these self-supporting airports run at an annual *deficit* that over the last three years has ranged from $90 million to more than $150 million. The 1973-74 expenditures from the fund include $103.9 million for the new Toronto international airport at Pickering and $94.4 million for the new Montreal international airport at Ste-Scholastique. Total annual revenues of $41.8 million don't even cover the $46.5-million cost of operating and maintaining the *existing* Toronto and Montreal airports, let alone contribute toward the outlay required for new facilities.[20]

Just how much of the air services deficit should actually be attributed to civil aviation is difficult to estimate. Some services that the government provides primarily to help commercial aircraft are of benefit elsewhere as well—meteorological services, for example, provide the weather forecast that you hear on the morning radio. In a study done for the Canadian Transport Commission, economists Z. Haritos and J.D. Gibberd attempted to separate out all these factors and calculate the costs directly attributable to civil aviation. Looking at the years 1954 to 1968, they found that "for the entire period under study revenues from user fees in addition to being less than total costs were also significantly less than current costs (operation and maintenance costs)."[21] In that period the government has never ever recovered the costs of operating the services that are already there. For 1968, total costs were at least $207.7 million, of which $128.8 million were current costs, while revenues were only $55.6 million.[22] For the whole fifteen-year period, revenues were $452.8 million, as compared with costs of $2.33 billion—a deficit of $1.88 billion on air services.[23]

The point of all this is that the airline industry is not even close to being economically self-sustaining. If the government attempted to recoup its expenses in landing fees and other user charges, it would drive the airlines deeply into the red, or else drive the price of airline tickets up so high that nobody could afford to fly. But subsidizing air travel is at best a questionable activity for the government, at least the way it is currently done.

The ability to travel from one place to another quickly is important primarily to businessmen, and at current airline prices businessmen are the only people who can afford it. One result of this is a promotional pitch heavily directed toward the business market. "Welcome," said a 1970 advertisement for CP Air's transcontinental Executive Jet, "to your office away from your office . . . . Some men aren't happy unless they're working. So we've put DeJur dictating equipment on all Executive Jet flights. Now, when that great business idea suddenly comes to you at 30,000 feet, you'll be able to record it instead of forgetting it." A promotional pamphlet for "CP Air's Orient" says, "If you're doing business there, it's time you met your partners . . . . Before you go we'll put you in touch with an expert specially appointed by the Department of Industry, Trade and Commerce to handle business arrangements for CP Air passengers. He'll help you with preliminary market analysis and pertinent information kits designed to maximize your advance investment of time and money. He'll set up meetings with your advance men in the Orient—Canada's Trade Commissioners.''

If the government is going to subsidize air travel, probably the most equitable thing for it to do would be to spend yet another two hundred million or so on it, so that fares—and especially fares on domestic flights—could be slashed to the point where a much wider range of people could afford to fly. Failing that, if the government is going to pour several hundred million dollars a year into aviation, it is at least reasonable to expect that whatever revenues accrue from aviation should go back to the government and not to a private company. Viewed in this context, the profits that CP Air makes are in effect an outright government gift. Whether or not CP Air's existence impedes Air Canada to the point where the public airline is actually driven into the red is not the main point. The point is that the money that goes to CP Air in the form of profits is money that could and should go to Air Canada and thus be saved to the Canadian taxpayer.

The amounts involved are small by the standards of the federal budget, but they are far from negligible. In the eleven years from 1962 to 1972, CP Air made net profits totalling $35.8 million, substantially more than the $27.8 million made by Air Canada.[24] This is despite the considerable difference in size between the two airlines; CP Air's annual operating revenue is less than a third that of Air Canada's. Even there, however, CP Air is slowly creeping up: in the years 1962 to 1968, when CP Air's transcontinental service was still small, its operating revenue was 27.9 per cent that of Air Canada's, while in the years 1969 to 1972, with CP Air's transcontinental flights increased to five and then seven a day, its operating revenue was 31.1 per cent of Air Canada's. In 1970, the worst year of the airline slump, Air Canada had a net loss of $1.1 million, while CP Air still managed a profit of just over one million dollars.

When the question of the Milan route arose in 1972, Air Canada and its chairman, Yves Pratte, were tired of the pattern of government decisions that had allowed CP Air to reach that position. Pratte was reported to be putting all the pressure he could on the Cabinet in a bid to get Milan, and threatening to resign if the route were awarded to CP Air. His campaign was squarely within the bounds of an Air Canada tradition that had seen the airline protest many times before under similar circumstances, generally without success. Pratte's predecessor, Gordon McGregor, was a bonny fighter who carried on a sniping match with his fellow Scotsman Grant McConachie that lasted for years.

McGregor fought CP Air's initial application for a transcontinental cargo flight, its 1957 application to leap headfirst into the trans-continental field, its attempt to obtain a flight to London. His battles were not entirely fruitless, but he knew that he was losing the long war of attrition. With both airlines losing money in the early 1960s, he proposed that they be merged. "The country can't afford it," he said. "The two airlines ran more than $13 million in the red last year, $25 million over the past three years. Merger is the only solution."[25] There was little response to his call, especially after both airlines moved back into the black in 1963. The next year Pickersgill proclaimed his policy of more "competition" rather than less.

While Air Canada would at times take an aggressive stance, CP Air would never be caught being apologetic or defensive. Probably wisely, it regarded a good offence as being the best defence. It purported to be not only seeking profits, but upholding the banner of free enterprise as well. "We must not be satisfied merely to recognize the superiority of our free-enterprise system," McConachie told a Chamber of Commerce audience in the mid-1950s. "We must also combat the forces working to threaten its very existence .... We must renew our dedication to free enterprise as a positive and dynamic faith." To do this, it was necessary to fight not only "the militant creeds of socialism and communism" but also—somewhat closer to home—"the encroachment of government in business and the trend to state control." And where better to start fighting state control than with Air Canada's monopoly of transcontinental traffic, at that point still untouched? This was, McConachie noted ominously, "the largest pool of air traffic anywhere in the world monopolized by a single carrier, with one exception . . . RUSSIA."[26]

The rhetoric of CP Air officials in the 1970s has more or less the same tone and sometimes exactly the same language. When Marchand, then still minister of regional economic expansion, first expressed the opinion that Milan should be given to Air Canada, John Gilmer, McConachie's successor as CP Air president, said that "it is obvious that CP Air has every right to expect the Government to assign Milan to it." He described the policy espoused by Marchand as "dear to the hearts" of New Democrats but one that "comes strangely from a member of our present Cabinet."[27] Air Canada's purchase of a one-third share of Wardair, the country's largest charter airline, provoked CP Air's vice-president for marketing and sales, Bryan Renwick, to warn of a "further encroachment of government in the private sector."[28] The charter-flight market is, of course, a most lucrative plum.

CP Air's goal, in its own words, is "fair competition." And what, in concrete terms, does that mean? "Being restricted to 25 per cent of the traffic in Canada is not what I call fair competition," Renwick said in early 1973. "We don't want to look a gift horse in the mouth, but nevertheless we won't be happy until we get to be 50-50.''[29] In that comment about looking a gift horse in the mouth there is a back-handed recognition, the merest suggestion, that because of the very nature of the airline business, all of CP Air's past accomplishments and any future growth it might enjoy have come about because of the goodwill of the government. CP Air still considers itself a soldier for unfettered Private Enterprise fighting the forces of Government Monopoly. McConachie, the freewheeling former bush pilot, saw himself as an entrepreneur in the great American tradition. His successors will tell you that CP Air got to be where it is because it has been run by smart businessmen, men who took the long view.

The corollary of that, and a correct one, is that the Government and its airline took the short view. Trans-Canada Air Lines had had inculcated into it from an early date, as had the CNR before, the idea that it was supposed to operate at a profit, and this placed a severe constraint on the kinds of decisions it could make. In 1949 it saw no prospect of being able to make a profit flying to the Orient, and so left an opening—the first of many—just wide enough for Canadian Pacific to slip in.

The Government, which had the power to close those openings, failed to see that if it did not do so the gradual but inevitable result would be the second national airline that everybody except Canadian Pacific wanted to avoid. By the time TCA started kicking up a fuss it was too late. It is useless to speculate on how TCA would have developed had there been no CP Air; however, it is certain that the same attitude that led the Government to allow the existence of a private airline also led it to create a business-oriented airline of its own.

One effect of this apparent identity of the two airlines is that public attention to the squabbles between them is almost nonexistent. And why should anyone pay attention? Only a small proportion of the population, coming mostly from the highest income group, flies on either airline. Even for those people, if price and service are identical, the matter of which airline provides the plane they fly on is of little concern. If Air Canada executives, with an obvious self-interest in the matter, can find little support for their continuing campaign to stop CP Air's encroachment on their territory, it is largely because of their own—and the Government's—failure to make the public airline a genuine public service.

The record of the development of Canadian civil aviation policy after 1944 does not cast credit on anyone. Although C.D. Howe's stock has been deservedly low in Ottawa for some time, a little of the spirit and determination he showed in his early years in the Cabinet would not be out of place in deciding that policy's future.

8 Phasing out people: The CPR and its employees

The Company believes that its labour relations in general are satisfactory.

Canadian Pacific bond issue prospectus,
February 1, 1971

Although the railways came out of the Second World War in the best financial position they had ever known, their future prospects were cloudy, unpredictable and potentially disastrous. Their costs, and particularly their wage bill, would rise steeply in the immediate postwar period. Their revenues would be affected by the loss of traffic to the newer modes of transport. It was one of those periods when the consequences of the unplanned growth of Canada's transportation system were blindingly clear.

There were three things the railways could do to try to collect what they regarded as their fair share of the postwar prosperity. The first, and least practicable, was to resist the wage demands of their employees, who were pressing their own claims to a bigger slice of the pie. Before the war, railway employees had been among the highest-paid workers, and now they wanted their wages at least to keep pace with the rapidly expanding incomes of workers who were putting together cars or fabricating steel. Resistance to those demands could awaken the previously somewhat docile railway unions, and lead to strikes that would do the railways no good.

A second expedient was to meet each increase in wages with a freight-rate increase. This meant that negotiations for higher wages would in effect become a three-way affair among the unions, the railways, and the Board of Transport Commissioners, which regulated freight rates. The BTC, in using the return on investment of the Canadian Pacific Railway as its yardstick for freight-rate determination, effectively accepted that role. (A rise in the cost of labour, leading to a smaller return on investment, would therefore justify an increase in freight rates.) But this was still only a partial solution to the railways' problem. Increased rates only accelerated the flight of traffic to other modes. Something else had to give.

That something was people. Employment on the Canadian Pacific Railway reached a peak of almost 84,000 in 1952, and has fallen steadily since then to only 44,000 in 1971, below even the lowest depression level of 1938.[1] A similar pattern, although not quite as dramatic, has prevailed on the Canadian National. That railway had a peak of 128,000 employees in 1952, and by 1971 the figure had fallen below 80,000.[2] A 1967 study of labour relations in the railway industry by University of Calgary economist Stephen Peitchinis warned: "Railway employment, which traditionally has been regarded as one of the most stable in the economy, has now become one of the most insecure."[3]

The railways have been phasing out people in two ways. One has been simply to get rid of the services where the most people are required—for instance, passenger service. Passenger runs require not only extensive crews on the trains, but also large numbers of station employees. Moreover, the measures that can be taken to cut down the number of people employed generally have the side-effect of driving passengers away. You can cut out several employees by eliminating the dining car and replacing it with a counter that serves cardboard hamburgers heated in infrared ovens, but passengers who complain that the service is not quite the same must be conceded their point.

Another area where the railways have cut down drastically is express and LCL freight. LCL (less-than-carload) traffic, which requires handling almost at every turn, once represented a substantial proportion of the railways' business, but in 1970, of the almost 208 million tons of freight carried by the railways, only a little over a million tons was express or LCL. Most of the railways' freight now consists of bulky commodities that require little handling such as coal, ore, grain, paper, sulphur, steel. If the old image of the CPR was a streamlined passenger train or a long, varied freight train, the new image is a train one hundred identical cars long, heading westward through southern British Columbia, carrying nothing but coal; coal from the fields of the Rocky Mountains, bound for the Pacific and eventually for the steel mills of Japan.

In those areas which the railways were not interested in eliminating, they have reduced their work force through the aggressive promotion of technological change. In 1950, only a small minority of the engines on Canadian railways were diesels; by 1960, the steam engine had all but vanished. Diesels require smaller engine crews, less servicing, fewer stops. More recent changes in railway operations have had similar effects. The best publicized and perhaps most important of these has been containerization, which has radically altered the intermodal carrying of freight. A container is a standard-sized (8 by 8½ by 20—or sometimes 40—feet), coffin-like box, that can be carried by truck, train or ship and transferred easily from one to the other. Before containers, freight arriving in port to be shipped to its eventual destination by rail had to be unloaded item by item, and then reloaded onto the trains. It was a slow, laborious process, and breakage and stealing were common. Containers, however, are sealed at the original shipping point and remain that way until they reach their destination. They are transferred from one mode to another by cranes.

A company like Canadian Pacific that is involved in several modes of transport is in a particularly good position to take advantage of containerization. The CPR introduced piggyback, a primitive form of containerization in which trailers can be carried by both truck and rail, as early as 1957. In the 1960s, it began to move toward a fully realized container system. CP Ships, which had once operated freighters and the luxurious Empress passenger liners on both the Atlantic and the Pacific, has phased out all these operations to concentrate on the Atlantic container trade. In 1970, Canadian Pacific opened its new container port at Wolfe's Cove in Quebec City, featuring a giant crane capable of handling forty containers an hour. The company is also involved in the operation of the four-million-dollar Brunterm container port in Saint John, New Brunswick (CP Rail's chief terminal in the Atlantic provinces), which handles traffic destined for the Caribbean, Australasia and other areas.

Another labour-saving device of which Canadian Pacific became enamoured in the 1950s was the computer. It installed a computer in the Montreal head office in 1955, a first in the Canadian transportation industry and one of the earliest large computers in any industry in Canada. By 1968, it had seven computers in Montreal as well as others scattered around the country. It uses them to keep track of where its freight cars and customers' shipments are, to do simulations of specific freight-shipment problems, and to handle financial data. The Montreal computer centre was reported in 1968 to be answering six to seven hundred queries about freight car locations every day.[4]

All these changes, and the resultant cut in the labour force by almost half, have constituted one of the main tasks of the new generation of Canadian Pacific managers that took over in the mid-1950s. The relation of their success in performing that task to the continued profitability of the railway has been direct. For despite the drastic drop in employment, the total payroll has still risen since 1952—from $269 million to $371 million in 1971.[5] The labour-saving devices have simply allowed Canadian Pacific to keep that payroll increase within manageable proportions: the payroll has risen by only slightly more in the twenty years since 1952 than it did in the five years preceding it. The proportion of operating expenses attributed to wages has dropped from a high of 53 per cent in 1954 to 46.7 per cent in 1971.[6] With the same amount of wealth, or a little more, to be divided among considerably fewer people, wages have not been the most contentious issue between labour and management in recent years (although, with railway wages falling behind those in other industries, they became the unions' main grievance in the fractious 1973 negotiations). Not surprisingly, the most notable collisions have arisen over conditions of work, technological change and changes in service.

One such transition that both railways handled with particular lack of attention to the people affected was the run-through, an operational change made possible by the introduction of the diesel. Originally, railway terminals were established at approximate intervals of 125 miles along the line, since this was roughly the distance that a steam engine could travel before it needed servicing. Diesels need less frequent servicing, especially when accompanied with other technological improvements that were introduced around the same time, and so it became possible to eliminate many of these terminal points. Since the railway was the only employer of any significance in many of these places, elimination of the terminal often meant the death of the town. The inevitability of run-throughs was more or less taken for granted, but how they were instituted became a question of considerable importance.

In 1958, Canadian Pacific proposed to run through from Toronto all the way to Smiths Falls, Ont., a distance of some 225 miles. It suggested that the run-through be negotiated at the union-local level between the railway and the Brotherhood of Railroad Trainmen, in accordance with a rule to be included in the collective agreement between the two parties. It came up with a proposal for such a rule that said that "in such negotiations each party will give full recognition to the other party's 'fundamental rights', with reasonable and fair arrangements being made in the interests of both parties."[7]

The matter was included in the usual drawn-out process of labour-management negotiations, and in due course was one of the items that was sent to a conciliation board, which proposed to help work out just what each party's "fundamental rights" were. Then, on June 13, 1960, the CPR withdrew its request for the inclusion of a rule regarding run-throughs in the collective agreement. It obtained an injunction preventing the conciliation board from dealing any further with the matter. When the injunction was quashed by the High Court of Justice of Ontario and the board started its hearings again, the CPR boycotted the proceedings. With its hands tied, the board gave up. The CPR proceeded with its run-through unilaterally.

Contrary to most labour-management disputes, the run-through controversy was one in which Canadian National was even less flexible than Canadian Pacific. Canadian National never even considered settling its run-throughs through negotiation. Manitoba Appeal Court Judge Samuel Freedman, who was appointed a one-man commission of inquiry when the problems caused by CNR run-throughs had become so serious that wildcat strikes had started breaking out, speculated that Canadian National's hard line may have been one of the factors causing Canadian Pacific to change its tack. "Negotiation of fundamental rights was abandoned by the C.P.R.," said Mr. Justice Freedman in his report, "when it was found that run-throughs could be carried through by the C.N.R. without negotiation."

Mr. Justice Freedman concluded, however, that run-throughs *should* be negotiated between management and labour. While admitting that the CNR had been within its legal rights in imposing run-throughs unilaterally, he contended that the law was a bad one and should be changed. He rejected the CNR's contention that management had an "inherent right" to introduce technological change without the agreement of its employees. "The institution of run-throughs should be a matter for negotiation," he said. "To treat it as an unfettered management prerogative will only promote unrest, undermine morale, and drive the parties farther and farther apart. In that direction lies disorder and danger. By placing run-throughs, on the other hand, within the realm of negotiation a long step will be taken toward the goal of industrial peace. More than that. Such a course will help to provide safeguards against the undue dislocation and hardship that often result from technological change."[8]

The Freedman report has proved a troublesome document for the railways. While agreeing to "consultation" on technological change, they never agreed to these changes being made a subject for negotiation; the unions, meanwhile, pressed for full implementation of the Freedman recommendations. It was thus the railways who were seen to balk at taking the long step toward the goal of industrial peace. In the early seventies, the issue is more or less in abeyance, since there has been no new operational change on the scale of the elimination of firemen in the fifties, or run-throughs in the sixties. When one does come up, as it must, the existence of the Freedman report could well be a major obstacle to the railways' getting their way quite so easily.

Passenger service has been another area of conflict between the railways and the unions. Worried about the jobs of their members and sensing an occasion on which they could take the leadership of a popular cause, the railway brotherhoods—and particularly the United Transportation Union (UTU), the Canadian Brotherhood of Railway, Transport and General Workers (CBRT), and the Brotherhood of Railway, Airline and Steamship Clerks (BRASC)—have carried on a spirited fight against the railways' attempts to abandon passenger runs. They have been the most active participants in whatever public hearings have been held and have run publicity campaigns on the issues involved for both their membership and the public at large. "There will be a hundred briefs," said one of the most vigorous union spokesmen on the issue just before the hearings on the *Canadian* began, "even if we have to write them all ourselves." As it turned out the unions got plenty of help, but Maurice Wright, counsel for the Canadian Railway Labour Association (a co-ordinating body of railway unions), was still one of the most visible figures and persistent questioners at the hearings.

At one point, he assailed J.C. Anderson, Canadian Pacific's vice-president for industrial relations, on the question of how much notice the affected employees would get if the railway's rationalization plan were implemented. According to the collective agreement, Anderson said, the CPR would be required to give four days' notice to non-operating employees (employees involved in jobs other than the actual running of the trains) before laying them off. It developed in the course of the discussion that that depended on a particular interpretation of the collective agreement. One clause said that the railway had to give an employee affected by "technological, operational and organizational changes" two months' notice, and three months if the change required the employee to move. But, Anderson maintained, the rationalization of the *Canadian* "is not an operational change, because it is a reduction in the existing operation. It is not an operational change as intended in the agreement." Therefore, the employees were not covered by that clause. They were covered by another clause that only required the railway to give them four days' notice.

"The men who would be involved," Wright said, "349 men, I believe it is, some of them would have seniority going back for a good many years."

"Some of them," Anderson agreed.

"And some of them really do not have any other function in life except as railway employees," Wright continued. "This is the only training they have. Isn't that right, surely you agree?"

"That is right," Anderson said.[9]

A representative of the Ontario government asked whether the CPR had consulted the unions in formulating its rationalization plan. The suggestion caught Anderson somewhat off guard. "I suppose that it hasn't been the general practice to go to the unions and expect them to negotiate jobs away with us," he said. "It just hasn't worked out over the years. We have had many talks of various kinds over the years. It just hasn't worked out."[10] His regret at the failure of the unions to negotiate reductions in jobs was, perhaps, somewhat feigned. It took a certain amount of cheek even to suggest that they should. It implied that there was some reason why labour should trust Canadian Pacific's good faith. But the unions have always known that in Canadian Pacific they were dealing with an adversary that wouldn't give an inch unless it had to. One union representative has referred to it as "the General Electric of Canada," in reference to one of the most notoriously anti-labour corporations in the United States. "Sometimes when negotiations are going nowhere," he said, "the CNR negotiators take us aside and say that if it were just up to them they would be more reasonable. Now it's hard to know whether that's true, but it is true that it's usually the CPR that takes the hard line."

The hard line has a long history: William Van Horne was not a man to suffer unions gladly. Any employee who was suspected of trying to organize one was fired. But this is not the labour policy that has remained longest in the memory. The policy that is most often associated with the construction of the railway was not one practised by the CPR itself. It was Andrew Onderdonk, the contractor on the government section of the line in British Columbia, who imported Chinese workers and paid them half the wages of white labourers. This was not a new procedure. Chinese had been employed on American railroads and in the mines in British Columbia. Their presence was regarded with suspicion and resentment by whites, and particularly by white workers, for whom the racism that they shared with the rest of the population was heightened by fear of unfair competition. Employers and other members of their class who testified before the Royal Commission on Chinese Immigration in the 1880s generally spoke highly of the new arrivals. "The proportion of depraved or immoral Chinamen is smaller than in any class I know of," Onderdonk told the Commission. "Ninety-nine percent of the Chinese here are industrious and steady." More to the point, he said that if the Chinese were to leave, "the development of the country would be retarded and many industries abandoned."[11]

The most articulate defender of the Chinese was Sir Matthew Begbie, the chief justice of British Columbia. "Industry, economy, sobriety and law-abidingness are exactly the four prominent qualities of Chinamen as asserted both by their advocates and their adversaries," he said in his submission to the Royal Commission. "Lazy, drunken, extravagant, and turbulent: this is, by the voices of their friends and foes, exactly what a Chinaman is not. This is, on the whole, the real cause of their unpopularity. If Chinamen would only be less industrious and economical, if they would but occasionally get drunk, they would no longer be the formidable competitors with the white man which they prove to be in the labor market; there would be no longer a cry for their suppression."[12]

To a modern ear, Begbie's gentlemanly detachment sounds remarkably civilized for the time and place, but it was a luxury he could afford. Not so the Knights of Labour, for whom Chinese labour was "confessedly of a low, degraded, and servile type, the inevitable result of whose employment in competition with free white labor is to lower and degrade the latter without any appreciable elevation of the former . . . . They are thus fitted to become all too dangerous competitors in the labor market, while their docile servility, the natural outcome of centuries of grinding poverty and humble submission to a most oppressive form of government, renders them doubly dangerous as the willing tools whereby grasping and tyrannical employers grind down all labor to the lowest living point."[13] This, said the Knights of Labour, and not their willingness to accept lower wages, was the chief reason for objecting to the Chinese. But whatever the reasons, and however valid they might be, white opposition to Chinese immigration created scars that would not heal easily or quickly. Just as the legacy of black slavery in the United States has not been wiped out in a mere hundred years, so the introduction of the Chinese into British Columbia as semi-indentured and low-paid workers created a climate which as late as 1935 allowed Mackenzie King's Liberals to campaign in B.C. on a promise that Orientals would not be given the vote.[14]

Nelson Bennett, a contractor for the Northern Pacific Railroad in Oregon, testified to the Commission that he actually preferred white to Chinese labour, and was particularly partial to Scandinavians, but he was employing Chinese "because we are at present shoving things."[15] The CPR and its contractors were always shoving things; the corollary of building the railway in five years was that labour was driven to the breaking point and any measures that might improve its lot were sternly opposed.

However, the CPR could not keep out unions forever. The railways, like most other industries, were first organized along craft lines: each separate trade within the industry had its own union. The running trades—engineers, firemen, trainmen and conductors—were organized as early as the 1890s, in fiercely independent craft unions, which did not join any central labour body until the 1960s.

Industrial unionism—the organization of all workers in an industry in one union regardless of craft divisions—made its first appearance on the CPR in 1902. The United Brotherhood of Railway Employees had started in San Francisco the previous year, and had quickly formed locals in western Canada as well. When attempts to win recognition were met with suspensions and dismissals from the CPR, the UBRE went on strike. The strike lasted through four months in 1903, but it was an unequal struggle; it was finally crushed, and the UBRE with it.[16] In the latter part of the decade, non-operating employees on the government-owned Intercolonial Railway in eastern Canada formed a similar organization. This was the Canadian Brotherhood of Railway Employees (CBRE), later the Canadian Brotherhood of Railway, Transport and General Workers. According to one old union hand, one of the major grievances of the workers on the Intercolonial was the practice of hiring a whole new slate of employees whenever the government changed hands.

In 1910, the CBRE made its first attempts to organize on the CPR. At that time, wages in the clerical departments of the railway averaged less than $45 per month. By 1912 the CBRE was ready to go to management with a proposed contract; it demanded a substantial wage increase, seniority rules, paid holidays, a grievance procedure and a ten-hour day. The CPR would have none of it. When the union applied to the Federal Minister of Labour for the appointment of a conciliation board, the CPR tried to block it. The company said that there was no evidence that the employees covered in the proposed agreement were actually members of the CBRE, and argued that if it did permit its clerks to join the union, confidential company documents might become public property. The Minister of Labour repeatedly refused to appoint a conciliation board, and in November 1912 the CBRE went on strike. Again the CPR was too strong for the union. The strike was lost after two months, and the CBRE's organizing attempt was a failure.[17] Strikers were rehired, often at better pay, but the words ''on strike'' were marked on their records.

A third and successful attempt to organize a union on the CPR that cut across craft lines came at the end of the First World War. The Brotherhood of Railway and Steamship Clerks, which had been rapidly expanding in the United States, signed up members on the CPR in western Canada and succeeded in winning a contract. By 1920, the divided and intricate structure of the railway unions in Canada was more or less in place; the only significant change since then has been the merger of all the running-trades unions except the Brotherhood of Locomotive Engineers into the United Transportation Union in 1970. But there are still a score of separate unions representing railway workers, and despite the presence of the CBRT and BRASC, industrial unionism, which on the whole has been the strongest and most militant form of organization, has not taken hold. Railway unions have also shown a tendency to fight among themselves: a jurisdictional dispute between the CBRE and BRASC in the early 1920s led to a split in the labour movement that was not fully healed until 1956.

Another factor in the relative quiescence of the railway unions has been the virtual elimination by the government of the strike weapon. Three times—in 1950, 1966, and 1973—has there been a national rail strike, and all those strikes were ended by the government after a short time. The government has always considered a railway strike to be a national emergency, and both unions and railways are aware that it will step in to stop such a strike either before it happens or as soon as it breaks out. A national railway strike is largely an exercise in theatre; the threat of a long strike, one which can actually inflict some damage on the railways, is simply not present. The proposition that a railway strike is a national emergency has never really been tested; in any case, the government's conviction that it is has been enough to take railway negotiations out of the realm of normal labour-management bargaining.

The unions, in making demands on the railways, are always at least equally making them on the government, since any dispute will likely be settled by government intervention of one sort or another. The railways, for their part, while ostensibly negotiating with the unions, are often effectively using their employees as tools in their own dickering with the government. When freight rates were regulated by the Board of Transport Commissioners, the railways expected that body to come up with a compensatory rate increase for any increase in pay they granted their employees. Their rejection of union wage demands was often directed as much toward the BTC as toward the unions. Since the passage of the National Transportation Act, the railways are in the happy position of being able simply to raise their own freight rates and thus compensate themselves for wage increases.

The settlement of railway wages by government intervention rather than by labour-management negotiation began as early as 1918. "Contrary to experience in other industries," said Stephen Peitchinis in his study, "whereby agreements were achieved through negotiation, railway managers flatly refused to negotiate wage advances. In fact, they proved so inept and so lacking in vision and policy that in early 1918 they found themselves in the most undesirable position of having to surrender the determination of Canadian railway wages to the United States."[18] The result was the McAdoo award, named for the American wartime director general of railways who, on the advice of a commission, granted a substantial increase in wages and an eight-hour day to railway workers on May 25, 1918. Disputes on the Canadian railways had been left in abeyance until the American commission reported, and now the federal government by order-in-council applied the McAdoo award without modification in Canada. Later that year, the railways were granted a twenty-five-percent increase in freight rates, disregarding even the guidelines established by the Crow's Nest Pass agreement of 1897. The next wage increase, in 1920, was also a direct spin-off from an American wage agreement, the Chicago award.

The practice of applying American wage settlements without amendment in Canada did not continue, but the government presence in labour-management negotiations on the railways did. It was a key factor in the recurring conflicts after the Second World War, three of which led to brief strikes. On August 29, 1950, Prime Minister Louis St-Laurent called a special session of Parliament to legislate striking railway employees back to work and appoint an arbitration board to impose a settlement. The arbitration board accepted the key demand of the unions, a forty-hour week; as usual, the increased costs to the railways were met by a freight-rate increase granted by the Board of Transport Commissioners. The cycle of higher wages and higher freight rates continued throughout the 1950s until at the end of the decade the Diefenbaker government decided the cycle must be broken.

On July 29, 1958, a conciliation board recommended increases in wages for railway employees, to which the railways said they would agree—if they could get an appropriate increase in freight rates. Meanwhile, the unions were taking the necessary action to get their increase: a strike vote was taken and a strike date set. On November 17, the BTC authorized a seventeen per cent increase in freight rates, effective December 1. Within ten days, the unions and railways had come to an agreement.

However, this practice of automatically passing on wage increases through higher freight rates had long grated on the areas that suffered most, the West and the Atlantic provinces. This time they protested heatedly to Ottawa. With no end to the freight-rate increases in sight, the Diefenbaker government introduced the Freight Rates Reduction Act, which called for a roll-back of the seventeen per cent increase to ten per cent, a temporary ban on further increases, and a subsidy to compensate the railways. The Government also appointed the MacPherson Commission to look into the whole problem.

The next negotiations two years later again came to the verge of a strike. The strike was stopped by legislation, this time in advance: Parliament forbade it on December 2, 1960, the day before the strike was to begin. The dispute was settled the following May, after the MacPherson Commission had issued the first volume of its report, when the Government accepted its recommendation of a temporary subsidy of $50 million a year to the railways while awaiting the passage of new legislation. It was to be a long wait, and in the meantime the railways insisted in every dealing with the unions that they couldn't grant wage increases unless the government would let them make more money.

In 1964, after a conciliation board had reported and a crisis had begun to build up, CPR President Buck Crump and CNR President Donald Gordon addressed a joint letter to Prime Minister Pearson in which they said that "the Railways find themselves by action of Government deprived of authority to raise added revenues to meet increased costs, and circumscribed in their ability to effect economies through the discontinuance of unremunerative operations. Under these conditions, they cannot undertake the responsibility of assuming added costs of the magnitude implicit in the majority report of the Munroe Conciliation Board. Even though the rejection of the report may inevitably lead to a railway strike, existing circumstances leave us no alternative."[19] The 1964 dispute was settled without a strike, but the 1966 negotiations, in which the railways took a similar position, led to the second railway strike in sixteen years. As in 1950, the Government legislated the strikers back to work after a few days, and set up a mediation process which, with the dark threat of arbitration at the end of the road, was successful in imposing a settlement.

The increasingly difficult position of the railway workers was well illustrated in the 1973 conflict. The railways manifested a renewed toughness on wages, particularly after the federal Liberal government, trying to strengthen its severely exposed western flank, imposed an eighteen-month freeze on freight rates. And while the wage dispute, easily expressed in hard figures, received the most public attention, the ultimately more critical question of job security lay just below the surface.

For a month, the non-operating railway unions carried on rotating strikes, closing down one area of the country at a time. But the railways did not budge, and the strain began to tell. At the end of August, the unions changed tactics and called a nationwide strike, with the full expectation that they would be legislated back to work, but with the hope—however faint—that the Government would decree a favourable settlement. The Government acted within a week, citing the existence of a national emergency and summoning members of Parliament back from their summer recess. The interim wage-settlement in the Government's back-to-work legislation was little different from the one the unions had rejected months earlier; it was only at opposition prodding that the Government, in a precarious minority situation, was forced to add on another four cents an hour, still considerably less than what the workers had wanted. There were noises from the unions about non-compliance with the legislation and a spirited demonstration on Parliament Hill in which windows were broken, but when the law actually went into effect most of the workers went back, and the remaining pockets of resistance gradually melted away.

Government involvement in labour-management relations on the railways was of course inevitable, and only reflected the heavy dependence of the railway industry generally on government support. But it has had some curious effects. The railways have not been required to negotiate with the unions except in the most perfunctory way. The unions have sometimes found themselves effectively supporting the railways in favouring the implementation of a wage-and-freight-rate-increase package deal. The situation even led some trade unionists to praise the MacPherson Report, a document which in the long term was severely inimical to their interests.

The events of 1973 showed how little the passage of the National Transportation Act had really "de-regulated" the railways. In a single summer, the Government was forced to intervene in questions both of freight rates and of wages. The closeness of the two occurrences in time was not a coincidence. The railways still give out in wage increases only what they can themselves collect in higher freight rates. Their wage policies continue to operate according to the Canadian Pacific Law of Railway Finance. That is the unofficial but nevertheless highly effective law which says that whatever adjustments may take place anywhere else in the economy, the CPR's profit position cannot be allowed to suffer.

9 The shy and timid old lady: The CPR becomes a conglomerate

I don't think we are too diversified—we would be if we didn't have a plan. You look closely and everything fits. You know, we didn't try to diversify just to look good.

Ian Sinclair, 1966
just after becoming
CPR president

There is a former railway union negotiator who likes to tell the story of the time in the early fifties when he sat across the bargaining table from a clutch of Canadian Pacific vice-presidents and listened to them moan about the railway's poor financial position. He examined their financial statements and said, "You haven't included all your profits in here. For instance, what about the dividends from the Belt Railway Company of Chicago?"

"But we don't own the Belt Railway Company of Chicago," said one vice-president with evident sincerity.

"Oh yes you do," shot back the union man. During a break in the negotiations he rechecked assorted financial reference books and found that, through a complicated chain of corporate interlocking, Canadian Pacific did indeed own a piece of the Belt Railway Company of Chicago.

The CPR at that time literally did not know what its assets were. Without ever really seeming to seek them, it had acquired substantial holdings in a dozen or so different business activities. It had its mining company, Cominco. It still had about a million acres of land left over from the grants of the early years. In the 1940s, some of that land had looked interesting to the great international oil companies, and the first oil strike in Canada had been made on Canadian Pacific land at Leduc, Alberta, in 1947. It was now receiving revenue on its oil lands in the form of royalties from the companies that had developed them. It had the ships, the airline, the hotels. The new Canadian Pacific executives who assumed the company's top positions in 1955 were motivated by the conviction that it could have a lot more.

These men—Norris R. (Buck) Crump, Robert Emerson and Ian Sinclair—would change the face of the company until it was all but unrecognizable. The changes that they instituted on the railway were only a small part of this. The railway played only a relatively minor role in their plans. Canadian Pacific in 1955 was a railway company that happened to have a variety of other interests. Canadian Pacific in 1973 is a conglomerate that happens to own a railway. Even the historic name, "Canadian Pacific Railway Company," has gone, replaced in 1971 by the new "Canadian Pacific Limited," more accurately reflecting the greater scope of the corporation. The railway was renamed "CP Rail," to put it on an equal footing with CP Air, CP Transport, CP Hotels, CP Oil and Gas, and the rest. In a memo to the Winnipeg *Free Press* in 1971, Canadian Pacific instructed the paper to "keep our identity clear, crisp and consistent. . . . If you are identifying the corporate parent (the company whose shares are traded on stock markets), then our first preference is Canadian Pacific or Canadian Pacific Ltd. If you must abbreviate, then we'd prefer CP Ltd. (not Canpac, not CP, not CPL—certainly not CPR)."

There is one key difference between Canadian Pacific and most other conglomerates. ITT and Litton Industries in the United States, and Power Corporation in Canada, have acquired most of their holdings through an aggressive policy of takeover. Canadian Pacific, while not being wholly reticent about taking over other companies, has developed into a conglomerate mostly through the development of properties it already had. Some of the more questionable business practices that have given American conglomerates a bad name have been largely absent in the case of Canadian Pacific.

A U.S. House of Representatives Subcommittee that investigated conglomerates in 1971 said of the corporations it had looked into, "These acquisition-minded managements frequently employed accounting practices which were designed to favorably influence the earnings per share of their company. The term 'conglomerate,' which in the 1950s and early 1960s connoted 'growth', 'enterprise', 'change' and 'glamour', in time generated doubt, apprehension, and dismay . . . . At the time [this] Subcommittee's investigation reached the hearing stage, all witnesses took great pains to explain various reasons that supported their contention that they were not 'conglomerate' corporations."[1]

The takeover by bushy-tailed young conglomerates, often based in the western or southern United States, of older, established, eastern-based companies such as Jones & Laughlin Steel and Reliance Insurance finally generated a reaction even in the American business community. But in Canada, the largest and most powerful conglomerate is also one of the most established and tradition-encrusted corporations. Does Canadian Pacific deserve to be linked with Litton and Ling-Temco-Vought? Are there similar dangers along its road to bigness as there are on the road taken by the American conglomerates?

First, there is no doubt that Canadian Pacific is in fact a conglomerate, if a conglomerate be defined as a company that is involved in a large number of different business activities. The most authoritative classification of industrial activities is the U.S. Office of Management and Budget's Standard Industrial Classification Manual, which divides corporate activity into eighty-five "major groups." Canadian Pacific is involved in at least twenty of them:

- Metal mining (Cominco)
- Bituminous coal and lignite mining (Fording Coal in the Rockies)
- Oil and gas extraction (PanCanadian Petroleum)
- Mining and quarrying of non-metallic minerals, except fuels (Cominco's potash mine at Vade, Saskatchewan)
- Lumber and wood products, except furniture (Pacific Logging)
- Chemicals and allied products (again through Cominco)

● Primary metal industries (Cominco again)
● Railroad transportation (CP Rail)
● Local and suburban transit and interurban highway passenger transportation (this category includes commuter railways, such as the one Canadian Pacific runs in Montreal)
● Motor freight transportation and warehousing (CP Transport and Smith Transport)
● Water transportation (CP Ships)
● Transportation by air (CP Air)
● Pipe lines, except natural gas (Canadian Pacific owns a crude oil line in Alberta, and is working on the development of solids pipelines)
● Communication (CP Telecommunications)
● Electric, gas, and sanitary services (West Kootenay Power and Light)
● Eating and drinking places (Canadian Pacific is involved in the restaurant business through CP Hotels)
● Business services (in 1970, the company set up Canadian Pacific Consulting Services Ltd. "to function as a broadly-based engineering and economic consultant on an international scale serving both government and business," according to the Montreal *Star*.)
● Credit agencies other than banks (CP Securities Ltd. is a subsidiary of Canadian Pacific Investments "engaged in raising money by way of short-term notes, bank loans and medium-term and long-term debt in order to provide funds for capital projects and working capital requirements of CPI's subsidiary and associated companies including CPR and subsidiaries of CPR.")
● Real estate (Marathon Realty)
● Hotels, rooming houses, camps, and other lodging places (CP Hotels)

This puts Canadian Pacific well in the ranks of the most highly conglomerated of North American corporations. In 1967, *Fortune* magazine examined its top 500 American corporations to find out their degree of diversification. Using a somewhat modified version of the Classification Manual's categories, it arbitrarily set involvement in eight categories as the cutoff point for conglomerates. By this standard, it found only forty-six conglomerates among the five hundred. The most highly diversified company, General Tire & Rubber, was in twenty-five categories, counting the operations of its non-consolidated subsidiaries; Litton Industries was second with eighteen. The next company (General Electric) was in fourteen categories, two companies placed in thirteen, and two others in twelve.[2] Allowing for the difference between *Fortune*'s categories and those of the Classification Manual, and for further trends toward conglomeration in the United States since 1967, it is still safe to say that Canadian Pacific is one of the seven or eight most diversified corporations in North America.

The House of Representatives investigation found that the dangers presented by conglomerates went beyond the practices of stock manipulation and unorthodox finance. The most serious dangers it cited were in the area of what it termed the "concentration of economic power." The report noted the increasing concern of many groups in the economy over that concentration: business groups in some of the smaller states were worried about the trend toward out-of-state control of corporations; organized labour was aware that the larger a corporation is the harder it would be to bargain with. "Union leaders fear a loss of bargaining power with huge diversified concerns," the report quoted the *Wall Street Journal* as saying. " 'If the outfit we bargain with provides only 20% of the conglomerate's profit, our strike doesn't hurt that much,' worries one."[3]

An AFL-CIO resolution submitted to the House Subcommittee warned, "The more diverse a company's business interests, the less pressure unions are able to bring in the collective bargaining process. The conglomerate is not responsive to any force except profit. Such issues as work force security, economic progress, purchasing power and human dignity—the concepts which labor has for years struggled to imprint on the corporate conscience—are swept aside in the conglomerate's insatiable search for profits, profits and more profits. The wave of corporate giantism in the United States poses another threat: the shutdown of a particular segment of the conglomerate solely for economic gain."[4]

The Subcommittee found little evidence for the claims that bigness and diversification enhanced efficiency and technological advance. It cited a whole host of examples of technological innovations, ranging from the jet engine and the computer to the self-winding watch, that were created by small firms or individual inventors rather than large corporations.[5] Closer to home, a Vancouver *Sun* reporter, Neale Adams, suggested that the Canadian Pacific empire ought to be broken up, "not simply because Canadian Pacific is huge" and "not because it is a monopoly," but "because it is trying to do too many things at once, and it isn't doing any of them well . . . .

"Size has as many advantages as disadvantages. The larger Canadian Pacific is, the more it can spend on research, top-notch accounting, outside consultants. Financing can be easier. But when diversity is put on top of size, problems begin to pile up. Canadian Pacific's management is under a double strain. The various divisions, because they are so diverse (really, mining has little to do with logging, less to do with railroading, less to do with real estate, and nothing to do with running hotels), are constantly straining for autonomy. The management is constantly struggling to keep everything under control. At this point, decentralization is more talked about than real,'' Adams said.[6]

By the yardstick that means most to Canadian Pacific, profit, Adams's thesis of the company as a bumbling bureaucracy or ''a shy and timid old lady''[7] is not really tenable. Although comparisons are difficult because of inflation and changes in the company's accounting practices, Canadian Pacific's net profit of $96.1 million in 1972 was a record, and was close to double what the CPR had made in the best pre-conglomerate year, 1956. All the arguments against an economy controlled by conglomerates, and they are strong ones, don't change one fact: diversification has paid off for Canadian Pacific. It will pay off still more. Ian Sinclair confidently expects the company's profit to pass the $100-million mark in 1973. And even then, results from the two new Canadian Pacific subsidiaries regarded as having the greatest profit potential, Marathon Realty and PanCanadian Petroleum, will have just begun to make their impact felt.

When Crump, Emerson and Sinclair took over in 1955, they set out to determine, once and for all, just what Canadian Pacific did own. While this inventory—which took seven years—was going on, they were also deciding what would be the most lucrative new fields for the company to enter. In 1958, Canadian Pacific incorporated a new subsidiary, Canadian Pacific Oil and Gas Ltd: henceforth the company would develop its oil lands on its own. That same year, it purchased Smith Transport, a trucking firm with 2,000 vehicles operating on routes covering 5,000 miles in eastern Canada. Along with the 200 vehicles CP Transport already had in western Canada, this made Canadian Pacific the largest trucking operator in the country. The protests from the existing trucking industry were vehement at first—Camile Archambault, assistant to the president of the Trucking Association of Quebec, muttered darkly about the ''growing transport monopoly of the CPR''[8]—but soon died down.

The clearest sign that Canadian Pacific was thinking conglomerate came in 1962, when it incorporated another new subsidiary, Canadian Pacific Investments Ltd. This was an umbrella company to hold all of its non-transportation interests, which were placed one by one into the hands of the new corporation. New subsidiaries were set up under CPI to manage them: CP Hotels, Marathon Realty, CanPac Minerals, Fording Coal, the reactivated Pacific Logging, CP Securities. Canadian Pacific's controlling interest in Cominco also was transferred to CPI. Two significant new acquisitions, the Great Lakes Paper Co., a large paper mill operator in Thunder Bay, Ont., and Central-Del Rio Oils, which was merged with CP Oil & Gas into PanCanadian Petroleum, rounded out CPI. The railway, CP Transport, CP Ships and a new shipbuilding subsidiary, Canadian Pacific (Bermuda) Ltd., continue to be operated under Canadian Pacific Ltd. The airline operates by itself as a third corporate nucleus. But despite the proliferation of companies and subsidiaries, the key decisions are still made centrally; if the right hand always seems to know what the left hand is doing, that is because they are really the same hand. The president of Canadian Pacific Investments is Duff Roblin, an amiable ex-politician who is useful mainly in public relations and maintaining liaison with Canadian Pacific's political friends. The chairman and chief executive officer of CPI is Ian Sinclair.

Aside from its controlled companies, CPI also has an investment portfolio worth more than $200 million, most of it in common stocks. The two largest chunks in the portfolio are its 12.3-percent interest in MacMillan Bloedel and a 13-percent interest in TransCanada Pipe-Lines Ltd., whose principal activity is operating the natural gas line from Alberta to Quebec. (This was the pipeline in question in the famous debate that was largely responsible for bringing down the St-Laurent government in 1957.) Canadian Pacific is the largest single shareholder in TransCanada and, along with the other large shareholder, Home Oil, appears to control it. There are three TransCanada directors directly associated with Canadian Pacific: John Taylor, the president of PanCanadian Petroleum; R.W. Campbell, PanCanadian's chairman; and Sinclair.

Among the other companies in the CPI portfolio are Husky Oil Ltd., The Investors Group (a holding company involved mostly in insurance, finance and real estate), Union Carbide Canada Ltd. and Rio Algom Mines. Great Lakes Paper and Central-Del Rio Oils both started out in the investment portfolio and eventually became controlled companies, but Canadian Pacific has shown little interest in doing the same thing with the companies in its current portfolio, with the possible exception of MacMillan Bloedel and TransCanada PipeLines. In the case of The Investors Group, CPI once held as much as 20 per cent of the company, but sold most of it off and now retains only a 4.4-percent interest.

In most of its activities, Canadian Pacific has used its initial holdings, usually obtained through government favours of one sort or another, as a base for further expansion. PanCanadian Petroleum, for instance, has now expanded far beyond the original Alberta oil lands. Although PanCanadian's production is still largely confined to Alberta (with some in Manitoba, Saskatchewan and the United States), exploration extends to the Gulf of St. Lawrence, the east coast of Nova Scotia, the Grand Banks of Newfoundland, the North Sea, offshore Tunisia, offshore Italy, Sicily and the Italian mainland. PanCanadian is still fairly small (it claims to be the largest Canadian-owned oil company, but that makes it picayune by international standards); however, it is one of the more lucrative stars on the Canadian Pacific horizon, with a 1972 net profit of $15.2 million on a gross income of $47.2 million.[9]

The chief reason for whatever excitement PanCanadian has generated is its nine per cent interest in Panarctic Oils Ltd., a joint private-public consortium set up to develop the petroleum reserves of the Canadian North. Through PanCanadian's interest, along with a nine per cent interest held by Cominco, Canadian Pacific is the largest private shareholder in Panarctic (the federal government holds 45 per cent). Although Panarctic started out as an alliance of small companies, the international giants have begun to show interest in it. Imperial Oil, the Canadian subsidiary of Exxon Corp. (formerly Standard Oil of New Jersey), the largest oil company in the world, has bought a fractional share. Four U.S. gas transmission companies, including the giant Tenneco, have poured $75 million into Panarctic's exploration program in return for a share of the gas produced. Although as yet Panarctic has no producing wells, since there is no existing way of getting the oil and gas out, its gas discoveries are rapidly approaching the threshold required to justify the construction of a pipeline to the south.[10]

The CPR's lands are another asset that has undergone a startling transformation. Canadian Pacific spokesmen tend to speak of the company's land policy in the past, or even pluperfect, tense. "Canadian Pacific had been put into a position of unparalleled influence and power," concluded J. Lorne McDougall in his chapter on lands, "and it had behaved wisely, temperately and in the national interest."[11] But Canadian Pacific land policy did not end with the virtual completion of western settlement by 1930. The million acres it retained in 1963, when Marathon Realty was incorporated, made it one of the largest landowners in the country. About half of this was rural land on the Prairies, which it rented out to farmers. The rest of it was urban land, much of it inherently very valuable and some of it made even more valuable over the years by tax advantages left over from the great days of railway handouts.

In Winnipeg, Canadian Pacific paid no municipal property tax at all until 1954. In that year, the railway signed an agreement with the city under which it paid an annual grant of $250,000 in lieu of taxes. Winnipeg Mayor Stephen Juba estimated in 1958 that it would be paying almost three times that if it were paying taxes on the same basis as everyone else, but the agreement with the city contained a clause that prohibited any review of the deal for ten years. When the agreement finally did come up for review, the provincial government of Premier Duff Roblin (the same Duff Roblin who became president of CPI), was under growing pressure from the city of Winnipeg to make the CPR pay more. The bill that it came up with, and that was passed by the Manitoba legislature in 1965, was a compromise: Canadian Pacific property would be taxed, but at a reduced assessment. The reduction would be fifty per cent until 1972, forty per cent until 1980, and so on down the line until the CPR would finally begin paying taxes at the full rate in 2005. Winnipeg Alderman Joe Zuken calculated that by the end of those forty years, the railway would have saved thirteen million dollars in taxes.[12]

Canadian Pacific's tax concessions in Vancouver were handled somewhat less openly. In 1957, CPR land in the Oakridge area of the city, between 41st and 45th Avenues east of Oak Street, was found to be assessed at $1,480 per acre for the land alone (there was a higher assessment for improvements). Homeowners' land in the same area was being assessed at $1,470 for a 33-by-100-foot lot, or roughly $19,400 per acre. When Canadian Pacific sold 35.5 acres in the area to the Woodward's retail interests for a shopping centre, that land was assessed at $483,900; 43.4 acres in the same block retained by Canadian Pacific was assessed at $64,255. Vancouver City Council submitted a proposal to the city's ratepayers in 1961 to buy the Shaughnessy golf course (named after the early-twentieth-century CPR president) from Canadian Pacific for $2,750,000. The land had been assessed in 1960 at $290,300. Either the city was offering far too much for the land, or else the CPR had been paying taxes on a scandalously low assessment, or possibly both. In any case, the ratepayers said no.

At one point, the CPR actually used much of its urban land for railway purposes, but by the 1960s most of it was far too valuable for that. In these railway properties—its station in the centre of Calgary, its freight yards on False Creek in Vancouver, its tracks on the Toronto waterfront—it had the makings of far more than a mere land company. The clever managers who hated to see properties lying idle saw the potential for Canadian Pacific to enter the glamorous and lucrative field of real-estate *development*. Since passengers weren't going to take the trains anyway, large stations were obviously a waste. Passenger terminals could be tucked into a corner of something else. One of the first large projects undertaken by Marathon Realty after its incorporation was Palliser Square in Calgary: the station was torn down and replaced with a complex of office buildings, apartments, shops, and the Husky Tower, which despite its name has been owned and operated by the CPR since Husky Oil, originally a full partner with Canadian Pacific, decided that the tower wasn't worth the effort and sold an undisclosed number of shares in it to Marathon. The passenger station is located in a lobby of one of the buildings, with a few perfunctory ticket windows to let you know that it's not just open space. Marathon also owns a one-third interest in the hotel part of the Convention Centre complex being built across the street from Palliser Square, while Canadian Pacific's Palliser Hotel is just over to one side. The initial impression a visitor to Calgary gets upon emerging from the railway station is composed entirely of Canadian Pacific buildings.

Marathon owns 21 shopping centres across the country (most of them in the West), five industrial parks, and a number of residential properties, but it is best known for its massive downtown complexes, among which Palliser Square is one of the less ambitious. Project 200, in which Marathon is the senior partner, was supposed to change the face of the Vancouver waterfront (the central part of which, it should be remembered, has been owned by Canadian Pacific since the original land grant in the 1880s); one large building has been built, but the project has since been stalled as a result of the city's at-least-temporary failure to build a proposed waterfront freeway and new crossing of Burrard Inlet that are vital to the project.[13] Canadian Pacific built Place du Canada, one of the endless series of multi-use complexes in downtown Montreal, and owns a six-block area immediately to the west which it plans to redevelop at an announced cost of $300 million. The development plan calls for demolishing Windsor Station and replacing it with a modern building to house Canadian Pacific's head office and a new, smaller passenger terminal. In Toronto, Marathon owns a 50-percent share of the most grandiose development project ever conceived in this country, Metro Centre.

Although Toronto fronts on Lake Ontario, the commercial section of the city ends more than a quarter of a mile from the actual shore of the lake. Between the harbour and Front Street are an expressway and a maze of tracks that belongs to both major railways. This area is the most obvious place for the rapidly-growing city to expand. Down at the waterfront, redevelopment has already begun: The Toronto *Star* has built its new building there, and an apartment complex has gone up across the street from it. The Liberal government, its once-solid Toronto base threatened, announced a new waterfront park during the 1972 election campaign. But that still leaves the railway tracks: in the 1970s, urban land devoted to railway purposes is considered "underused".

Since it was the railways that owned most of that land, it was the railways that would develop it: Canadian Pacific (through Marathon) and Canadian National agreed to go halvers. The result was Metro Centre, which the railways said would cost a billion dollars, a nice round figure and an impressive one. The western half of it would be residential, with living space for 22,000 people. The eastern half would contain office buildings, shops, a downtown air terminal, a bus terminal, a new railway terminal to replace Union Station which would be demolished, a concert hall, radio and television studios, and a radio and television transmission tower that would be the tallest structure in the world.

The philosophy that biggest was best was in its heyday in 1967 when the railways first announced their proposal, and for its adherents Metro Centre was the millennium. From the beginning, however, the plan contained some problems. Once problem was that much of the land on the proposed 190-acre Metro Centre site was not actually owned by the railways. Canadian Pacific, in fact, owned only a few meagre parcels of the land, although it will be a one-half owner of the project if it is ever completed. It had, however, been using three large portions in the heart of the site, almost forty acres in all, on lease from the Toronto Harbours Commission. Up until 1968, according to the terms of the lease, that land could be used for railway purposes only. In that year, however, the Harbours Commission agreed to an extra-ordinary deal with the CPR and the lease was renegotiated to remove that clause. Also taken out was a provision that the Harbours Commission could set the annual rental on the land at five per cent of the value of the buildings on it, which could have proved expensive for Canadian Pacific after the property was redeveloped. In exchange, the CPR paid the Harbours Commission $1½ million in cash and continued to pay exactly the same rental as it had before: $7693.68 a year.

Canadian National may be running into more serious problems with some of the land on the site to which it lays claim. The western portion of the site, an area of 55 acres, has been used by Canadian National for years, but its title to the land has never been clear. In June 1973 the Ontario government indicated that it considered the land to be owned by the province. There has been some speculation that it may press the claim in court, but at the time of writing no action had been taken.

Also in the Metro Centre area is 13.6 acres owned by the city of Toronto, the most important part of which is the 7.2-acre site of Union Station. The city has agreed to trade that land to Metro Centre Developments Ltd. (a consortium of the railways) for railway-owned land elsewhere in Toronto. According to Toronto Alderman John Sewell,[14] the city land in Metro Centre is worth approximately $88.8 million, while the value of the parcels of land the city is getting in exchange is at most $46 million and perhaps considerably less. The Metro Centre deal has been pointed to as an example of the lengths to which development-oriented civic politicians are willing to go in order to obtain showy projects for their cities; a comparison with the lengths to which railway-oriented federal and provincial politicians in the last century were willing to go in order to obtain railways is perhaps not out of place.

The behaviour of most Toronto politicians over Metro Centre has made a mockery of the word negotiation. Even if they had harboured any private doubts, they would have been outgunned by the heavy artillery that has been mounted in support of the project by the railways. CP and CN have considered Metro Centre a matter of sufficient importance to be handled from the very top. In April 1971, Toronto Mayor William Dennison, Executive Committee member David Rotenberg and Development Commissioner Graham Emslie went to Montreal to meet with Crump and CNR president Norman MacMillan about the land trade, and returned to Toronto with glowing reports of how well they had made out.

"One of the most disastrous effects of Metro Centre," said Toronto Alderman Karl Jaffary, "will be that transportation facilities will be worse than they were before, not better. In designing the new railway station, they have assumed that the rail transportation that exists now is the maximum that will ever be needed." This is the familiar pattern that has occurred in other cities, and opposition to Metro Centre in Toronto has centred largely on a fight to preserve Union Station, both as a convenient passenger terminal and as a historic building. But the site of Union Station, right across the street from Canadian Pacific's Royal York Hotel and the portion of Metro Centre closest to Toronto's existing downtown core, may be the only part of the deal that the railways are really interested in. Metro Toronto's chief planner, Wojceich Wronski, once expressed surprise at Jaffary's naive acceptance of the railways' plans for Metro Centre at face value; "you don't actually think they're going to build all that stuff, do you?" he asked the alderman. Jaffary's speculation is that the railways want to get their hands on Union Station, now owned by the city, demolish it, and put up some office buildings on the site; but that the riskier and more imaginative parts of Metro Centre will never be built.

It is a tactic that other developers have used before, and it is the sort of thing that has helped give them a bad name. Now, Marathon spokesmen are talking about a "people-oriented" approach to development. In 1972 John Webster, planning manager for Marathon's project to redevelop the CPR freight yards on False Creek in Vancouver, told a public meeting in the city that the purpose of the company's proposal for the area was just to get discussion going. "We can't afford to do things the way we used to," he said. "We can't get things pushed through city council."[15] J.D. Puddicombe, Marathon's chief public relations spokesman, said that "we used to build something and say, 'There it is—come on over.' Now we say, 'We have a piece of property to develop—what do you want?' When we work that way nobody is surprised and fewer are angry." With the election in 1972 of city councils in Toronto and Vancouver whose approval of development schemes is somewhat less catatonic than that of previous councils, manifestations of Marathon's people-orientation can be expected to multiply. But its basic purpose in building buildings, which according

to Puddicombe, is "to bring us the greatest rate of return on our investment," cannot be expected to change. Real-estate development is now
one of the most serious activities of the top echelons in Canadian business. The richest families in the country, the Bronfmans and the Eatons,
are involved in it on a massive scale. So, with its unfailing eye for
the main chance, is Canadian Pacific. And with this one special advantage: most of the land to develop already belongs to it.

As a natural consequence of diversification, Canadian Pacific has
begun to spread out geographically as well. Some Canadian Pacific
operations have by their nature been multinational for a long time:
Cominco, as we have seen; Canadian Pacific Steamships and, after
1949, CP Air. The railway itself has long had a number of lines in
the United States. But in recent years the undertaking of activities
outside Canada has been much more the result of a deliberate policy.
The latest subsidiary to go international is CP Hotels: "There is no
way in any business that you can remain domestic and survive," said
Donald Curtis, its Ohio-born president, soon after announcing its first
international venture in 1973.

The first effort was a management contract for a hotel in Mexico
City owned by former Mexican President Miguel Alémán. It used to
be operated by Hilton Hotels International and was called the Continental Hilton; Canadian Pacific is renaming it the Château Royal. At the
time of writing, two more international projects had been announced,
both of them joint ventures with Canadian and local foreign capital.
In one of these, Canadian Pacific and Baron Edmond de Rothschild,
to whom Curtis was once an adviser, are building a 415-room luxury
hotel on Baron de Rothschild's grandfather's estate near the Long-
champs racetrack in Paris. The other venture involves CP Hotels in
a three-way partnership with the Israeli Corporation (in which Baron
de Rothschild has a major interest) and a Toronto group of Jewish
businessmen, in a new hotel in Tel Aviv. Although Curtis said that
"it is not a primary objective of ours to co-ordinate with CP Air,"
it is significant that two of the three new hotels (Mexico City and
Tel Aviv) are in CP Air destinations. In the United States, as in Canada,
the railroads were once the operators of the largest hotel chains; that
position has largely been taken over in recent years by the airlines.
A similar transition is occurring within Canadian Pacific, except that
here it can happen very quietly since, conveniently, no change in
ownership is required.

The most interesting multinational venture Canadian Pacific has so far
undertaken is an enigmatic little company called Canadian Pacific (Bermuda) Ltd. The company was first incorporated in the tiny North Atlantic island colony as Cerium Investments Ltd. in July 1964; its name
was changed to CP (Bermuda) later that same year. All except a handful

of CP (Bermuda)'s shares are owned by Canadian Pacific Ltd. in Montreal; a number of Bermudian nationals own one share each, presumably to satisfy local requirements. The act under which the company was incorporated gives it wide powers, ranging from "to engage in and carry on the business of insurance, re-insurance, co-insurance and counter-insurance of all kinds" all the way to "to carry on outside these Islands from a place of business in these Islands all or any of the businesses of farmers, livestock keepers, livestock breeders, graziers, slaughtermen, butchers, tanners . . . ."[16] Whether CP (Bermuda) actually plans to use the powers granted to it or whether they are just there to help fudge its true purpose is impossible to say. In any case, CP (Bermuda) gives Canadian Pacific a corporate umbrella under which it can do virtually anything virtually anywhere in the world.

Most of the clauses in the act contain the provision that the business in question be carried on "outside these Islands." It is a surprising condition; why then bother with Bermuda at all? The probable reason lies in Bermuda's unusual corporate tax structure: unlike most other countries, Bermuda does not tax corporations on the basis of a percentage of their yearly profits. Companies incorporated in Bermuda pay a flat rate. If a company is principally engaged in insurance or the management of a unit trust it pays one thousand Bermudian dollars a year (the Bermudian dollar is approximately equal to the Canadian dollar); other companies—such as CP (Bermuda)—pay BD$650.

So far, the only activity carried on by CP (Bermuda) has been a very traditional one for Canadian Pacific, shipping, but one part of the tradition has not been adhered to. Its ships have not been built in Britain, where most CP ships were previously constructed (only a few small ones have ever been built in Canada); rather the eleven oil tankers and bulk carriers that CP (Bermuda) leases to various users around the world have been built in Japanese shipyards. The ships are commanded by British officers, and the crews are Spanish or Hong Kong Chinese. About the only connection with Canada, other than ownership, is that several of the ships are carrying Canadian lumber and other bulk commodities from British Columbia to Japan. Two of them, the W.C. Van Horne and the T. Akasaka, are built to carry raw materials to the steel mills on the coast of Japan, mostly coal from their major suppliers: Australia, the Appalachian region of the United States, and western Canada (although they have so far not seen the shores of B.C). CP Rail is also involved in this deal, carrying the coal from the Rocky Mountains to the coast, and one of the suppliers is the Canadian Pacific subsidiary Fording Coal. The government of Canada kicked in five million dollars to build a new superport at Roberts Bank south of Vancouver.

The W.C. Van Horne was launched in Yokohama in March 1970, and a number of Canadians flew to Japan for the ceremony, among them Ian Sinclair and his wife, and also journalist Charles Lynch of Southam News Services. "We were outnumbered about a thousand to one by Japanese dignitaries and shipyard workers," Lynch described the scene, "but the Maple Leaf flag flew proudly in the breeze and it was a great Canadian occasion." Sinclair was asked how Canadian Pacific ever got into such a business. "Sharp figuring," was his answer. "After the band played O Canada," Lynch went on, "they sailed through God Save the Queen—the national anthem of Bermuda—followed by the stirring national anthem of Japan. Mrs. Sinclair rattled through a nifty paragraph of Japanese that she had been rehearsing for a month, naming the ship the W.C. Van Horne."[17]

For Canadian Pacific, the occasion symbolized the emergence of the company as a major force in the highly competitive international shipping business. For the Marine Workers' and Boilermakers' Industrial Union, the symbolism was somewhat different. "The 'Dollar Patriots'," said a 1971 issue of *Ship Shop*, the organ of its Vancouver local, "are the main force that stands in the way of the development of the shipbuilding industry in Canada and the formation of a Canadian marine. This fact is nowhere better illustrated than in the case of the Canadian Pacific Railway."[18]

10 Life at the top:
The men behind the CPR

*I don't run a railroad. I work for the Canadian
Pacific Railway Company.*

Ian Sinclair, 1966,
just after becoming CPR president

An annual meeting of Canadian Pacific Ltd. is an exercise in efficiency rather than democracy. Although the meeting is run according to the usual rules of order and democratic procedures, some of the healthy parry-and-thrust is taken out of it by the circumstance that one man is voting more shares and proxies than all the other people at the meeting combined. On May 2, 1973, Ian Sinclair, presiding over his first annual meeting as chairman and chief executive officer, was asked how many proxies he was voting; he replied that he was voting just under thirty-seven million of them. That's out of a total of 71,662,280 common shares issued.

Those proxies, more than the relatively few shares Sinclair owns himself, and perhaps even more than his position as chairman of the board, are the real expression of his power within Canadian Pacific. For they represent the confidence of the owners of the company in him to carry out their wishes. He is their public face; his presence allows them to stay in the background. "Who owns Canadian Pacific?" is in fact one of the most closely guarded secrets in Canadian finance. Canada has no equivalents of the Rockefellers, the Du Ponts, the Mellons, the Morgans and the other American corporate dynasties. The closest analogue to the position of those families is occupied in Canada by the chartered banks—but that leaves open the question of who controls the banks. Control of the Canadian economy is in large measure anonymous. Well-known Canadian financiers such as E.P. Taylor and K.C. Irving (both since 1971 resident in the Caribbean because of the generous tax laws in that area of the world) are the possessors of substantial individual fortunes, but are relatively small in the overall scheme of things. Even the richest Canadian families, the Eatons and the Bronfmans, are somewhat outside the financial mainstream, the former having chosen to remain there and the latter having been excluded because of their religion.

Within this secretive web, Canadian Pacific is perhaps the most secretive of all. Most federally-incorporated companies are required, by a clause in the Corporations Act, to keep a list on file enumerating every shareholder and the number of shares he owns. This list must be open to the inspection of any shareholder, so that someone who is sufficiently curious can, for the price of one share, find out who owns how much of whatever corporation he is interested in. Canadian Pacific, however, is not incorporated under the Corporations Act. It is incorporated under the Railway Act; this act contains a similar clause, except it leaves out the provision that the list must say how many shares each shareholder owns. The owner of one share and the owner of half a million could be listed one underneath the other, and no one could tell the two apart.

One thing that is clear is that, in the literal sense, Canadian Pacific is owned by a large number of people; there is no one individual who owns a majority of its shares. As a result, even if someone did find out how many shares each shareholder owned, he might still be unable to tell which was the controlling block. And even if he found out which was the controlling block, he couldn't be sure that the ostensible owner of that block was not holding it in trust for some other individual or group. In any case, the controlling block is probably fairly small, and large numbers of shares have changed hands in recent years without any real effect on control of the company.

It is also clear that Canadian Pacific is not owned by its board of directors. At the 1973 annual meeting Elmer Sopha, a former Liberal member of the Ontario legislature from Sudbury, stood up during a discussion of the wording of the proxy form and pointed out that he represented a shareholder who owned more shares than all twenty-four directors of the company put together. It was true, but it was also irrelevant; through their proxies the board of directors, and in fact Sinclair alone, could easily outvote any recalcitrant shareholder. Sopha had to be satisfied with a promise from Sinclair that the company would *consider* his proposal to change the proxy form.

Sinclair, an intense, rather humourless man, is the first non-railwayman to head Canadian Pacific, and represents a distinct change in style if not in substance from his predecessor, Buck Crump. Crump was the son of a CPR employee in the CPR town of Revelstoke, B.C., who joined the company as an apprentice machinist at sixteen and who even after becoming chairman of the company forty-one years later still projected a crusty and rough-edged image. When he retired, being unilingual and having never liked Montreal, he scouted all the major Canadian cities in search of a place to live and finally chose Calgary for its "cowtown" atmosphere. His only regret after a year of living there was that some people were trying to introduce some culture into the city.[1]

But it was Crump who presided over the changes that made his own style obsolete. By the time he retired, Canadian Pacific was emphatically not a company to be run by a railwayman off the track. While Crump liked to look back on his early days and say that he "wore overalls longer than most union leaders,"[2] Ian Sinclair can look back only on his years of service in the company's legal department. Trained as a lawyer, he joined the legal department in 1942 as an assistant solicitor, and later headed the department before becoming senior vice-president, president, and then in 1972 chairman of the board. He was the brightest of the bright young men Crump gathered around him, and first rose to prominence in preparing the company's presentation to the MacPherson Commission. The appointment to the top position of someone whose training has nothing to do with running a railway is a reflection of the changes that have taken place in the company, but in one respect Sinclair's elevation to the chairmanship is entirely in line with Canadian Pacific tradition.

Like Crump, Edward Beatty, Lord Shaughnessy and all the other top men before him, Sinclair comes from within the company. Outside influences are channelled through the board of directors. Of the twenty-four directors, only Crump, who will soon retire from the board, Sinclair, CP Ltd. President Fred Burbidge (also a lawyer by training), and Senior Vice-President Keith Campbell, are company men. The other twenty are on the board as representatives of institutions or geographical areas which maintain a mutually valuable contact with Canadian Pacific. And among those institutions, the most important is the Bank of Montreal.

The few studies that have been done of the Canadian ruling class —such as John Porter's *The Vertical Mosaic* and Frank and Libby Park's *Anatomy of Big Business* in the early 1960s and, more recently, the work of Leo Johnson of the University of Waterloo—all agree on the central position of the major chartered banks. In the picture that emerges, each of the five largest banks—the Royal Bank of Canada, the Canadian Imperial Bank of Commerce, the Bank of Montreal, the Bank of Nova Scotia and the Toronto-Dominion Bank—is at the nexus of a group of companies linked by common directors and common access to a pool of capital. The largest of these groups, the one surrounding the Bank of Montreal, controls assets of more than twenty billion dollars. Its major component companies, apart from the Bank, are the Royal Trust Company, the Sun Life Assurance Company, International Nickel, the Steel Company of Canada and Canadian Pacific.

The 1960s and early 1970s have been a period in which the concentration of economic power has grown rapidly. "An examination of the directorships held by the directors of the Bank of Montreal in 1968," according to Leo Johnson, "shows that the degree of interconnection between the major components of the Bank of Montreal network has, if anything, increased [since 1957]. In addition, the network has widened to include several other important corporations. A similar situation exists among the other banks."[3] While the banks as a group have increased their control, the dividing lines between the different networks have become more and more blurred. A large corporation will maintain a primary relationship with one bank, and secondary relationships with one or more of the others.

In the case of Canadian Pacific, while its links with the Bank of Montreal are the most intimate, and have been ever since the company was founded, all five of the major banks are now represented on its board of directors. There are five Canadian Pacific directors who are also directors of the Bank of Montreal, including Bank Chairman Arnold Hart and Canadian Pacific President Fred Burbidge. Ian Sinclair is one of four Canadian Pacific directors on the board of the Royal Bank of Canada; another is Earle McLaughlin, chairman and president of the Royal Bank. There are two Bank of Commerce directors on the Canadian Pacific board, while the Bank of Nova Scotia and the Toronto-Dominion are each represented by a single director.

These links are not accidental and do not depend upon the individuals involved. When Buck Crump retired from the board of the Bank of Montreal in 1972, Burbidge was appointed to succeed him, fulfilling the requirement that one of the top officers of Canadian Pacific always sits on the Bank's board. Max Bell, a Calgary oilman and newspaper-owner who sat on the boards of both Canadian Pacific and the Bank of Nova Scotia, died in 1972; Canadian Pacific appointed F.H. Sherman, another Bank of Nova Scotia director, to succeed him. J.V. Clyne of MacMillan Bloedel was one of the Bank of Commerce directors on the Canadian Pacific board but retired from the Commerce board in 1972; among the new Canadian Pacific directors appointed in 1972 was Jake Moore of Brascan, also a director of the Bank of Commerce. The appointment of an additional director from one of the banks occurs only as a consequence of an increase in that bank's power within the company, while the failure to appoint another director from the same bank when a bank director retires or dies would represent a waning of that bank's influence.

The relationship with the banks comes out of a basic need of the modern corporation: access to capital. The interlocking directorships with other companies, such as International Nickel, Stelco, Dominion Foundries and Steel Ltd., the Iron Ore Company of Canada, Du Pont of Canada or Eaton's, represent communication between organizations with basically similar interests and, often, between buyer and seller. One director, Allan Findlay, represents the CPR's law firm of Tilley, Carson & Findlay (he succeeded Cyril Carson on the board in 1973). Occasionally, directors earn their place on the board simply by virtue of owning a large number of shares, but there are no such directors on the board now; the largest shareholder on the board is Norman Whitmore of Regina, who owns 22,500 common shares or roughly $350,000 worth of stock, a sizeable investment but hardly anything in relation to the total worth of the company. Max Bell, by contrast, owned several million dollars worth of stock, as does Clifford Fielding of Sudbury, a former director who resigned from the board in 1971. Fielding was the man Elmer Sopha was referring to at the annual meeting when he said he represented a shareholder who owned more stock than all the directors put together. James Richardson of Winnipeg was another director with an investment in the several-million-dollar range, until, in an example of the toing-and-froing that has long characterized business-government relations, he resigned from the board in 1968 to become a minister in the Cabinet of Prime Minister Pierre Elliott Trudeau.

One apparently anomalous director is Allard Jiskoot of Amsterdam, a partner in the Dutch investment firm of Pierson, Heldring & Pierson. The presence of a Dutch director on the board is particularly striking now that there is no American director and, with the retirement of Sir George Bolton in 1972, no British director for the first time in the history of the company. Jiskoot was first appointed a director in 1964, and much was made at the time of the fact that Jan Lodewyk Pierson, the founder of the investment firm and Jiskoot's grandfather, had helped sell a CPR bond issue during one of the railway's financial crises in 1883. But there were more pressing reasons for the appointment of Jiskoot to the board as Canadian Pacific's first director from continental Europe. It came at a time of intense speculation about an attempt to take over the CPR; most of the rumours included least some Europeans as being involved in the takeover attempt. "Clues are few," reported the *Financial Post* on March 21, 1964. "It is known that CPR management was approached by two groups which expressed interest in accumulating substantial holdings of CPR shares. It has been reported that last year CPR officials visiting in Europe had occasion to discuss the company's affairs with European investment bankers. And this week, Jiskoot's appointment to the CPR board of directors was jumped on as a potentially important clue by Canadian investment bankers familiar with the financial powers of Europe."

If there was a European attempt to take over Canadian Pacific, it ultimately failed, getting just far enough to merit the appointment of one director. But there have been other, perhaps related, changes in ownership which seem to have resulted in the consolidation of control in the same hands as before. When Crump was asked, on the occasion of his retirement as chairman of the board, what he thought had been his greatest achievement in office, he paused for a moment, started to say dieselization, then pulled back and paused again, and finally settled upon the repatriation of ownership into Canadian hands. When Crump became president in 1955, only 14.5 per cent of the voting stock of the company was owned in Canada; by the time of his retirement in 1972, the figure had risen to 63 per cent. The largest parcel of shares, totalling 45.5 per cent, was owned in Britain at the time of Crump's accession, while 31.3 per cent was owned in the United States. In 1972, the British share had declined to 10.5 per cent and the American share to 18.1 per cent.[4]

That much Canadian Pacific makes public, but it does not say what this change actually represents. Control of the company has always been exercised, or has appeared to be exercised, from Montreal, not from London. The controlling block of shares has probably always been held in Canada, even when the Canadian portion of the whole company was small. The most likely explanation for the "repatriation of ownership" is a move on the part of the owners of that controlling block to accumulate more shares in order to meet takeover threats such as the one coming from Europe in the early sixties. Another possibility, not incompatible with the first, is that the owners of the company considered it prudent to give Canada's most prestigious company more of a Canadian face. In any event, there was a series of changes all through the sixties designed to make the company more enticing to Canadian investors.

Most of these changes concerned the company's preferred stock, which originally was sold in units of five pounds sterling. Unlike most preferreds, this was a voting stock, with each unit of five pounds conferring one vote. Much of the British interest in Canadian Pacific was held through the preferred. In August 1965, the stock was listed on Canadian stock exchanges for the first time. Two years later, Canadian Pacific announced that it was converting the preferred into a Canadian dollar stock at a rate of $3 for 1 pound; this was just before a devaluation of the pound and investors who made the switch in time avoided a substantial loss. Finally, in 1971, it announced a new conversion: both the Canadian dollar and the remaining sterling preferred would be exchanged for shares of a new preferred stock, which would pay a higher dividend than the old but have no voting rights.

Whether this was aimed at a specific takeover attempt or simply designed to forestall any such attempt in the future is not clear, but it did have the effect of closing off the most likely avenue anyone wanting to take over the company would follow. At that time, one voting right could be bought through the preferred for approximately $10, while a common share conferring one vote cost about $65 (this was before a five-for-one split in 1972). For Clifford Fielding, for example, the $2,160,000 worth of dollar preferred stock that he owned (that's par value; he had likely bought it for considerably less) conferred more voting power than his roughly $6½-million investment in common stock. Understandably, he and other shareholders were not pleased at the new exchange offer.

The offer caused a flurry in the financial community that lasted for several months. A Canadian Pacific Preference Stockholders Information Committee was formed; each side came up with charges and legal opinions. Investors watched closely to see what the two large preferred shareholders on the board of directors, Fielding and Max Bell, would do. Sinclair rather testily announced that after the deadline for acceptance of the offer had passed, "as a matter of policy, the company will not in the future make an offer on more favourable terms to preference shareholders who do not take advantage of the exchange.''[5] While Bell finally accepted the offer, Fielding did not and resigned from the board in protest. The whole episode left a bitter taste but it succeeded in accomplishing its purpose of consolidating control, and a bitter taste was something Canadian Pacific could afford.

Now that the proper hands are firmly on the tiller, the question remains: what do the owners of Canadian Pacific (whoever they are) plan to do with the company? There has been evidence over the last ten years, chiefly the development of Canadian Pacific Investments, that indicates that their plans may not be entirely straightforward. When CPI was incorporated in 1962, Canadian Pacific presented it as a natural consequence of diversification. The company's non-transportation interests had grown to the point where they needed a separate corporation to take care of them. It was not, upon examination, a terribly convincing argument. If a real-estate developer, an oil and gas company, a hotel chain and a logging firm could all be managed under the same corporate umbrella, then surely a railway, an airline and a trucking company could be thrown in too. The formation of CPI might have the beneficial side-effect of distracting attention from the anomaly of all these diverse businesses being owned by a railway company, but it was strongly suspected that there was more to it than that.

A more likely reason was to help conceal Canadian Pacific's growing non-railway profits, a valuable undertaking when the company was going to the government for subsidies every year. Until the early 1970s, Canadian Pacific included the profits of its subsidiaries in its net income figures only if they were formally paid out to the parent company in the form of dividends. By the simple device of retaining profits in its subsidiaries, Canadian Pacific could avoid declaring them. CPI, by acting as yet another buffer between the parent company and most of the subsidiaries, opened up still more possibilities. Presumably feeling that its subsidies are safe, the company now includes in its income statement an item called "equity in earnings retained by subsidiaries." This item, as stated in the company's annual reports, amounted to $7 million in 1971, and $23.7 million in 1972. There is little doubt, however, that some profits are still unstated; real estate firms, in particular, are notoriously modest in declaring how much money they've made.

Probably the most important reason for the creation of CPI concerned the uncertain future of the railway. For Buck Crump and his associates, the railway was the least interesting of Canadian Pacific's properties. They were willing to hang on to it if the government would either free it from regulation or prop it up with subsidies or—as actually happened—some combination of the two, but they wanted to prepare themselves against the day when it would become a liability rather than an asset. Governments change, and transportation policies and attitudes toward business change with them. The nationalization of the Canadian Pacific Railway has a sufficiently long and honourable history as a political issue that the possibility that some future government may actually try to carry it out has to be seriously considered. And the owners of Canadian Pacific wanted to be in a position where, if that day did come, they could magnanimously say to the government, "It's all yours."

However, only if the company's other interests were secure could Canadian Pacific greet a government in a nationalizing mood quite so cheerfully. It could be cumbersome and untidy to nationalize part of a corporation and not the rest of it. Any government that had the teeth to undertake nationalization in the first place might well go for not just the railway but also all its latter-day fruits, and nationalize Canadian Pacific as an entity, down to the last oil well, lead-zinc mine and shopping centre. For Canadian Pacific, the trick was to separate off the company's lucrative new investments to the greatest extent possible without losing control of them.

The first step toward this goal was the actual creation of Canadian Pacific Investments, but this did not go far enough. At the beginning, CPI was 100-percent owned by the Canadian Pacific Railway Company, as it was then still known. In that situation, CPI was just another Canadian Pacific asset. It was Canadian Pacific's intention from the beginning to turn CPI eventually into a public company, listed on the stock exchanges, and to sell off a nominal percentage of it to Canadian Pacific shareholders and outside investors and hence complicate any possible government takeover. That step was actually taken in 1967, five years after the company was set up. This raised the possibility of a third, and more drastic, step—the total spinoff of Canadian Pacific Investments. That would entail Canadian Pacific's totally divesting itself of its formal interest in CPI, selling it to Canadian Pacific shareholders to make sure that the company doesn't fall into the wrong hands. There would then be no legal connection between Canadian Pacific Ltd. and CPI, although the control and the profits would remain exactly where they were before. So far such a step has proved unnecessary. In 1971 Robert Jamieson, who has covered Canadian Pacific for the *Financial Post* for years, commented that "ten or twelve years ago ... the possibility existed that the company might at some time want to turn over to the government the railway, or the railway and other transportation assets, without having to turn over the non-transportation assets in CPI. There seems little possibility of this in today's climate."[6] But climates change, and the rumours that Canadian Pacific will at some point spin off CPI persist.

Another move it could make would be to spin off CPI's subsidiaries directly. Cominco, PanCanadian Petroleum and Great Lakes Paper are already public companies and have minority shares owned by outside investors. In 1973 Sinclair told a Vancouver newspaper reporter, "I look forward to the day when we will have participation directly in the hotels, the airline, Marathon Realty and the shipping."[7] This would have the effect of insulating some of Canadian Pacific's most valuable assets. It would also, however, have one unfortunate side-effect: public companies are required to disclose certain information, like profits and assets, that private companies can keep secret. These things can always be fudged a little, but it's always simpler not to have to say anything at all. This is a particular advantage for Marathon Realty, engaged in a highly competitive and highly sensitive business. It may help explain why, while affirmations of Marathon's intention to go public abound, the company has appeared in no hurry to make those professions good.

The asset Canadian Pacific has been most successful in hiding, and the one whose importance to the company is most difficult to assess, is not ostensibly intended to promote the enrichment and aggrandize-ment of Canadian Pacific at all. Its purpose, rather, is the security of the company's employees: it is the CPR's pension fund. Pension funds do not just sit around, receiving contributions from the employer and employees and paying out benefits to superannuated workers. That would be silly. They are invested. And the more wisely they are in-vested the higher the pensions that can be paid out for the same amount in contributions, and the better it is for everybody. Not just for the employees; there can be little side-benefits for the employer too.

The pension fund of a large corporation encompasses a substantial sum of money. In the case of Canadian Pacific it is $551.8 million; if parts of the pension funds of CP Air and other Canadian Pacific subsidiaries that are administered along with the parent company's fund are included, that figure rises to $581.4 million. Any questions about control of the pension fund, therefore, are not quibbles over peanuts. The pension fund is a pool approximately three-quarters the size of the total retained income of the company. The portion of it invested in common stocks, $198.7 million, is greater than the total amount invested in common stocks of non-controlled companies by Canadian Pacific Investments.

In some companies, the pension fund is operated jointly by manage-ment and unions. Even in companies where management has sole con-trol of the fund, in most cases it is required to turn it over to a friendly trust company for administration. Canadian Pacific has the unique advantage of being able to administer its own fund. This is, if not expressly forbidden, at least strongly frowned upon by Canadian pen-sion legislation, which says that "the funds of a pension plan shall

be administered by a life insurance company, a corporate trustee, individual trustees, a society established under the *Pension Fund Societies
Act* or by the Government of Canada.''[8] A corporate trustee is usually
understood to mean a trust company; no, said the CPR—it was a corporation, it would be its own corporate trustee. And just in case that
wasn't enough, it argued that its pension plan was not in fact a pension
plan under the meaning of the legislation and therefore was not governed by it. There is a clause exempting pension plans if "under the
terms of the plan the employer is not required to make contributions
to or under the plan."[9] Although Canadian Pacific makes contributions
to its plan, it is not *required* to, it argued, since it was not required
to set up the plan in the first place. By that argument no pension
plan in the country is a pension plan, but it was accepted by the federal
Superintendent of Insurance, who administers such matters, in 1973
and the pension fund remained in the CPR's hands.

Thus, while money paid into the pension fund appears in the company's books as money spent, either directly in the case of the
employer's contribution (which, until a recent change in legislation,
was small) or as wages in the case of the employees' contribution,
it is not in fact spent at all. It is as firmly controlled by the company
as it would be if it were in its retained income account, with the added
advantage that Canadian Pacific does not have to disclose where these
monies are being invested. The occasional hints that have trickled out
indicate that the welfare of the employees has not always been upper-
most in Canadian Pacific's consideration.

In 1964, Canadian Pacific Investments acquired its initial holdings
of TransCanada PipeLines and Central-Del Rio Oils, as well as a six
percent interest in the Provincial Bank of Canada which it later sold.
All three of these were acquired in purchases from the holdings of
the Canadian Pacific Railway pension fund.[10] Was the pension fund,
figuring that the investments had outlived their usefulness, picking a
good time to sell? Or was CPI, betting that the investments were good
ones, picking a good time to buy? Difficult to say, since both decisions
were ultimately the responsibility of the same body: the board of directors of Canadian Pacific. If it was in fact a good time to buy (as
it turned out in at least two of the three cases), then it was to the
advantage of Canadian Pacific to have the stocks in the hands of CPI
rather than the pension fund, since the company does not profit directly
from the fund's investments. It was not, however, to the advantage
of the employees for whom the plan was supposedly set up.

Whether or not there were other deals like the three that were revealed
in 1964 is not known, but the possibilities involved in such deals may
help to explain why for many years the yield of the pension fund
was less than four per cent, startlingly poor for a company of Canadian

Pacific's unquestioned business acumen. It is also the reason why such transactions are illegal. The company apologized and in so many words promised not to do the same thing again. And perhaps it hasn't. Even if it were, however, continuing to undercut the pension fund of its own employees, we probably would never know. But then it doesn't really have to resort to such tactics to get its money's worth out of the pension fund.

There are other, subtler ways in which the fund's investments can be co-ordinated with those of CPI. Pension funds traditionally do not vote their shares in the companies they own chunks of, although there is no inherent reason why they couldn't vote them if they wanted to. Suppose that the CPR pension fund owned a ten-percent block of shares, the maximum permitted under the law (making the assumption that the fund would stick to the law), in, say, MacMillan Bloedel. Added to the 13 per cent held by Canadian Pacific Investments, that would mean that 23 per cent of the company was under the control of Canadian Pacific. Even if the pension fund did not vote its block, neutralizing ten percent of the shares, in a company with such widely dispersed ownership as MacMillan Bloedel, would make CPI's 13 per cent loom a lot larger. Now all of this is conjecture. The individual investments of the pension fund are not known. But it is a conjecture based on the circumstance that the investments of the pension fund and those of CPI are controlled by the same people. There would be nothing unusual in co-ordinating them. It isn't even illegal. It just makes good business sense.

In terms of the benefits it confers on the company's employees, the CPR's pension plan is considered a reasonably good one. The company and the unions regularly bicker about it at negotiation time, but the unions are generally successful in getting the improvements they ask for. In return, they are expected not to ask too many questions about what is done with the fund. Sometimes there are direct trade-offs, as when Canadian Pacific granted increased pension benefits in 1971 in exchange for union support for the company's bid to be allowed sixty years to pay in its full share of the plan's fund (other privately-owned corporations had only twenty-five years). The arrangement at least superficially serves the purposes of both sides. If the railway comes up with a good pension plan the unions see no reason to complain. For Canadian Pacific, the pension fund isn't really about pensions at all.

If the pension fund advantages that Canadian Pacific has managed to chisel out seem minor for a company of its size, it must be remembered that those benefits do not exist in isolation. Canadian Pacific's position is made up of a whole pattern of advantages, some of them large like the original land grants, cash subsidies and loans, but most of them fairly small. The most remarkable ability of Canadian Pacific management has been the capacity to develop those advantages to the fullest. It is an achievement of which Canadian Pacific is proud, and it is perhaps the root of the continuing note of complacency in Canadian Pacific public statements: not really arrogance, simply complacency. "We don't go after major successes in this company," Ian Sinclair answered one questioner at the 1973 annual meeting, "but we avoid major failures too." If you accumulate the pennies, eventually they will become dollars. That is the Canadian Pacific way of life. It has survived depressions and changes of government and outlived younger and cheekier rivals. While preparing itself against all eventualities, Canadian Pacific would never seriously entertain the suggestion that it won't go on for a lot longer still.

11 The myth revisited:
And a modest proposal

Be it understood the CPR, Clifford Sifton and the Almighty comprise the Trinity of Canada, ranking in importance in the order named.

Bob Edwards, Calgary *Eye Opener*,
early twentieth century

One of the more disturbing phenomena of political life is the ease with which certain words lose their meaning and become merely a jumble of euphonious sounds. This happened long ago to the words "peace with honour," for instance. Or "national security." In a Canadian context, "fluently bilingual." Or one of the most venerable and least examined of catchwords, "private enterprise."

Just as the Holy Roman Empire was neither holy nor Roman nor an empire, so is most private enterprise beyond the corner-store level neither private nor enterprise. It is not private because government grants, government contracts, easygoing government regulation and other fruits of government favour are often crucial elements determining a corporation's success. It is not enterprise because enterprise implies some degree of risk, and government involvement has in many cases advanced to the extent where virtually all elements of risk are removed. The only risk that, say, Bell Canada runs is that the government will fail to approve its annual rate increase, and even that risk is virtually eliminated by the presence of a friendly federal government and a friendly Canadian Transport Commission.

Canadian Pacific operates under similar circumstances. Profitable railway services it can operate as it pleases; for unprofitable services, it gets government subsidies. It has long since reached a live-and-let-live arrangement with a government-owned railway. The airline operates routes allocated to it by the government, with the government supplying the necessary support services on the ground. The real-estate arm, created from federal-government land granted to the company in the 1880s, builds the projects that malleable city councils will permit it. If the mining company needs a railway which the railway arm is not interested in building for fear it might lose money, no matter: the government will build it. Even labour disputes are rarely settled without government intervention.

It is not surprising, therefore, that the two identities, that of the CPR and that of the state, sometimes get confused, especially in western Canada, where the CPR's presence is most strongly felt. When the federal government refused to share prairie premiers' sense of urgency about correcting freight-rate inequities at the Western Economic Opportunities Conference in July 1973, it was not speaking only for itself. It was speaking for the railways that profit from those inequities: its own railway, Canadian National, and the "private" one, Canadian Pacific. Sometimes, as in this case, the state appears to be an arm of Canadian Pacific. At other times Canadian Pacific appears to be an arm of the state. In reality, the relationship is much more complex than either of those assertions implies.

The interests of a corporation are easily defined: the goal of a corporation, simply stated, is to make money. Anything that enhances its ability to make money is in the corporation's interests; anything that hinders that ability is not. The interests of a government are much more difficult to pin down. In theory, a government, as an elected instrument of the people at large, is not supposed to have special interests as such (except perhaps its own survival), but most governments listen more closely to some sectors of the population than to others. The interests of a government tend to become identified with the interests of the most powerful segments of the community, especially if those segments provide the financial support to keep that government in office. Corporations that contribute to a political party are not necessarily seeking a direct return, in the form of a subsidy or other plum, although that often comes as a side-benefit. They are seeking a government that will view a favourable business climate, economic growth under private enterprise, stability and encouraging new investment as being among its goals. Since a government also has goals of its own, high among which is getting itself re-elected, it is subject to certain public pressures from which corporations, which are not even nominally responsible to anybody, are insulated. This accounts for the occasional conflict between the two. On most important matters, however, government and corporate interests can be reconciled without too much difficulty.

This identity of interests is enhanced by a frequent identity of personnel at the top levels. Robert Bonner, a former Attorney General of British Columbia, heads MacMillan Bloedel; Mitchell Sharp, a former vice-president of Brascan, heads the Department of External Affairs. The late Robert Winters bounced back and forth from the St-Laurent Liberal government to Brinco to the Pearson Liberal government to Brascan. Former provincial premiers such as John Robarts and Jean Lesage acquire collections of corporate directorships.

This same two-way flow operates in the specific case of Canadian Pacific. In 1968 Duff Roblin, having resigned the premiership of Manitoba and having sought unsuccessfully first to become leader of the federal Progressive Conservative party and later to win a federal seat, was looking around for something to do. Canadian Pacific came to the rescue: Roblin was offered, and accepted, the presidency of Canadian Pacific Investments, a rather meaningless position, since control of the entire Canadian Pacific empire is centralized in the top management of Canadian Pacific Ltd., but one that carried with it the prestige due a former Conservative provincial premier and did not unduly tax Roblin's less than overwhelming talents (there was wide speculation that his reason for abandoning provincial politics was the strong suspicion that he would lose the next election; instead it was left to his successor, Walter Weir, to fall to the forces of social democracy).

At almost exactly the same time, another prominent Manitoban was heading in precisely the opposite direction. James Richardson, from the richest and most powerful Winnipeg grain-trading family, had just been elected to the federal House of Commons by a Winnipeg constituency, and was giving up his formal corporate connections to accept a position in the Liberal Cabinet. Among these corporate connections was a directorship, and a substantial holding of stock, in Canadian Pacific. His main achievement in public life has been a substantial increase in the flow of federal patronage to the Winnipeg area.

It is not entirely true that people's views cannot change as they change jobs. The views of, say, Charles Dunning no doubt mellowed in the course of his career as he moved from being a farmers' leader and spokesman through various Liberal cabinets to the corporate boardrooms. But the regularity of migrations between the Cabinet room and the boardroom and the ease with which they take place suggests that, in most cases, a change in outlook is not required. Business and business-oriented politics are not two different careers, but two different aspects of the same career. In the case of James Richardson, who will be able to move back into the business world when his political career is over as easily as he moved out of it in 1968, we are talking not of conflict of interest but of something much more fundamental. We are talking of an identity of interests of the most disturbing kind.

Canadian Pacific is unusual here only in that its size, the manner in which it was established, and the nature of the activities it operates make its relationship with the government particularly close. Other companies have to satisfy themselves with DREE grants, tax concessions, incentives from the Department of Industry, Trade and Commerce, and maybe the appointment of one of their executives to a government board or commission. But by and large, the pattern holds; the relationship the federal government has established with Canadian Pacific is the relationship it has established with broad sectors of Canadian business.

A transcontinental railway would be an important instrument of national policy for any government, no matter what its political orientation or base of support. A different government, however, might attempt to carry out a different national policy. It might place a high value on economic equity between different regions, or the maintenance of adequate passenger transportation at reasonable cost all across the country, or ensuring that technological change brings benefits without unduly disrupting people's lives. It might require Canadian Pacific to operate without external subsidies on the grounds that a railway should use its profitable operations to subsidize internally the ones it is required to maintain at a loss in the public interest. If it did any of these things, it would come into serious conflict with Canadian Pacific. Canadian

Pacific would not stand for being used as an instrument of national policies with which it did not agree. And its intransigence might force a government to consider nationalization.

In doing so, it would have to overcome the substantial prejudice against public ownership that has been built up in this country, a prejudice that is not entirely without foundation. The record of public ownership in Canada is by and large a sorry one. Business propaganda usually identifies government-owned corporations with inefficiency, petty patronage and corruption, and there is enough truth to those allegations that the message sinks home. The best that can ever be said about a publicly-owned corporation is that it operates on "sound business principles"—that is, just like a private corporation.

One of the crown corporations that comes closest to that ideal is the Canadian National Railways. From the beginning, the CNR was a national railway by necessity rather than by design; the basic reason for its establishment was to bail out the shareholders of the Grand Trunk and Canadian Northern and assume their huge debt. It seems to regard making good that debt, which in 1973 was more than a half billion dollars, as one of the major reasons for its existence. Its board of directors is made up of private businessmen, some of them—like their counterparts at Canadian Pacific—directors of banks, insurance companies, and other large corporations. The national railway is, as the CPR's Ian Sinclair said, "operated on a commercial basis."[1]

As a result of the manner in which it was set up, the CNR has always had something of an inferiority complex, for which it can only compensate by trying to beat Canadian Pacific at its own game. It can't quite succeed, but it can come pretty close, and just making the effort has the desired effect. As a result, any suggestion that a railway should be run as a public service is an immediate casualty—that was never the idea anyway. Canadian National still feels some need to demonstrate that it is no less tough with its employees than Canadian Pacific, no more tolerant of quixotic schemes such as passenger service, no less ready to seek out fields such as trucking and real-estate development in order to add to its profits. That Canadian National could get involved in a project like Metro Centre in Toronto has not even been cause for surprise. Here was our publicly-owned railway cast in the role of profit-hungry, soulless developer, and giving a performance that was, to say the least, convincing. The experience of Canadian National suggests that a business railway and a public railway cannot coexist. A business railway belonging to private owners and a business railway belonging to the government can, and do. If we want a public railway, it will be necessary to have *only* a public railway.

Even then, there is no certainty that public ownership will make any difference. One can, however, be sure that no real changes will take place *without* the nationalization of Canadian Pacific. Even after nationalization, the Canadian railway problem will still be a difficult one. A logical and equitable freight-rate structure will not magically appear overnight. The question of how to balance the different modes of transportation will still admit of several answers, and it will not always be clear which is the best one. The most that nationalization will do is remove an essentially irrelevant consideration from the discussion: the profit margin of a private company. It will make it possible for government-owned utilities to operate without constant reference to the profit motive. It will create the *opportunity*—an opportunity that does not now exist—for Canada's transportation system to be put on a rational basis. It will then be the responsibility of the new owners of Canadian Pacific to take advantage of that opportunity.

Any discussion of nationalization inevitably raises the question of compensation. It would be very easy to say that as a matter of principle all corporate assets belong to the people and hence no compensation should be given, but that would ensure that the project would never be carried out, except perhaps in some far-off millennium. It would be equally easy to say that Canadian Pacific should be paid in full for its assets, but that too would ensure that the project would never be carried out. It would be too expensive, and governments always have other priorities. There are many other possible formulas for determining compensation, and which one is used will no doubt depend on the circumstances under which nationalization is carried out.

There is, however, at least one strong argument for paying, at most, a sharply reduced indemnity to the owners of Canadian Pacific. That is that the government has already made a very substantial down payment, in the form of subsidies, direct and indirect, to the company over the years. One logical formula would be to subtract the total of those subsidies from the value of the assets of Canadian Pacific to determine the amount to be paid as an indemnity. The result would probably come very close to zero. If so, we might feel queasy about taking over something so large and powerful as Canadian Pacific with little or no compensation. But we needn't. There is no particular moral imperative requiring us to pay for Canadian Pacific. We have already paid for Canadian Pacific, many times over.

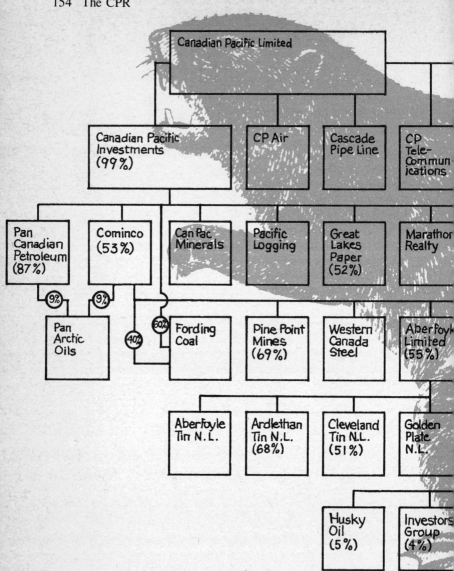

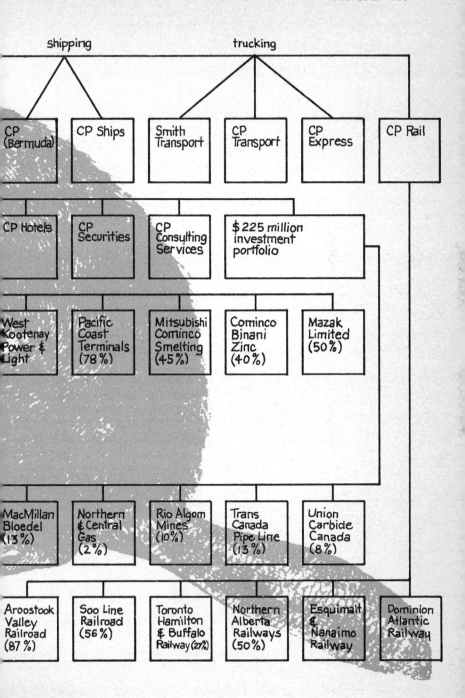

Appendix 1

**Aid granted for construction to Canadian Pacific Ltd.
and other companies now in the Canadian Pacific system**

	Federal	Provincial	Municipal	Total
Cash subsidies and expenditures on construction, dollars				
Canadian Pacific Ltd.				
Main line:				
Cash subsidies	25,000,000	—	263,600	25,263,600
Expenditures on construction of lines turned over to CPR	34,041,082	—	—	34,041,082
Branch lines:				
Cash subsidies	2,840,514	369,658	86,733	3,296,905
Expenditures on construction of lines turned over to CPR	1,076,070	—	—	1,076,070
Acquired & leased lines				
Cash subsidies	12,122,385	2,649,366	1,136,155	15,907,906
Total	75;080,051	3,019,024	1,486,488	79,585,563
Other companies (All cash subsidies)				
Main line	—	11,990	1,400	13,390
Acquired & leased lines	13,357,129	9,551,076	3,773,176	26,681,381
Total	13,357,129	9,563,066	3,774,576	26,694,771
Grand total	88,437,180	12,582,090	5,261,064	106,280,334
Land grants, acres				
Main line	25,000,000	—	—	25,000,000
Branch lines	1,609,024	—	—	1,609,024
Acquired & leased lines	6,239,453	11,114,069	—	17,353,522
Total	32,848,477	11,114,069	—	43,962,546

Appendix 2

Selected Canadian Pacific profit figures

	Net railway profit, before payment of fixed charges	Net profit from railway and miscellaneous sources, after fixed charges	Total profits, including dividends and income retained in subsidiaries	Total federal subsidies, estimated
1967	$39.6 million	$32.9 million	$84.2 million	$45 million
1968	$41.3 million	$42.8 million	$77.3 million	$40 million
1969	$34.6 million	$31.4 million	$75.8 million	$35 million
1970	$38.4 million	$28.8 million	$65.7 million	$30 million
1971	$45.8 million	$38.6 million	$75.5 million	$40 million
1972	$57.6 million	$44.7 million	$96.1 million	$40 million

The first three columns represent three different profit figures (or income figures, in the more neutral term the company prefers) presented by Canadian Pacific in its annual reports. The first one isolates railway profits, but does not take into account the payment of interest on the CPR's railway debt ('fixed charges'). The second column adds profits from non-railway activities operated directly by Canadian Pacific Ltd., such as trucking and shipping, and subtracts the fixed charges. The third adds dividends from CP Air and CP Investments, and the item "income retained by subsidiaries" which Canadian Pacific only began declaring in the early 1970s (figures from previous years are obtained from the company's five-year summaries).

The difficulty of obtaining an exact figure for federal railway subsidies has been noted in Chapter 2.

Appendix 3

Canadian Pacific Ltd.
Board of Directors
as of May 1973

W.A. Arbuckle
Chairman of the Canadian Board
The Standard Life Assurance
  Company
Director
Bank of Montreal

W.J. Bennett
President
Iron Ore Company of Canada

Fred Burbidge
President
Canadian Pacific Ltd.
Director,
Bank of Montreal

Keith Campbell
Vice-president
Canadian Pacific Ltd.

J.V. Clyne
Retired Chairman of the Board
MacMillan Bloedel Ltd.

Norris R. (Buck) Crump
Retired Chairman of the Board
Canadian Pacific Ltd.

Allan Findlay
Partner
Tilley, Carson & Findlay

G. Arnold Hart
Chairman of the Board
Bank of Montreal

Allard Jiskoot
Partner
Pierson, Heldring & Pierson

David Kinnear
Chairman of the Board
The T. Eaton Co. Ltd.
Director
Bank of Montreal

H.J. Lang
Chairman
Canron Ltd.
Director
Canadian Imperial Bank
  of Commerce

Herbert H. Lank
Director
Du Pont of Canada Ltd.
Director
Toronto-Dominion Bank

W. Earle McLaughlin
Chairman and President
Royal Bank of Canada

J.H. Moore
President
Brascan Ltd.
Director
Canadian Imperial Bank
  of Commerce

Paul Paré
President
Imasco Ltd.
Director
Royal Bank of Canada

158

Claude Pratte
Counsellor
Letourneau, Stein, Marseille,
    Delisle & LaRue
Director
Royal Bank of Canada

Lucien Rolland
President
Rolland Paper Company, Ltd.
Director
Bank of Montreal

A.M. Runciman
President
United Grain Growers Ltd.

F.H. Sherman
President
Dominion Foundries and
    Steel, Ltd.
Director
Bank of Nova Scotia

Ian D. Sinclair
Chairman
Canadian Pacific Ltd.
Director
Royal Bank of Canada

H. Greville Smith
President
Canadian International
    Investment Trust Ltd.
Director
Royal Trust Co., Steel Co.
    of Canada and other companies
    in the Bank of Montreal group

Norman E. Whitmore
President
Wascana Investments Ltd.

Henry S. Wingate
Director, Chairman of the
    Advisory Committee and Re-
    tired Chairman of the Board
International Nickel Company
    of Canada, Ltd.

Ray D. Wolfe
President
The Oshawa Group Ltd.

Footnotes

Chapter 1

1 Pierre Berton, "What we once did we can do again", *Maclean's*, September 1971, p. 79.

2 E.J. Pratt, *Towards the Last Spike* (Toronto, Macmillan, 1952) p. 53.

3 The *Risorgimento*, or "resurgence" of Italian culture and national awareness in the 1860s, is supposed to have led to the founding of modern Italy.

4 Luigi Barzini, "Romance and the Risorgimento", *New York Review of Books*, October 5, 1972, p. 16.

5 From "Canadian Railroad Trilogy", words and music by Gordon Lightfoot; M. Witmark and Sons (ASCAP), 1967.

6 Pratt, *op. cit.*, p. 4.

7 *Ibid.*, p. 34.

8 Pierre Berton, *The National Dream: The Great Railway 1871-1881* (Toronto, McClelland & Stewart, 1970) p. 249.

9 *Ibid.*, p. 305.

10 ITT owns Avis-Rent-a-car and the Rayonier paper company; Brascan owns John Labatt Ltd. and the main supplier of electric power in Brazil: Light—Serviços de Eletricidade.

11 Arthur J. Cordell, *The Multinational Firm, Foreign Direct Investment, and Canadian Science Policy*, Special Study No. 22 for the Science Council of Canada (Ottawa, Information Canada, 1971) p. 73.

12 "Volvo Grows Up", *The Economist*, July 10, 1971, p. 89, cited in Cordell, *op. cit.*, p. 76.

13 W.T.R. Preston, *The Life and Times of Lord Strathcona*, cited in "The Life of Lord Strathcona", by "Ironquill", *Grain Growers' Guide*, April 28, 1915.

Chapter 2

1 Government of Canada, Estimates, 1973-74, p. (27-70).

2 Montreal *Star*, October 28, 1960.

3 Question No. 1476, March 8, 1973, answered by Jean Marchand,

Minister of Transport, May 16, 1973.

4 Statistics from J.C. Lessard, *Transportation in Canada*, background study for the Royal Commission on Canada's Economic Prospects (Ottawa, Queen's Printer, 1956) pp. 76, 101.

5 Royal Commission on Transportation (MacPherson) Report (Ottawa, Queen's Printer, 1961) Vol. II, p. 3.

6 *Ibid.*, Vol. I, p. 13.

7 *Ibid.*

8 *Ibid.*

9 *Ibid.*

10 Montreal *Star*, January 25, 1962, p. 35.

11 Royal Commission on Transportation (MacPherson), *op. cit.*, Vol. I, p. 5.

12 *Ibid.*, Vol. I, p. 5.

13 Montreal *Star*, editorial, September 1, 1967.

14 See, for example, Peter C. Newman, *The Distemper of Our Times: Canadian Politics in Transition: 1963-1968* (Toronto, McClelland and Stewart, 1968) pp. 231-240.

15 Canadian Transport Commission, Hearing on the *Canadian*, Winnipeg, August 17, 1970, Transcript, p. 64.

16 In conversation with Saskatchewan Liberal Leader Davey Steuart. Winnipeg *Free Press*, January 19, 1973.

17 Canadian Pacific Railway Co., Report of Shareholders' Meeting, May 14, 1966.

18 Macdonald to Stephen, September 17, 1889. Cited in G.P. de T. Glazebrook, *A History of Transportation in Canada* (Toronto, McClelland and Stewart, 1964) Vol. II, p. 107.

19 Stephen to Macdonald, May 8, 1882, cited in Donald Creighton, *John A. Macdonald: The Old Chieftain* (Toronto, Macmillan, 1955) p. 336.

20 *Ibid.*, p. 362.

21 Vernon C. Fowke, *The National Policy and the Wheat Economy* (Toronto, University of Toronto Press, 1957) p. 52.

22 Statistics from N. Vallerand, "Histoire des faits économiques de la Vallée du St-Laurent, 1760-1866", *Economie Québécois*, Montreal, 1969, cited in R.T. Naylor, "The rise and fall of the third commercial empire of the St. Lawrence", in Gary Teeple, ed., *Capitalism and the National Question in Canada* (Toronto, University of Toronto Press, 1972) p. 11; and from T.C. Keefer, "Railways", in H.V. Nelles, ed., *Philosophy of Railroads and Other Essays* (Toronto, University of Toronto Press, 1972) p. 147.

23 Royal Commission to Inquire into Railways and Transportation in Canada (Drayton-Acworth) Report (Ottawa, King's Printer, 1917) p. xxvii.

24 William Pearce, "A brief history of the lands set apart for the construction of the railways, particularly the main line of the Canadian Pacific Railway, also a history regarding the settlement of lands in the immediate vicinity of Calgary," Pearce papers, Archives of Saskatchewan, Regina.

25 Van Horne to Rogers, December 8, 1884. Public Archives of Canada, Van Horne letterbook 9.

26 Pierre Berton, *The Last Spike: The Great Railway 1881-1885* (Toronto, McClelland and Stewart, 1971) pp. 11-21.

27 Keefer, *op. cit.*, p. 144.

28 *Ibid.*, p. 141.

29 Charles Horetzky, *Startling Facts!!: Canada Pacific Railway and the North-West Lands, also a Brief Discussion Regarding the Route, the Western Terminus and the Lands Available for Settlement* (Ottawa, 1880) p. 72.

Chapter 3

1 George Bernard Shaw, *The Intelligent Woman's Guide to Socialism and Capitalism* (New York, Brentano's, 1928) p. 272.

2 Van Horne to Macdonald, February 28, 1891, cited in Pierre Berton, *The Last Spike* (Toronto, McClelland and Stewart, 1971) p. 266.

3 I am indebted to a paper by John A. Eagle of the University of Alberta, "Lord Shaughnessy and the Railway Policies of Sir Robert Borden, 1903-1917", presented at the meeting of the Learned Societies, Montreal, June 9, 1972, for much of the information about the relations between Shaughnessy and Borden.

4 *Grain Growers' Guide*, editorial, May 9, 1917.

5 Shaughnessy to Borden, Montreal, May 16, 1916, enclosing five-page "Memorandum", unsigned, undated. Cited in Eagle, *op. cit.*

6 *Ibid.*

7 *Ibid.*

8 *Ibid.*

9 *Borden Diaries*, May 17, 1916, cited in Eagle, *op. cit.*

10 *Grain Growers' Guide*, editorial, April 4, 1917.

11 *Grain Growers' Guide*, editorial, May 9, 1917.

12 Royal Commission (Drayton-Acworth) Report (Ottawa, King's Printer, 1917) p. lxv.

13 *Ibid.*, p. lxii.

14 *Ibid.*, p. li.

15 G.P. de T. Glazebrook, *A History of Transportation in Canada* (Toronto, McClelland & Stewart, 1964) Vol. II, p. 184.

16 Statistics from Glazebrook, *op. cit.*, p. 202.

17 Statistics from Statistics Canada document No. 52-201 (1971): "Canadian National Railways 1923-1971" (Ottawa, Information Canada, 1973) pp. 14, 22.

18 Citied in Glazebrook, *op. cit.*, p. 205.

19 Canadian Pacific Railway Co., Report of Shareholders' Meeting, 1935; cited in Glazebrook, *op. cit.*, pp. 210-211.

20 Statistics from Statistics Canada 52-201 (1971), *op. cit.*, p. 14.

21 Edmonton *Journal*, December 31, 1960.

22 Toronto *Star*, September 27, 1961.

23 Cominco Ltd., Annual Report, 1972.

Chapter 4

1 Ronald A. Keith, *Bush Pilot with a Briefcase: The Happy-go-lucky Story of Grant McConachie* (Toronto, Doubleday Canada, 1972) p. 233.

2 Canadian Transport Commission, Railway Transport Committee, Decision "In the matter of the Application and Appeal of Saskatchewan Wheat Pool, Agra Industries Limited, Co-Op Vegetable Oils Ltd. and Western Canadian Seed Processors Ltd., pursuant to Section 23 of the *National Transportation Act*." June 27, 1973, File No. 30637.2, p. 44.

3 Hu Harries & Associates Ltd., Economic Consultants, "A Review and Summary of Western Canadian Freight Rate Inequities", a report prepared on the instruction of Robert A. Boulware, Chairman, Transportation and Development Authority of Calgary, November 10, 1971, p. 30.

4 *Ibid.*, p. 26.

5 *Ibid.*, p. 25.

6 *Ibid.*, pp. 34-35.

7 *Ibid.*, p.7.

8 Vernon C. Fowke, *The National Policy and the Wheat Economy* (Toronto, University of Toronto Press, 1957) p. 93.

9 *Ibid.*, p. 93.

10 Schedule to 44 Victoria, Chapter I, an Act respecting the Canadian Pacific Railway, Article 15.

11 Glazebrook, *A History of Transportation in Canada* (Toronto, McClelland & Stewart, 1964) Vol. II, p. 114.

12 Laurier speech to CMA, Quebec City, 1905, cited in *Canadian Annual Review of Public Affairs*, 1905, pp. 149-150, and in Fowke, *op. cit.*, p. 66.

13 I am indebted to an unpublished paper by Henry Dyck, University of Manitoba, "Agrarian Political and Economic Attitudes Mani-

fested in the *Grain Growers' Guide* 1908-1918'', April 17, 1972, for much of the information about the *Grain Growers' Guide*.

14 *Grain Growers' Guide*, December 6, 1911, p. 5.

15 *Grain Growers' Guide*, editorial, September 22, 1920.

15 *Grain Growers' Guide*, January 17, 1912.

17 *Grain Growers' Guide*, January 27, 1915, p. 21.

18 *Grain Growers' Guide*, editorial, May 4, 1921.

19 Harold A. Innis, *A History of the Canadian Pacific Railway* (Toronto, University of Toronto Press, 1971) p. 294.

20 Horetzky, *Startling Facts!! op. cit.*, p. 72.

21 Van Horne to Hon. Sir D.L. MacPherson, Minister of the Interior, March 14, 1885. Public Archives of Canada, Van Horne Letterbook 10.

22 Van Horne to Smithe, September 23, 1884. Public Archives of Canada, Van Horne Letterbook 7.

23 Vancouver *Province*, December 19, 1964.

24 Martin Robin, *The Rush for Spoils: The Company Province 1871-1933* (Toronto, McClelland and Stewart, 1972).

Chapter 5

1 Winnipeg *Free Press*, December 15, 1959.

2 J. Lorne McDougall, *Canadian Pacific: A Brief History* (Montreal, McGill University Press, 1968) p. 82.

3 Province of Saskatchewan's *Submission to the Royal Commission on Transportation, 1960: An Historical Analysis of the Crow's Nest Pass Agreement and Grain Rates: A Study in National Transportation Policy* (Regina, Queen's Printer, 1960) pp. 23-24.

4 Canadian Pacific Railway Company. Annual Report, 1892, p. 12, cited in Province of Saskatchewan's submission, *op. cit.*, p. 31.

5 Canada, House of Commons, Debates, 1897, p. 4514, cited in Province of Saskatchewan's submission, *op. cit.*, p. 34.

6 Canadian Pacific Railway Company. Annual Report, 1897, pp. 7-8, cited in Province of Saskatchewan, *op. cit.*, p. 44.

7 Conversation with the author, April 1973.

8 Royal Commission on Transportation (Turgeon) Report (Ottawa, King's Printer, 1951) p. 245.

9 Cited in Royal Commission on Transportation (Turgeon), *op. cit.*, p. 245.

10 Cited in Royal Commission on Transportation (Turgeon), *op. cit.*, p. 244.

11 Royal Commission on Transportation (Turgeon), *op. cit.*, p. 244.

12 *Ibid.*, p. 249.

13 *Ibid.*, p. 250.

14 *Ibid.*, p. 252.

15 Royal Commission on Transportation (MacPherson), Report (Ottawa, Queen's Printer, 1961) Vol. I, pp. 28-30.

16 Canada, House of Commons, Standing Committee on Transport and Communications, Minutes of Proceedings and Evidence, November 1, 1966, Appendix A-22, p. 2240.

17 *Ibid.*, p. 2240.

18 E.P. Reid, "Statutory Grain Rates" (Ottawa, 1960), in Royal Commission on Transportation (MacPherson), *op. cit.*, Vol. III, p. 380.

19 *Ibid.*, p. 404.

20 Profit statistics from Canadian Pacific Railway Company, Annual Reports, 1962-1970, and Canadian Pacific Ltd., Annual Report, 1971. Wheat statistics courtesy of Canadian Pacific Ltd.

21 Harold A. Innis, *A History of the Canadian Pacific Railway* (Toronto, University of Toronto Press, 1971) p. 294.

22 Reid, *op. cit.*, pp. 400-403.

23 *Ibid.*, p. 402.

24 Cited in Winnipeg *Free Press*, December 8, 1959.

Chapter 6

1 Toronto *Globe and Mail*, October 28, 1960.

2 Toronto *Star*, August 30, 1968.

3 Vancouver *Sun*, August 31, 1970.

4 Vancouver *Sun*, August 31, 1970.

5 Canadian Transport Commission, Railway Transport Committee, Decision "In the matter of the Application of the Canadian Pacific Railway Company on behalf of Esquimalt and Nanaimo Railway Company for authority to discontinue the passenger train service between Victoria and Courtenay, in the Province of British Columbia, provided by trains 1 and 2 of Esquimalt and Nanaimo Railway Company", October 30, 1970, File No. 49466.31, pp. 18-19.

6 *Ibid.*, p. 16.

7 *Ibid.*, p. 16.

8 Canadian Transport Commission. Sixth Annual Report, 1972.

9 Vancouver *Sun*, August 31, 1970.

10 Winnipeg *Free Press*, September 20, 1958.

11 Toronto *Globe and Mail*, October 28, 1960.

12 Board of Transport Commissioners. Order No. 118362 and Notice "In the matter of the Canadian Pacific Railway Company's trains Nos. 3,4,13 and 14, known as 'The Dominion', and related

matters", August 1965, File No. 27563.479, pamphlet no. 21, p. 397.

13 Canadian Transport Commission, Railway Transport Committee. "Reasons for Order No. R-6313 concerning Costs Regulations", August 5, 1969, pamphlet no. 15, p. 398.

14 14-15-16 Elizabeth II, Chapter 69, An Act to define and implement a national transportation policy for Canada, to amend the Railway Act and other Acts in consequence thereof and to enact other consequential provisions, Section 42, amending Section 314I, Subsection (6) of the Railway Act.

15 Statistics from J.C. Lessard, *Transportation in Canada* (Ottawa, Queen's Printer, 1956), *op. cit.*, p. 101.

16 Statistics from Dominion Bureau of Statistics, Document no. 50-001 (Ottawa, Queen's Printer, 1970).

17 Government of Canada, Estimates, 1973-74, pp. (27-22)—(27-27).

18 Statistics from Dominion Bureau of Statistics, Documents no. 53-201 (1968) "Road and Street Mileage and Expenditure", and 53-220 (1968) "The Motor Vehicle, Part IV: Revenues" (Ottawa, Queen's Printer, 1969).

19 Canada, House of Commons, Standing Committee on Transport and Communications. Minutes of Proceedings and Evidence, July 5, 1966, p. 1635, cited in H.L. Purdy, *Transport Competition and Public Policy in Canada* (Vancouver, University of British Columbia Press, 1972) p. 280.

20 Ron Haggart, "The great railroad debate", *Saturday Night*, April 1969, p. 31.

21 Dominion Bureau of Statistics. Documents no. 52-207 (1968) "Railway Transport: Part I", and no. 53-206 (1968) "Motor Vehicle Traffic Accidents" (Ottawa, Queen's Printer, 1969).

22 Claiborne Pell, *Megalopolis Unbound: The Supercity and the Transportation of Tomorrow* (New York, Frederick A. Praeger, Inc., 1966) p. 131.

23 *Ibid.*, p. 132.

24 Canada, House of Commons, Standing Committee on Transport and Communications. Minutes of Proceedings and Evidence, May 12, 1966, p. 993.

25 Canadian Transport Commission, Research Branch. *Intercity Passenger Transport Study* (Ottawa, Information Canada, 1970) p. 76.

26 Canadian Transport Commission, Hearing on the *Canadian*, Calgary, August 24, 1970, Transcript, pp. 111-112.

27 Interview with Amy Booth, *Financial Post*, May 14, 1966.

28 Statistics Canada, Document No. 52-201 (1971): "Canadian National Railways 1923-1971" (Ottawa, Information Canada, 1973) p. 22.

29 For a full discussion of the death of the Newfie Bullet and Canadian National's behaviour in Newfoundland, see Denys Mulrooney, "CN's 'involvement' in Newfoundland", *St. John's Alternate Press*, July 14, 1971, pp. 17-37.

30 Canadian Brotherhood of Railway, Transport and General Workers, "Submission to the Canadian Transport Commission In the matter of passenger train services in the Quebec City-Windsor Corridor and in the Mid-Canada Area", 1972, p. 6.

31 *Financial Post*, May 14, 1966.

Chapter 7

1 Leslie Roberts, *C.D.: The Life and Times of Clarence Decatur Howe* (Toronto, Clarke Irwin, 1957) p. 44.

2 Winnipeg *Free Press*, May 12, 1943.

3 Canada, House of Commons, Debates, April 2, 1943, pp. 1776-1778.

4 Canada, House of Commons, Debates, March 17, 1944, pp. 1573-1574.

5 Canada, House of Commons, Debates, August 17, 1946, pp. 5000-5002.

6 Canada, House of Commons, Debates, August 17, 1946, pp. 5002-5003.

7 Ronald A. Keith, *Bush Pilot with a Briefcase* (Toronto, Doubleday Canada, 1972) pp. 254-257.

8 International Civil Aviation Organization, *Digest of Statistics*, 1955-66 (Montreal, International Civil Aviation Organization), cited in Robert L. Thornton, *International Airlines and Politics: A Study in Adaptation to Change* (Ann Arbor, University of Michigan, Graduate School of Business Administration, 1970).

9 Toronto *Globe and Mail*, November 5, 1953.

10 Toronto *Globe and Mail*, November 12, 1953.

11 Toronto *Globe and Mail*, November 17, 1953.

12 Canada, House of Commons, Debates, November 17, 1953, p. 99.

13 Toronto *Globe and Mail*, November 21, 1953.

14 Toronto *Globe and Mail*, February 8, 1958.

15 Toronto *Globe and Mail*, February 8, 1958.

16 Toronto *Globe and Mail*, January 22, 1959.

17 Pickersgill, Hon. J.W. "Statement of Aviation Policy Principles", April 24, 1964.

18 Pickersgill, Hon. J.W. "Statement of Aviation Policy Principles", March 27, 1967.

19 Government of Canada, Estimates, 1973-74, p. 27-26.

20 *Ibid.*, pp. (27-40)—(27-41).

21 Z. Haritos, and J.D. Gibberd, *Civil Aviation Infrastructure Annual Costs and Revenues 1954-1968: A Study of the Air Transport Mode in Canada*, paper done for the Canadian Transport Commission, Economics Branch (Ottawa, Information Canada, 1972) p. 17.

22 *Ibid.*, pp. 20, 35.

23 *Ibid.*, p. 20.

24 Statistics from Air Canada, Annual Reports, 1971-72; Canadian Pacific Railway Company, Annual Reports, 1962-70; Canadian Pacific Ltd., Annual Reports, 1971-72.

25 Cited in Keith, *op. cit.*, p. 307.

26 *Ibid.*, p. 295.

27 Toronto *Globe and Mail*, August 17, 1972.

28 Vancouver *Province*, December 8, 1972.

29 Cited in John van der Feyst, "The case for responsible air policy", *Canadian Business*, March 1973, p. 10.

Chaper 8

1 Statistics Canada. Document no. 52-202 (1971) "Canadian Pacific Limited 1923-1971" (Ottawa, Information Canada, 1973) p. 19.

2 Statistics Canada. Document no. 52-201 (1971), "Canadian National Railways 1923-71" (Ottawa, Information Canada, 1973) p. 25.

3 Stephen G. Peitchinis, *Labour-Management Relations in the Railway Industry,* Task Force on Labour Relations Study No. 20 (Ottawa, Information Canada, 1971) p. 49.

4 Winnipeg *Free Press*, March 23, 1968.

5 Statistics Canada, Document no. 52-202 (1971), *op. cit.*, p. 19.

6 *Ibid.*

7 Cited in Industrial Inquiry Commission on Canadian National Railways "Run-Throughs" (Freedman) Report (Ottawa, Queen's Printer, 1966) p. 22.

8 *Ibid.*, p. 24, pp. 91-92.

9 Canadian Transport Commission. Hearing on the *Canadian*, Ottawa, October 26, 1970, Transcript, pp. 78-82.

10 *Ibid.*, p. 90.

11 Royal Commission on Chinese Immigration. Report and Evidence (Ottawa, 1885) p. 149.

12 *Ibid.*, p. 71.

13 *Ibid.*, p. 150.

14 See Liberal party advertisement, Vancouver *Sun*, October 7,

1935, p. 11.

15 Royal Commission on Chinese Immigration, *op. cit.*, p. 171.

16 See Paul Phillips, *No Power Greater: A Century of Labour in B.C.* (Vancouver, B.C. Federation of Labour, 1967) pp. 39-41.

17 See W.E. Greening and M.M. Maclean, *It Was Never Easy 1908-1958: A History of the Canadian Brotherhood of Railway, Transport and General Workers* (Ottawa, Canadian Brotherhood of Railway, Transport and General Workers, 1961) pp. 23-34.

18 Peitchinis, *op. cit.*, p. 104.

19 Cited in Peitchinis, *op. cit.*, p. 221.

Chapter 9

1 United States House of Representatives, Antitrust Subcommittee of the Committee on the Judiciary, *Investigation of Conglomerate Corporations* (Washington, U.S. Government Print Office, 1971) p. 4.

2 Thomas O'Hanlon, "The Odd News about Conglomerates", *Fortune*, June 15, 1967, pp. 175-177.

3 United States House of Representatives, Antitrust Subcommittee, *op. cit.*, p. 54.

4 *Ibid.*, p. 54.

5 *Ibid.*, pp. 56-58.

6 Vancouver *Sun*, June 6, 1970, p. 5.

7 *Ibid.*

8 Winnipeg *Free Press*, February 6, 1958.

9 PanCanadian Petroleum Ltd. Annual Report, 1972, p. 1.

10 See "A Tale of Treasure", *Forbes*, March 1, 1972, pp. 26-27.

11 J. Lorne McDougall, *Canadian Pacific* (Montreal, McGill University Press, 1968) p. 142.

12 Joe Zuken, Brief presented to the NDP caucus of the Manitoba Legislature on behalf of the Labour Election Committee, 1972.

13 For a full discussion of Project 200 and its implications, see Vancouver Urban Research Group's *Forever Deceiving You: The Politics of Vancouver Development* (Vancouver, 1972) pp. 14-37.

14 See Mr. Sewell's book, *Up Against City Hall* (Toronto, James Lewis and Samuel, 1972) pp. 96-116, for a full discussion of Metro Centre.

15 Vancouver *Sun*, May 4, 1972.

16 Bermuda, 1964: No. 143, The Cerium Investments Company Act, 1964, Section 4, Subsections (a) and (j).

17 Charles Lynch, "Canada's Aristotle Onassis", Ottawa *Citizen*, March 12, 1970.

18 "To Get A Canadian Merchant Fleet: The 'Dollar Patriots' Must

Be Stopped'', *Ship Shop*, Official Organ of the Marine Workers' and Boilermakers' Industrial Union No. 1, Special Edition, August 1971.

Chapter 10

1 Iris Naish Fleming, ''The Informal Buck Crump'', Toronto *Globe and Mail*, July 16, 1973.

2 Ron Grant, ''CPR's Crump recalls 50 years of railroading'', Montreal *Gazette*, August 18, 1970.

3 Leo A. Johnson, ''The Development of Class in Canada in the Twentieth Century'', in Gary Teemple, ed., *Capitalism and the National Question in Canada* (Toronto, University of Toronto Press, 1972) p. 155.

4 Canadian Pacific Railway Co., Annual Report, 1955, and Canadian Pacific Ltd., Annual Report, 1972.

5 Cited in Jamieson, Robert. ''Would CP stock offer have amused Victoria?'', *Financial Post*, September 25, 1971.

6 *Ibid*.

7 Montreal *Gazette*, April 26, 1973.

8 Pension Benefits Standards Act, Pension Benefits Standards Regulations, Order in Council 1967-1289, *Canada Gazette Part II*, July 12, 1967.

9 Pension Benefits Standards Act, 1966-67, c. 92, Section 6, Subsection (2).

10 Alastair Dow, ''CPR: Another stock deal with its pension fund'', Toronto *Star*, December 24, 1964, and ''CPR steps into Trans-Canada'', Toronto *Star*, January 30, 1965.

Chapter 11

1 Toronto *Star*, September 3, 1973.

Index

Acworth, W.M., 34-35
Agrarian protest movement, 50, 52-53. See also *Grain Growers' Guide*
Air Canada, 100-102. *See also* Trans-Canada Air Lines
Air routes, Pickersgill division of, 97-98
Air services program, 81, 82-83, 98-99; subsidies to, 99-100
Air Transport Board, 96,97
T. Akasaka, 130
Alberta, 46, 47, 50, 125-26
Alberta Railway and Coal Company, 62
Anderson, J.C., 108-109

Bank of Montreal, 20, 136, 137
Bank of Nova Scotia, 137
Bayley, Howard, 65
Beatty, Edward, 36, 37-38, 72, 136
Begbie, Sir Matthew, 110
Bell, Max, 137, 139-40
Belt Railway Company of Chicago, 118
Bennett, Nelson, 111
Benson, Edgar (Ben), 17
Blair, A.G., 31, 63
Board of Railway Commissioners, 32, 36, 66
Board of Transport Commissioners, 16, 78-79, 104, 112-13
Bonner, Robert, 149
Borden, Robert, 31-35
Brascan, 137
British Columbia, 44, 75-76; CPR influence in, 3, 20, 29, 53-57, 125, 126, 128; mineral wealth of, 62; southeastern, CPR expansion in, 61-64
British Columbia Southern Railway, 62-63
Brotherhood of Locomotive Engineers, 112
Brotherhood of Railroad Trainmen, 107
Brotherhood of Railway, Airline and Steamship Clerks, (BRASC), 108, 112
Brown, George, 21
Burbidge, Fred, 136

172   The CPR

Calgary, 25, 44-46, 125-26
Calgary *Herald,* 43
Campbell, Keith, 136
Campbell, R.W., 123
Canadian, 74, 77-78, 83-85, 108-109
Canadian Bank of Commerce, 30
Canadian Brotherhood of Railway Employees (CBRE), 111-12
Canadian Brotherhood of Railway, Transport and General Workers
    (CBRT), 108, 112
Canadian Imperial Bank of Commerce, 137
Canadian National Railways, 10, 28, 148, 151; and Metro Centre,
    126-28, 151; and Trans-Canada Air Lines, 90; employment statistics
    for, 104; formation of, 35-36; Great Slave Lake Railway, 39-40;
    passenger service, 38-39, 76, 80, 82, 85-86; subsidies to, 10, 12,
    14, 16, 80, 114; treatment of unions, 107-108
Canadian Northern Railway, 30, 66
Canadian Pacific Air Lines, 13, 90-102, 120, 142; international routes,
    93-95; transcontinental routes, 95-98
Canadian Pacific (Bermuda) Ltd., 123, 129-31
Canadian Pacific Consulting Services Ltd., 120
Canadian Pacific Hotels, 120, 129, 142
Canadian Pacific Investments Ltd., 34, 122-23, 124, 149; role of, 140-42
Canadian Pacific Ltd., 118, 119-23; subsidiaries, 119-20, 140-42
Canadian Pacific Oil and Gas Ltd. *See* PanCanadian Petroleum
Canadian Pacific Railway, 28, 118, 120, 122; and Trans-Canada Air
    Lines, 90-91, 100; Crow's Nest Pass Agreement, 61, 63, 66 *(see
    also* Crow's Nest Pass Agreement); directors of, 136-40; employment
    statistics for, 104, 106; expansion into southeastern B.C., 62; Euro-
    pean takeover attempt of, 138-40; Great Slave Lake Railway, 39-40;
    land holdings of, 22, 24, 48, 54-57, 61-64, 124-29; land holdings,
    taxation of, 23, 51-52, 124-25; as instrument of national policy,
    4, 10-12, 19, 21, 43, 150; ownership of, 134-35, 138-40; pension
    fund, 142-44; public ownership of, 25, 28, 32-33, 52, 140-42, 150-2;
    subsidiaries, 6, 7 *(see also* Canadian Pacific Investments Ltd.; Cana-
    dian Pacific Ltd.); subsidies to, 10-14, 17, 22-24, 47, 61, 63, 68-70,
    80, 84, 114; treatment of unions, 107, 109-12
Canadian Pacific Railway Act, 23, 29, 48
Canadian Pacific Securities Ltd., 120
Canadian Pacific Ships, 120, 122, 142
Canadian Pacific Telecommunications, 120
Canadian Pacific Transport, 13, 120, 122
Canadian Railway Labour Association, 108
Canadian Transport Commission, 17, 44, 46, 148; passenger service
    decisions of, 75-76, 77, 79, 80, 83, 84, 86, 108-109

Caribou. See "Newfie Bullet"
Cartier, George Etienne, 20
Central-Del Rio Oils, 122, 123, 143
Champagne, F.S., 75
Chinese labourers, 109-11
Clyne, J.V., 56-57
Columbia and Western Railway, 64
Cominco, 39-40, 64-66, 118, 119-20, 124, 142
Competition Act, 46
Conglomerates, 119-22
Conservatives, 3, 29, 30, 35
Co-operative Commonwealth Federation (CCF), 40, 50, 52
Crow's Nest Pass Agreement, 43, 49, 55, 60-61, 63-64, 66-70, 113; abrogation of, 67; benefits to CPR of, 66; importance to western farmers of, 71-72; provisions of, 61; railway project, 62-3. *See also* Freight rates, on grain
Crump, Norris R. (Buck), 18, 56, 78, 114, 118, 120, 128, 135-38, 140; on passenger service, 74, 87
Curtis, Donald, 129

Delagrave, Pierre, 85
Dennis, J.S., 55-56
Dennison, William, 128
Depression, effect on railways of the, 37
Diefenbaker, John, 38, 40, 96
Dinsdale, Walter, 40
Dominion, 78-79, 83, 84
Dominion Atlantic Railway, 75
Douglas, Tommy, 50
Drayton, Sir Henry, 34-35
Drayton-Acworth Royal Commission, 34-35
Drew, George, 96
Dunning, Charles, 52-53, 150
Dunsmuir, James, 55

Emerson, Robert, 11, 74, 78, 79, 118, 120
Emslie, Graham, 128
Esquimalt and Nanaimo Railway, 55-57, 75-76

Fielding, Clifford, 137, 139-40
Findlay, Allan, 137
Fording Coal, 119
Freedman, Judge Samuel, 107, 108
Freight Rates Reduction Act, 114

Freight rates, 29, 32, 36-7, 42-47, 49, 50-1, 148; and wages 104,
   113; inequities of, 45-47; on grain, 11, 14, 43-44, 60-61, 64, 65,
   66-72; Turgeon Commission recommendations on, 47
Freight transport, railway share of, 13

Galt, Alexander Tilloch, 20
Gilmer, John, 101
Gordon, Donald, 114
Graham, George, 67
Grain Growers' Grain Company, 50
Grain Growers' Guide, 33, 50-52
Grain rates. *See* Freight rates, on grain
Grand Trunk Railway, 20-21, 25, 30-36
Grand Trunk Pacific Railway, 31-35
Great Lakes Paper Company, 122, 123, 142
Great Northern Railroad, 62
Great Slave Lake Railway, 39-40
Great Western Railway, 20
Green, John, 75

Hamilton, Lauchlan, 54
Harries, Hu and Associates, 44-46
Hart, Arnold, 137
Hees, George, 96
Heinze, F. Augustus, 63-64
Hill, James J., 4
Hincks, Francis, 20, 25
Home Oil, 123
Howe, Clarence Decatur, 90-93, 96, 98, 102
Hudson Bay Railway, 36
Hudson's Bay Company, 21, 22
Husky Oil Ltd., 123, 125

Intercolonial Railway, 19, 20, 25, 31, 111
Interstate Commerce Act, 19
Investors Group, the, 123

Jaffary, Karl, 128
James, Thomas, 74, 78, 84
Jamieson, Don, 17
Jiskoot, Allard, 138
Juba, Stephen, 124

Keefer, Thomas, 25

Keith, Ronald, 93-94
Kelsall, John, 75, 84
Kerr, Rod, 78
King, Mackenzie, 45, 66
Knights of Labour, 110
Knowles, Stanley, 92
Kootenays. *See* British Columbia, southeastern

Lake Manitoba Railway and Canal Company. *See* Canadian Northern
    Railway
Land holdings, CPR. *See* Canadian Pacific Railway, land holdings of
Laurier, Sir Wilfrid, 30-31, 49, 63
Lessard, J.C., 81
Liberals, 30

McAdoo award, 113
McConachie, Grant, 93-94, 101, 102
Macdonald, Sir John A., 4, 18-19, 25-26, 29, 48
Macdonnell, J.M., 96
McGill, Peter, 20
McGregor, Gordon, 95, 100-101
Mackenzie, Alexander, 25-26
Mackenzie, William, 30
McLaughlin, Earle, 137
MacMillan, H.R., 57
MacMillan, Norman, 128
MacMillan Bloedel, 5, 55-57, 123, 137; CPR interest in, 55-57
MacNab, Allan, 20
MacPherson Royal Commission on Transportation, 13-15, 60, 65, 74,
    114; on Crow rates, 69-70; reasons established, 38; and Turgeon
    Commission, 47
Manitoba, 23, 52, 66; CPR influence in, 3, 124-25; objections to
    monopoly clause, 48-49
Mann, Donald, 30
Marathon Realty, 22, 120, 124, 125-29, 142
Marchand, Jean, 14-15, 17, 90, 101
Maritime Freight Rates Act, 12, 69
Metro Centre, 126-28
Monopoly clause, 23, 29, 49
Montreal, 20, 76-77, 99
Moore, Jake, 137
Munroe Conciliation Board, 114

National Farmers' Union, 53

National policy. *See* Canadian Pacific Railway, as instrument of national policy

National Transcontinental, 31

National Transportation Act, 12, 13, 17, 70, 115; and freight rates, 47; passenger service provisions of, 79, 80; effect on wages, 113

New Brunswick, 21

New Democratic Party, 52

"Newfie Bullet", 86

Newfoundland, 86

North West, CPR influence in, 2-3, 23-24, 48

North West Territories, railway to, 40

Northern Alberta Railways, 39

Northern Pacific Railroad, 62

Nova Scotia, 21, 75

Onderdonk, Andrew, 109

Ontario, 76-77, 126-28

Ottawa, 76-77

Pacific Logging, 56-57, 119

Palliser Square, 125-26

Panarctic Oils Ltd., 124

PanCanadian Petroleum, 119, 123-24, 142

Passenger service, railway, Chapter 6; abandonment of, 16; share of traffic, 13, 81. *See also* Canadian National Railways, passenger service; Canadian Transport Commission, passenger service decisions of

Pearson, Lester, 114

Pell, Claiborne, 82

Pickersgill, Jack, 16-17, 40, 80, 90, 97, 101

Pine Point Mines Ltd., 39-40

Port-aux-Basques, 86

Port Moody, 54

Prairies, the: CPR influence in, 21, 43 (*see also* Alberta, Manitoba, Saskatchewan); CPR route through, 24; era of railway expansion, 36

Pratte, Yves, 100

Prince Edward Island, 20

Princess Marguerite, 76

Progressive Party, 50, 52

Provincial Bank of Canada, 143

Puddicombe, J.D., 128-29

Quebec, 20, 76-77, 99

Railway passenger service. *See* Passenger service, railway
Railway unions, 11-12, 107-112; use of strike, 112-15
Railways, amalgamation of. *See* Canadian Pacific Railway, public ownership of
Rapeseed rates, 43-44, 72
Rapido, 76, 85
Red River Rebellions, CPR role in, 23-24
Red River Valley Railway, 48
Reid, E.P., 71
Reid, J.D., 51
Renwick, Bryan, 101
Richardson, James, 137, 150
Riel, Louis, 24
Rio Algom Mines, 123
Roblin, Duff, 122, 124, 149
Rogers, Major A.B., 24
Rotenberg, David, 128
Royal Bank of Canada, 137
Royal Commission on Chinese Immigration, 110-11
Royal Commission on Transportation (1931), 37-38. *See also* entries for Drayton-Acworth, MacPherson, Turgeon Royal Commissions

St. John's, 86
St-Laurent, Louis, 113
Saskatchewan, 3, 52, 62, 70
Saskatchewan Co-operative Elevator Company, 52
Saskatchewan Grain Growers, 53
Sewell, John, 127
Sharp, Mitchell, 149
Shaughnessy, Lord, 31, 32-36, 52, 136
Sherman, F.H., 137
Ship Shop, 131
Sinclair, Ian, 56, 79, 85, 87, 118, 120, 123, 131, 134-35, 139, 142
Smith, A.H., 34
Smith, Donald A. (Lord Strathcona), 3, 6-7, 20, 22
Smith Transport, 13, 120, 122
Smithe, William, 54-55
Sopha, Elmer, 135
Stephen, George, 18-19, 20, 23
Strathcona, Lord. *See* Smith, Donald A.
Subsidies, railway. *See* Canadian National Railways, subsidies to; Canadian Pacific Railway, subsidies to
Super Continental, 80

Taylor, John, 123
Technological change, 105-108
Thornton, Henry, 36
Tilley, Carson and Findlay, 137
Toronto, 20, 76, 99, 126-28
Toronto-Dominion Bank, 137
Toronto Harbours Commission, 127
Trans-Canada Air Lines, 15, 90, 102. *See also* Air Canada
TransCanada PipeLines Ltd., 123, 143
Tupper, Charles, 63
Turbo, 85
Turgeon Royal Commission, 47, 67-69, 71

Union Carbide Canada Ltd., 123
United Brotherhood of Railway Employees (UBRE), 111
United Farmers of Alberta, 50, 51
United Transportation Union (UTU), 108, 112

Van Horne, William, 3, 24, 29, 30, 48, 54; and Crow's Nest Pass
   Agreement, 60-1, 66, 72; and unions, 109
W.C. Van Horne, 130-1
Vancouver, 22, 24, 53-55, 125, 126, 128

Wardair, 101
Webster, John, 128
West Kootenay Power and Light Company, 65, 120
Western Economic Opportunities Conference, 148
Wheatcroft, Stephen, 96, 97
Whitmore, Norman, 137
Winnipeg, 124-25
Winters, Robert, 149
Wisconsin Corporation, the, 57
Woodard, J.M., 84
Wright, Maurice, 17, 108-109
Wronski, Wojceich, 128

Zuken, Joe, 125

Also from James Lewis & Samuel

Quebec: A Chronicle 1968-1972
An account of five crucial years in Quebec's history which records the events of October 1970 and the emergence of the labour movements as a major political force. Paper $1.95.

Corporate Canada
Fourteen articles on major Canadian corporations like Eaton's, branch-plant industries like computers, and major economic policy issues like regional incentives grants and energy, drawn from the pages of Last Post magazine. Paper $1.95.

Louder Voices: The Corporate Welfare Bums
David Lewis puts together the information about what he calls the corporate welfare system, in a book which will be of interest to Canadians as long as government policies and the tax system remain unchanged. Paper $1.95.

Read Canadian
A book which introduces Canadian books in more than thirty areas, from urban problems to the history of the West. Paper $1.95.

Up Against City Hall
Toronto's most controversial alderman, John Sewell, reports on his attempts to win victories for citizens' groups and to reduce the power of the land development industry at city hall. Paper $2.95.

She Named It Canada
A witty, entertaining, attractive illustrated history of Canada written by the Corrective Collective, a Vancouver-based women's group. Paper $1.00.

A History of Canadian Wealth
Gustavus Myers' classic of Canadian economic and political history-writing, exposing our own home-grown robber barons and con-men, the wheelers and dealers in land and votes and lives. Written in 1913 and never before published in Canada, Myers' book has been acclaimed. Paper $2.95.

Quebec in Question
A short, lucid separatist's history of Quebec written by sociologist Marcel Rioux and translated by James Boake. Paper $3.50.

The Citizen's Guide to City Politics
The first practical and realistic guide to how city hall operates and why, which focusses on the links between city government and the real estate and land development industry. Written by James Lorimer. Paper $3.95.

An Unauthorized History of the RCMP
The Browns recount the role of the RCMP in Canadian history — in the Winnipeg General Strike and other labour disturbances in 1919, in intelligence work and infiltration of the Canadian Communist Party, in strikebreaking in the late 1920s and early 1930s, in persecuting immigrants and radicals during the Depression, in waging war on the unemployed during the 30's, in intelligence during the Second World War, and in dealing with students, draft dodgers and farmers during the 60s. Paper $1.95.

Working People
An account by James Lorimer and Myfanwy Phillips of life in a working-class neighbourhood of Toronto. Paper $4.95

The Real World of City Politics
Six accounts by James Lorimer of issues in Toronto city politics which define the realities of civic government in Canada and illustrate how these realities are being challenged by citizen groups. Paper $2.95

Grass Roots
Heather Robertson's remarkable second book about the farms and small towns of western Canada. "Since I didn't go east," she writes, "I went west, an accidental city slicker looking for roots, a third-generation Canadian in need of a history and a sense of place." $10.00 cloth